Pascal

COMPUTER SOFTWARE ENGINEERING SERIES

ELLIS HOROWITZ, Editor

University of Southern California

CALINGAERT

Assemblers, Compilers and Program Translation

EVEN

Graph Algorithms

FINDLAY and WATT

PASCAL: An Introduction to Methodical Programming

HOROWITZ and SAHNI

Fundamentals of Computer Algorithms

HOROWITZ and SAHNI

Fundamentals of Data Structures

Pascal
An Introduction to Methodical Programming

William Findlay & David A. Watt
Computing Science Department,
University of Glasgow

COMPUTER SCIENCE PRESS, INC.

Published simultaneously in the United States of America and Great Britian by:

Computer Science Press, Inc.
11 Taft Court
Rockville, Maryland 20850 U.S.A.
ISBN 0-914894-19-6

Pitman Publishing Ltd.
39 Parker Street
London WC2B 5PB
Great Britain
ISBN 0 273-01 220-7

6   82 81

Library of Congress Cataloging in Publication Data

Findlay, William.
    Pascal, an introduction to methodical programming.

    (Computer software engineering series)
    Includes index.
    1. PASCAL (Computer program language) I. Watt, David Anthony, joint author. II. Title. III. Series: Computer software engineering series (Potomac, Md.)
QA76.73.P35F56   001.6'424   78-11540
ISBN 0-914894-19-6

Preface

This book is intended for use in conjunction with a first course in computer programming based on the programming language Pascal. The reader is assumed to have had no previous exposure to computers, and to have only elementary mathematics. Programming principles, good style and a methodical approach to program development are emphasized, with the intention that the book should be useful even to those who must later write programs in a language other than Pascal. Thus our primary objective is simply to teach readers how to write good programs.

A secondary objective is to present an introduction to Pascal. In this respect the book should be useful not only to novices but also to readers with some limited experience of programming in another language.

Pascal was introduced in 1971 by Professor Niklaus Wirth. His aim was to make available a language which would allow programming to be taught as a systematic discipline and in which the techniques of both "scientific" and "commercial" programming could be convincingly demonstrated. The adoption of Pascal has been rapid and widespread, to the extent that it has become the lingua franca of computing science.

For our present purposes what is really important is the clarity with which fundamental programming concepts may be expressed in Pascal. Most of the book is devoted to a treatment of these fundamentals, presented in such a way that the reader should be convinced of the need for each language feature before he is shown how it is realized in Pascal. Since Pascal contains only a few features which are not truly fundamental, these remaining features are also covered, briefly, for the sake of completeness.

Use of the book

The best way to acquire a methodical approach to programming is subconsciously, by imitation, and the best time to start is right at the beginning. The technique of programming by stepwise refinement is therefore imparted mainly by consistent example throughout the book. Nevertheless, two chapters are devoted exclusively to programming methodology. The first, Chapter 7, introduces the methodology by means of a case study, and is placed early enough to encourage good programming habits from the start. The second, Chapter 20, applies the methodology to realistically-sized problems, by means of two further case studies. Although this chapter comes at the end of the book, the case studies can and should be read at an earlier stage: Case Study II after Chapter 16, and Case Study III after Chapter 17.

The main text falls naturally into six parts. Part I (First Steps in Programming) aims to bring the novice as soon as possible to the stage of writing and testing complete programs in a methodical manner. This part covers the INTEGER and BOOLEAN data types, input and output, and the basic control structures of sequencing, selection and repetition. Its highlights are the first complete program, in Chapter 4, and the introduction of a methodology, in Chapter 7. Part II (More Data Types) covers the remaining simple data types, such as CHAR and REAL, and arrays. Part III (More Control Structures) completes the treatment of control structures. Part IV (Subprograms) introduces functions and procedures. This is the pivot of the book - the reader who has mastered the material up to this point can reasonably call himself a programmer. Part V (More Data Structures) completes the coverage of Pascal's rich variety of data structures with records, strings, files, sets and pointers. Most of these features are not found in many other programming languages, but they contribute substantially to Pascal's expressive power. Part VI (Programming Methodology) consists of the chapter of case studies.

Some of the topics could be skipped on a first reading, and are so marked in the list of contents and in the text. These same topics may be omitted altogether if time presses.

Examples

Every non-trivial example used in this book has been tested on a computer. We challenge readers to find any errors in them!

Exercises

Each chapter is followed by a set of exercises. The more difficult exercises are marked with asterisks (*). Some of the exercises are intended to be answered on paper, to provide practice in the use of the language features introduced in the chapter. Answers to a selection of such exercises are provided. The remaining exercises are designated programming exercises, which involve the writing of complete programs to be be run and tested on a computer. Practical experience of this nature is essential to every programmer. (Not all the programming exercises need be attempted.)

A programming course should be supplemented by a programming laboratory, in which a series of programming exercises selected by the course organizer should be undertaken. The programming exercises herein may be used to assist in such a selection.

References

We have not attempted to write a work of reference, but we hope that the arrangement of the material, together with the appendices and the index, will assist the reader to find information on specific points. The standard reference on Pascal is "Pascal User Manual and Report" by Kathleen Jensen and Niklaus Wirth (Springer-Verlag, New York-Heidelberg-Berlin, 1975). For those wishing to study programming further we can wholeheartedly recommend "Algorithms + Data Structures = Programs" by Niklaus Wirth (Prentice-Hall, Englewood Cliffs, New Jersey, 1976).

Acknowledgments

Like all programmers, we owe a great debt to Professor Edsger Dijkstra, whose insights into the creative aspects of programming we have attempted to reflect. Equally, we wish to acknowledge the work of Professor Niklaus Wirth, whose programming language Pascal is by far the best tool available today for teaching the fundamental concepts of programming.

We also wish to thank our colleagues in the Computing Science Department of Glasgow University for their encouragement and advice, and in particular Dr John Jeacocke whose perceptive comments were of great assistance. Our gratitude goes to Professor D.C. Gilles for allowing us ready access to the Department's PDP 11/40 computer, which we used to prepare and type camera-ready copy.

W. Findlay
D. A. Watt

April 1978

Contents

PART IV   SUBPROGRAMS

PART V   MORE DATA STRUCTURES

I First steps in programming
1 Computers and programming

1.1 INTRODUCTION

There can be few people, at least in the industrialized countries of the world, who have never had any contact with computers. Computers are now routinely used for mundane tasks such as producing bank statements, financial reports, electricity bills and payslips. Hotel and airline reservation systems have been made possible by computers. In industry, computers control machine tools and chemical plant. Scientists use computers to analyse experimental data, doctors generate "cross-section" X-ray pictures, psychologists simulate mental processes. Manned and unmanned space exploration would hardly be possible without the assistance of computers. On the frivolous side, computers have been programmed to play games such as backgammon and chess (but not very well). More ominously, military applications have a long history.

Computing has grown from nothing, just thirty years ago, to a position as one of the world's largest industries. There no sign that this expansion is slowing down. Indeed the development of cheap integrated circuits means that domestic and personal computers are now becoming practical. These will more and more invade everyday life as domestic appliances, motor vehicles, communications systems and the like come increasingly to depend on them. This accelerating process has rightly been called the Second Industrial Revolution. Nobody can yet foresee with any certainty what the ultimate consequences for society may be, but it is already clear that vast changes lie ahead for us all.

Consider the impact of personal calculators on accepted ideas about education and numeracy. Computer technology will soon have a similar effect in all areas of clerical and skilled manual work. This book was prepared using a computer, making it considerably less expensive than would be possible with traditional printing technology. On the other hand the craft of the compositor has been made redundant, and the end product lacks the elegance he might have given it. Concerns like these make it imperative that computers be understood as widely as possible.

One of the most common misconceptions is that computers are "problem-solving" machines. Nothing could be further from the truth. In fact the succesful application of computers is made possible only by finding solutions to problems which computers themselves have created. The most obvious of these is that a computer is useless without a program to control it. The writing of good computer programs is both a vital part of the modern economy and a fascinating intellectual exercise. Such is the topic of this book.

1.2 HARDWARE AND SOFTWARE

Early computers filled large rooms with tall metal racks on which were fixed thousands of vacuum tubes, tanks of hot mercury and panels of flashing lights. The resemblance to an ironmonger's store was so compelling that the computer engineers of the time wryly talked about their creations as "hardware". Nowadays a considerably more powerful computer fits easily in a briefcase, but the principles of its operation are the same.

The hardware of every digital computer consists of a processor, a store and an assortment of peripheral devices. The processor is the unit which actually performs the calculations. It contains a control unit to direct operations, as well as an arithmetic unit. The latter is equivalent to an electronic calculator, but much faster, being capable of a million or more operations per second. To make use of this speed the processor must be able to access its data equally quickly. Retaining data for rapid access by the processor is the job of the computer's store. Some calculators have a handful of "registers" in which numbers can be kept. The store of a modest computer contains tens of thousands of registers. A calculator's numeric keys and display correspond to the peripherals or input/output devices of a computer. These allow data to be placed in the store and results to be taken out. Though very fast by human standards, peripherals are usually much slower than the processor and store.

A calculator is given instructions by pressing its function keys. However the great speed of a computer would be wasted if it could not be supplied with instructions as quickly as it obeys them. To make this possible the computer's instructions, encoded in numerical form, are held in store along with the data. The computer works in a cycle as follows.

(1) The control unit fetches the next instruction from store.
(2) The instruction is decoded into electronic signals by the control unit.
(3) In response to these signals the arithmetic unit, the store, or a peripheral device carries out the instruction.
(4) The whole cycle repeats from step (1).

In this way long sequences of instructions can be obeyed automatically at the full speed of the processor. Such a sequence of instructions is called a program.

Computer instructions are very simple in their effect, the following examples being typical.
(a) Read an item of data into store from an input device.
(b) Copy an item of data from one register to another.
(c) Add the contents of two registers and place the sum in a third.
(d) If the content of a register represents a negative number, take the next instruction from a different part of the program; otherwise continue with the next instruction in sequence.
(e) Write an item of data from store to an output device.

It has been proved that anything which can be computed, in principle, can be computed in a finite number of steps by a program consisting of elementary operations such as these. Such a program is called an algorithm. It has also been proved that there are results which are not computable by any machine whatsoever. In these cases it may be possible to compute an approximation to the desired result. A program to do this is called a heuristic. Heuristics are also useful when an algorithm exists but is impractically slow or needs too much store.

The collection of all the programs available in a computer system constitutes its software. This word was invented to emphasize that the programs are just as important as the hardware. It also contrasts them effectively. Hardware is visible, solid and substantial; software is somewhat intangible. The hardware of a computer system is not easily changed; the software is usually in a state of flux.

One of the most important parts of the software is the operating system, a set of control programs which are kept permanently in store. The operating system carries out many of the routine tasks needed to prepare and run a user's job, e.g. deciding which job to run next, making ready its input, bringing the user's program into store, allocating it some processor time, and so on.

1.3 PROGRAMMING LANGUAGES

The earliest computers were programmed in machine code: i.e., by giving them instructions directly in numerical form. However the drawbacks were soon recognized.

(a) Because of the very primitive nature of machine instructions, machine-code programming is both tedious and error-prone.

(b) For the same reason, machine-code programs are difficult to understand and to modify.

(c) Programming is a time-consuming and expensive business. It would be a great saving to be able to transfer programs between computers, but a machine-code program is specific to one model of computer and will not work on any other.

Why not write programs in English? Computing is not unique in requiring the detailed description of sequences of actions: there are many similar examples in daily life. However, anyone who has ever struggled with the often mystifying instructions in motor maintenance handbooks, do-it-yourself manuals, or recipe books will readily agree that English is far from ideal for the job. In fact the glories of English - its vast scope, its subtlety, its potential for ambiguity and metaphor - must be considered severe disadvantages when the aim is literalness, accuracy and completeness. A programming language must aim at the truth, the whole truth, and nothing but the truth.

English is at the opposite extreme from machine code and precisely for that reason must be rejected as a medium for practical computer programming. What is needed is a middle way: one which combines the readability and generality of English with the directness and precision of machine code. Because of their position relative to machine code, languages of this sort are called high-level languages.

Knitting patterns offer an interesting example where a similar problem has been faced. A knitting pattern is comparable in complexity with a modest computer program, so it is understandable that a special "knitting language" has evolved. It borrows many words from English, but these are used in stereotyped ways and with definite meanings. Another noteworthy feature of a knitting pattern is its division into two parts: a list of the materials and tools needed, followed by a list of instructions stating how to use them. The programming language used in this book, Pascal, shares both of these characteristics.

Any language can be studied from two points of view: that of its grammar, or syntax, and that of its meaning, or semantics. A good understanding of both is needed to use it properly. We will find that the semantics of Pascal can be described adequately in English. On the other hand a description of its syntax in English would be very tedious. Instead we will use a pictorial device, the syntax diagram. This is best explained by an example. Stated in English, the Pascal definition of an Integer Number is the following. "An Integer Number is a sequence of one or more Decimal Digits. A Decimal Digit is the character '0', or '1', or '2', or '3', or '4', or '5', or '6', or '7', or '8', or '9'." Exactly the same information is conveyed by Figure 1.1.

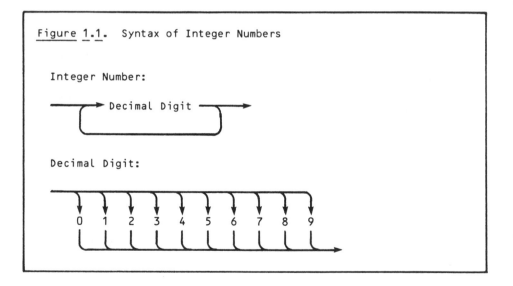

Figure 1.1. Syntax of Integer Numbers

Integer Number:

Decimal Digit

Decimal Digit:

0 1 2 3 4 5 6 7 8 9

This can be understood by following the arrows through the diagram, from entry to exit, and writing down a specimen of everything you pass. When you come to a fork, either path may be chosen. As a slightly more complicated example, Figure 1.2 defines an Identifier, widely used in Pascal to give things names. The English equivalent of this diagram is "An Identifier is a sequence of characters beginning with a Letter and followed by zero or more Letters or Decimal Digits." The definition of Letter is omitted: it is tedious in any form.

4

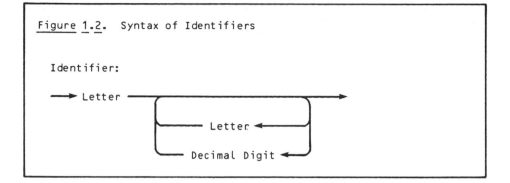

Figure 1.2. Syntax of Identifiers

Identifier:

Letter

Letter

Decimal Digit

A program written in Pascal cannot be directly performed by the hardware of a computer. To make it executable it must be translated from Pascal into an equivalent set of machine code instructions. This translation can be specified rigorously enough to make it a suitable task for a computer program. Three programs are involved here: the translator program, or compiler; the user's Pascal text, or source program; and the equivalent machine code, or object program. Thus a Pascal program is run in two distinct stages.

(1) The Pascal compiler is brought into store and activated. It causes the computer to read the source program, check it for errors, and convert it into the corresponding object program.
(2) The object program is left in store as the result of stage (1). It is activated in turn and reads input, performs computations, and writes output in exactly the manner described by the original Pascal program.

Programs often contain errors in the use of the programming language and these are reported by the compiler during stage (1). The report usually takes the form of an error message or a number which refers to a list of error messages. These error messages are often helpful in finding the cause of the trouble. (However, the compiler may be misled by an error into taking later, perfectly correct, parts of a program as erroneous. Thus one genuine error can cause a whole group of messages to be output, many of which are spurious. Nothing more forcefully reminds a programmer that computers do not understand the programs which drive them.)

EXERCISES 1

1.1. Which of the following are valid Identifiers, according to the syntax of Figure 1.2?

(a) SEVEN, (b) VII, (c) NMR7, (d) 7, (e) KERMIT, (f) JOE 90,
(g) ABCDEFGHIJKLMNOPQRSTUVWXYZ

1.2. Write down examples of Sentences generated by the following syntax diagrams.

Sentence:

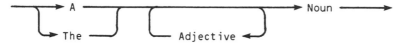

Subject:

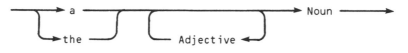

Object:

Adjective:

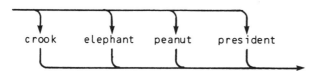

Noun:

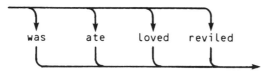

Verb:

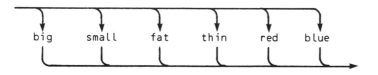

1.3. Which of the following are valid Sentences, according to the syntax of the previous exercise?

(a) The big fat president was a crook.
(b) The reds reviled the president.
(c) The elephant ate peanuts.

(d) The small, thin president loved a peanut.
(e) The thin crook was a red.
(f) A elephant was a elephant.

1.4. Write down examples of Chemical Formulas generated by the following syntax diagrams.

Chemical Formula:

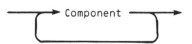

Component:

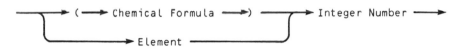

Element:

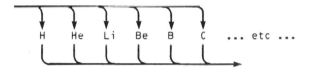

2 Data: types, constants and variables

2.1 DATA AND DATA TYPES

The word "data" means "the things given". We use the term to refer to the values which must be supplied to a piece of program before it can produce any results. Data may originate outside the computer, in which case it must be read from an input device, or it may already be available in the computer's store, having been placed there as a result of some computation.

An item of data represents some fact, observation or idea about the world. People can recognize data in speech, in pictures, in printed text and in many other forms. However, the input devices of a computer are much less adaptable than human sensory organs and almost all data presented to computers is in the form of a text, a string of characters from some character set. Such texts are usually punched on cards for input by means of a card reader, or typed directly into the computer at a terminal. There are devices which permit the input of sound and pictures to computers, but they are not common, and even these devices work by converting the data to what is basically a form of text.

Printed material has traditionally used a large set of symbols. The alphabet is often available in bold letters, in italics, and in many sizes and styles. There is also a huge assortment of symbols for use in mathematics and other specialized fields. For economic reasons computer input is much more restrictive. In fact most computers can process only a small, fixed set of characters. This will certainly include the capital letters, the decimal digits, the usual punctuation marks and a few of the mathematical signs.

Even this restricted set of characters allows a vast range of data to be input to the computer. The digits alone allow us to write integer numbers and these can represent a great variety of things, for example populations, votes, dates, sums of money, and so on. The digits together with the decimal point allow us to write numbers containing fractions (real numbers). Thus we can represent smoothly-varying quantities such as distances, times, weights, volumes and probabilities. With the letters and mathematical symbols we can input formulas. Finally, the punctuation marks allow us to input human languages: both "natural" languages such as English and "programming" languages such as Pascal.

A very important characteristic of a data item is its type, as this determines how it can be represented and processed. Each of the examples in the previous paragraph is of a different type. To pick just two: populations and sums of money have nothing in common, apart from the fact that they can both be counted. It would make no sense to add the population of London to the cash holdings of the Bank of England. The addition would give a numerical result that did not correspond to any "fact, observation, or idea about the world". By contrast, adding the population of London to that of Paris does make sense. The result corresponds to "the total population of the capital cities of the U.K. and France". It is very easy to make a computer do entirely meaningless calculations and one of the best ways to avoid this mistake is type checking: ensuring that the types of the data involved are compatible with the operations to be performed upon them.

In programming languages such as Pascal every item of data is considered to be of some specific type and there are rigid rules about how each type may be used. When a program is being translated into machine code the compiler checks it to verify that these rules have been obeyed. For practical reasons it is not possible to implement as many types as there actually are in the world - only radical differences of type are recognized. To take an extreme example: in most programming languages numbers are treated quite differently from characters of text. Thus the compiler would reject an attempt to find the logarithm of the ampersand symbol. However most programming languages (Pascal among them) treat all integer numbers alike. Adding a population to a sum of money would not be detected as an error. (Pascal does, however, permit finer distinctions of type to be made than any other important programming language. This is a major factor contributing to its popularity.)

A consequence of this is that the data items processed by a program are imperfect representations of the world, because they lack many of the properties of the original information. At best they are more or less approximate models. Much of the interest of programming lies in choosing good models of the objects and processes the program is meant to represent, then seeing their behaviour when the program is run on a computer.

2.2 CONSTANTS AND VARIABLES

Some of the data used in a program never change. For example, the ratio of the circumference of a circle to its diameter is approximately 3.14159 and this is an invariable fact. Other data change very slowly by comparison with the frequency of their use. For example, the speed of light is measured more accurately every few years, but between measurements the current estimate is used in millions of calculations. Such data are modelled in a program by constants, in other words by stating their values literally. It is often useful to give a symbolic name to a constant. The name can then be used throughout the program whenever the value of the constant is required. A suggestive name such as PI, rather than the obscure 3.14159, makes a program easier to read.

Other data are intrinsically subject to change. For example, in a program summing a list of numbers, the running total changes every time an item from the list is added to it. In a salary calculation the nett pay starts out equal to the gross pay and changes as income tax, union dues and other deductions are taken from it. Such data are modelled in a program by variables.

In programming a variable is best thought of as a container for a value. We will speak loosely about "the value of a variable", but we should really say, in more precise language, "the value contained in a variable". Like a physical container a variable may be empty, in which case we will say that its value is undefined. Attempting to use an undefined value from an empty variable is one of the most common mistakes in programming. Variables can be both created and destroyed in a program: the value of a newly-created variable is undefined. Once a value has been placed in a variable it stays there until specific action is taken by the program to replace it, or until the variable itself is destroyed. Values of different types require variables of corresponding types to hold them. Again, we speak loosely of "an integer variable" when we really mean "a variable capable of holding an integer value".

Like constants, the variables in our programs have names. This is essential, not a convenience as it was with constants. We must be able to refer to specific variables independently of their values, since their values may change. In a program a variable is created by a declaration. To declare a variable it is necessary to specify both its type and its name. The instruction which alters the value of a variable is called an assignment statement. An assignment statement specifies a variable and an expression. When it is obeyed the expression is evaluated and the result is copied (assigned) to the variable. There are many other kinds of statement: some of them can be used to change variables, others use the existing values of variables.

More generally, definitions and declarations convey information about data types and data objects to the compiler; whereas statements specify actions to be taken by the computer when the program is run. (The term "statement" is rather misleading but unfortunately has become universal, for historical reasons. Statements would better be called "commands" or "instructions".)

You may like to think of the various types of data as each having a characteristic shape. Variables would then be thought of as suitably-shaped boxes. We will often represent variables by boxes in this book. Unfortunately it is not practical to print boxes of several shapes, so all our boxes will be rectangular, regardless of type. When we picture a variable as a box, we will attach its name to the box as a "label".

2.3 DEFINITIONS AND DECLARATIONS IN PASCAL

In Pascal constant definitions and variable declarations come at the head of a program, before any of the statements which make use of them. Furthermore, the constant definitions precede the variable declarations. This strict order tends to make the program easier to understand (both for the human reader and for the compiler).

It is a general rule of Pascal that every identifier must be defined or declared before it is used.

A constant definition looks like an equation. On the left is the name to be defined, this is followed by the "=" sign, and this is followed in turn by the value to be ascribed to the constant. All of this can be summarized very concisely in pictorial form, by means of a syntax diagram: see Figure 2.1. This diagram does not give the syntax of Constant, as that would take us into other matters prematurely. For the time being, assume that any number is allowable.

Several constant definitions may be given, or none. If there are any they must be separated from each other by semicolons, and the complete group must be introduced by the symbol CONST.

{The semicolon is widely used in Pascal to form lists of definitions, declarations and statements, so it is wise to be quite clear about its function. The Pascal semicolon does not "terminate" things, unlike the full stop at the end of this paragraph. Rather, it separates them, more like the commas in this sentence; or the semicolon for that matter. Note that Example 2.1 does not end with a semicolon. Attention to this point will avoid much grief from trivial syntax errors in your programs.}

Figure 2.1. Syntax of Constant Definitions

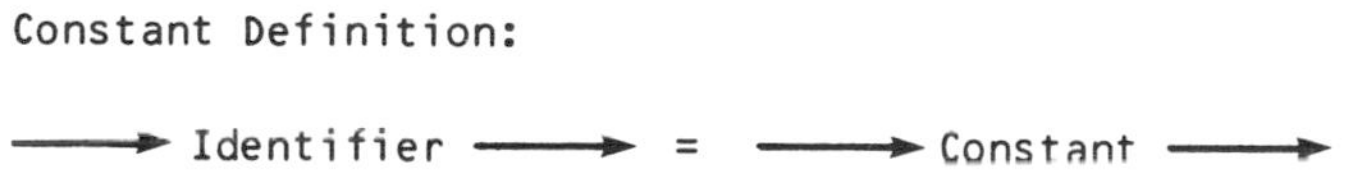

Constant Definition:

⟶ Identifier ⟶ = ⟶ Constant ⟶

Example 2.1

```
CONST
   WORKINGDAYS = 5;
   WEEKSPERYEAR = 52;
   PI = 3.14159;
   SPEEDOFLIGHT = 299792.0
```

These constant definitions establish two identifiers for integer constants (WORKINGDAYS and WEEKSPERYEAR) and two identifiers for real constants (PI and SPEEDOFLIGHT).

There is no ambiguity about the type of a constant identifier. It is the same as the type of the value to the right of the "=" sign and Pascal has been designed so that this type is always obvious to the compiler.

Variable declarations are a little more complicated than constant definitions and quite different in appearance. The variable declaration part of a program begins with the symbol VAR. This is followed by a group of one or more variable declarations, these being separated by semicolons. Each variable declaration consists of a list of identifiers, separated by commas, then a colon, and finally a type. See Figure 2.2 for the syntax diagram. Again, it would be premature to disclose the syntax of Type, so take it on trust that INTEGER and REAL are allowable.

{The following is a reliable general rule in Pascal: <u>within</u> definitions, declarations and statements, commas are used to separate the components of a list.}

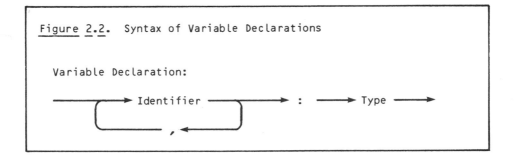

Figure 2.2. Syntax of Variable Declarations

Variable Declaration:

Example 2.2

```
VAR
    WEEKLYPAY, YEARLYPAY : INTEGER;
    RADIUS, CIRCUMFERENCE, ORBIT : REAL;
    RATEOFPAY : INTEGER
```

Here we declare three INTEGER variables (WEEKLYPAY, YEARLYPAY and RATEOFPAY) and three REAL variables (RADIUS, CIRCUMFERENCE and ORBIT). In terms of our "boxes", we can picture the effect of these declarations as follows, where the question marks act as reminders that the values of newly-declared variables are undefined:

WEEKLYPAY [?]   YEARLYPAY [?]   RATEOFPAY [?]

CIRCUMFERENCE [?]   RADIUS [?]   ORBIT [?]

2.4 ASSIGNMENT STATEMENTS

A value is copied into a variable when the computer obeys an assignment statement. In Pascal assignment statements have a simple syntax. On the left is specified the variable whose contents are to be replaced, following this is the ":=" sign , and on the right is an expression whose value is to be assigned to the variable. This reads naturally if the ":=" sign is pronounced as "becomes equal to". Figure 2.3 contains the syntax diagram. (An expression is a formula by which a value is computed. The syntax of Expression is probably the most complicated part of any programming language, and Pascal is no exception. This syntax is defined fully in Appendix 1.3, but it is inadvisable to study that until rather more of the background has been covered. We begin by looking at INTEGER expressions in Chapter 3.)

Figure 2.3. Syntax of Assignment Statements

Assignment Statement:

⟶ Variable ⟶ := ⟶ Expression ⟶

Example 2.3

Using the constants and variables introduced in Examples 2.1 and 2.2, the assignment statements

    WEEKLYPAY := 100;
    YEARLYPAY := WEEKLYPAY * WEEKSPERYEAR

(where "*" is the multiplication sign of Pascal) will leave the values of the variables WEEKLYPAY and YEARLYPAY as follows:

WEEKLYPAY [100]   YEARLYPAY [5200]

Now consider the curious-looking assignment statement

    WEEKLYPAY := WEEKLYPAY + 5

This assignment statement takes the current value of WEEKLYPAY, adds 5, and finally assigns the result to WEEKLYPAY. Thus the effect of this assignment statement is to increase the value of WEEKLYPAY by 5:

WEEKLYPAY [105]   YEARLYPAY [5200]

There are two important points to note here.
(a) When a value is assigned to a variable, its previous value (if any) is lost forever.
(b) The computer does not automatically change the value of YEARLYPAY when we change the value of WEEKLYPAY. The computer will obey only explicit instructions. If we wish the value of YEARLYPAY to be changed accordingly, we must ensure that the assignment statement YEARLYPAY := WEEKLYPAY * WEEKSPERYEAR is obeyed again.

13

It is important not to be misled by the superficial similarity of assignment statements and constant definitions. The latter are static, giving a name to a fixed value (at "compile time"), and have no effect when the program is obeyed by the computer. Assignment statements on the other hand are dynamic. Each time an assignment is performed by the computer (at "run time") the value copied into the variable may be different. It is precisely to point out this crucial difference that the ":=" sign is used in assignments in place of the "=" sign.

Type checking is particularly effective at finding errors in assignments. The type-compatibility rule for assignments is quite simple: any value of any type may be assigned, but generally only to a variable of the same type. Thus we are guaranteed that the value always "fits" its container. For example, we can assign the value 100, but not PI nor the ampersand character, to the INTEGER variable WEEKLYPAY.

3 The data type INTEGER

3.1 INTEGER CONSTANTS AND VARIABLES

The INTEGER type in Pascal allows us to represent, store and process
integer numbers. In theory the set of integer numbers extends outward
from zero to numbers with arbitrarily large positive or negative values.
But this is a finite world, modelled by an even more finite computer,
and infinite sets must be cut down to a practical size. Pascal
recognizes this fact of life by providing, automatically, a constant
identifier MAXINT, whose value is the largest integer number which can
be handled by the computer. (MAXINT is an example of a predefined
constant; you can use it without defining it yourself.) Thus the Pascal
INTEGER type contains all the integer values in the range:

   -MAXINT, ... , -1, 0, +1, ... , +MAXINT

(Typical values of MAXINT are 32767 on a minicomputer and 2147483647 on
a large computer.)

Pascal is so defined that the outcome of any arithmetic on INTEGER
values will be correct only if all the operands, and all the
intermediate results, lie in the range from -MAXINT to +MAXINT. It is
the programmer's responsibility to ensure that this is the case. If the
allowable range is exceeded the result of the arithmetic is
unpredictable. This is called overflow and the program must be
considered to have failed.

INTEGER constants are written as a sequence of decimal digits,
optionally preceded by a sign: "-" indicates a negative number, "+" or
no sign indicates a positive number. See Figure 3.1 and Example 3.1.
Chapter 2 showed how INTEGER variables are declared. No more need be
said here.

Example 3.1

```
CONST
   POSITIVE = +1;
   NEGATIVE = -POSITIVE;
   BIGGEST = MAXINT;
   SMALLEST = -MAXINT;
   EMERGENCY = 999
```

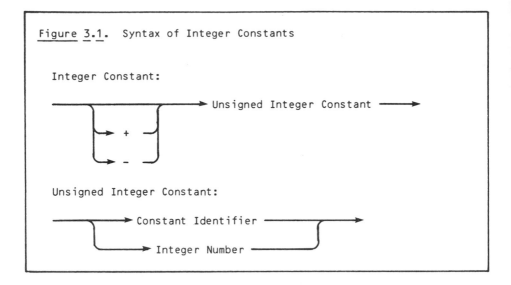

Figure 3.1. Syntax of Integer Constants

Integer Constant:

Unsigned Integer Constant

Unsigned Integer Constant:

Constant Identifier

Integer Number

3.2 INTEGER EXPRESSIONS AND ASSIGNMENTS

Given any two INTEGER values we can calculate a new INTEGER value by addition, subtraction, multiplication or division. Pascal uses the conventional notation for arithmetic operators, modified to suit the computer's character set. Addition is denoted by "+", subtraction by "-", multiplication by "*" and division by the symbol DIV. It is also possible to obtain the remainder from a division, using the symbol MOD (short for "modulo") in place of DIV.

Dividing one integer number by another does not always give an integral result: there may be a fractional part. To ensure that DIV always yields an integer any fractional part in the result is discarded (e.g. 7 DIV 2 = 3). The MOD operator is then defined precisely by:

    a MOD b = a - (a DIV b)*b

The normal priorities of these operators apply in Pascal, so any multiplications or divisions in an expression are performed before any additions or subtractions. If this is not what is wanted then parentheses, "(" and ")", can be used to override the priority rules.

It is allowable to prefix a sign to the first term of an expression. The "-" sign is the negation operator: the value of -x is the negative of x. The "+" sign is the identity operator: the value of +x is the same as the value of x, so the "+" may always be omitted.

Pascal has no operator for raising one number to the power of another, chiefly because it is very difficult to specify such an operator in a way that is both simple and consistent with the type rules. In partial compensation SQR(x), a function which returns the square of x, is provided. It will nearly always be more efficient to evaluate SQR(x) than (x*x). One other useful function is ABS(x), which

16

returns the absolute value of x (i.e. if x is negative ABS(x) = -x; otherwise ABS(x) = x).

SQR and ABS are examples of <u>predeclared</u> <u>functions</u>, which are provided in Pascal to augment the more common operators.

Example 3.2

On each of the following lines is a group of three equivalent expressions. The first in each group is written in the simplest way possible, the rest show some alternative formulations. As these examples illustrate, the sparing use of parentheses may clarify a complicated expression and overuse may have the opposite effect. Judicious spacing further improves readability.

```
-X                  (-X)                (-(X))
X+Y                 (X+Y)               ((X)+(Y))
X*Y+Z               (X*Y) + Z           (((X)*(Y))+(Z))
P*V DIV R * T       (P*V) DIV R * T     ((P*V) DIV R) * T
A*B*C*D-I-J*K*L     (A*B*C*D)-I-(J*K*L) (A*B*C*D)-(I+J*K*L)
SQR(SQR(X))         SQR(X*X)            X*X*X*X
```

Assignment statements can be used to alter the values of INTEGER variables, as for every other type. The right-hand side of such an assignment statement must be an INTEGER expression. See Example 2.3.

EXERCISES 3

3.1. Write constant definitions for the INTEGER constants DAYSINWEEK and YARDSPERMILE (or METRESPERKM).

3.2. Write declarations for the INTEGER variables GROSSPAY, TAX, UNIONDUES and NETTPAY.

3.3. What are the resulting values of the variables when the following assignment statements are obeyed in sequence? Draw suitable box diagrams.

```
UNIONDUES := 20;   GROSSPAY := 4800;   TAX := GROSSPAY DIV 3;
NETTPAY := GROSSPAY - TAX - UNIONDUES
```

3.4*. Write declarations and statements to calculate the minimum number of bank-notes and coins needed to pay out SUM in cash, assuming SUM is given as a multiple of the basic unit of your currency.

4 Input and output; the complete program

4.1 INPUT AND OUTPUT OF DATA

So far we have seen how to write constant definitions, variable declarations and assignment statements. The latter can be used to compute new values from values which have been computed previously and from constants. These program elements allow us to specify computations of a restricted kind, but they provide no means to vary the data on which the computations are performed.

Example 4.1

Assuming the variable declaration

    A, D, N, SUM : INTEGER

the following statements, obeyed in sequence, compute the sum of the first N terms of the arithmetic series A, A+D, A+2*D, ..., given the values 1 for A, 2 for D and 10 for N:

    A := 1 ;
    D := 2 ;
    N := 10 ;
    SUM := N * (2*A + (N-1)*D) DIV 2

If we wish to compute the series sum for different values of A, D and N, we have no alternative but to modify the "program" itself, specifically its first three statements.

Now, the whole point of programming a computer is to be able to write a program once, and then make it work with many different sets of data. In our example, we would prefer the values stored in A, D and N to be supplied somehow each time the program is run, rather than being part of the program itself and therefore fixed. This would allow us to supply different values each time.

Another limitation of our "program" is that the computed value is simply placed in a storage location (SUM), where it remains out of sight. Thus we also need a means of getting results out of the computer while our program is running.

18

The separation of a program and its data is a fundamental idea in computing. We should perceive a program as a general set of instructions for performing some computation. A program can be run many times, each time being supplied with different data upon which this computation is to be performed. The individual data items supplied in this way are "read" into the computer in response to explicit input instructions in the program; and results of the computation are "written" out, in some suitable form, in response to explicit output instructions in the program. All computers are equipped with "input devices" which allow data to be read by a program, and with "output devices" which allow data to be written.

Most commonly all the input data to be read by a program is prepared in advance by the computer user, perhaps by punching the data on cards. These cards are read by a card-reader when the program is run on the computer. The output written by the program will be printed on paper, by a line-printer, and the printed results returned to the user after the program has completed its run. This mode of computing is called "batch" computing.

Alternatively the computer user might use a terminal connected to the computer. While his program is running, the user types the input data on the terminal's keyboard. This data is read by the program, and the output written by the program returns directly to the terminal, where it is either printed on paper or displayed on a screen. The terminal acts as a combination of an input device (the keyboard) and an output device (the printer or screen). This mode of computing is called "interactive" computing.

Whatever mode of computing you will use, your programs will contain input instructions which cause data to be read from some input device, and output instructions which cause data (results) to be written to some output device.

4.2 BASIC INPUT

The role of an input instruction is to read an item of data and store it in a variable, so that subsequently it can be used in some computation. In Pascal this role is performed by the READ statement.

Example 4.1 (continued)

We can vary the data on which our "program" works by replacing the first three assignment statements by READ statements:

```
READ (A) ;
READ (D) ;
READ (N) ;
SUM := N * (2*A + (N-1)*D) DIV 2
```

Now if we supply the following input data, for example:

        -3 4 100

the data item -3 will be read and assigned to A, then the data item 4
will be read and assigned to D, then the data item 100 will be read
and assigned to N. We can make the "program" perform a different
calculation simply by running it again with different input.

    In general, the effect of the READ statement READ(V), where V is an
INTEGER variable, is to scan forwards through the input data (skipping
blank characters) until a data item is found; the value of this data
item (which must be an integer number, possibly signed) is then assigned
to V.
    The three consecutive READ statements in Example 4.1 could be
combined into a single READ statement with the same effect:

    READ (A, D, N)

A, D and N are called parameters of the READ statement. A READ
statement may have any number of parameters, all of which must be
variables, and for each of these variables one data item is read.

4.3 BASIC OUTPUT

The role of an output instruction is to get results out of the computer
in some suitable form, e.g. printed on paper or displayed on a screen.
In Pascal this role is performed by the WRITE statement.

Example 4.2

    Continuing from Example 4.1, we could write out the value of the
series sum by the following WRITE statement:

    WRITE (SUM)

    The following statements, executed in sequence, will read values
for A, D and N, compute the series sum, and write out the values of
A, D, N and the series sum:

    READ (A, D, N) ;
    SUM := N * (2*A + (N-1)*D) DIV 2 ;
    WRITE (A, D, N, SUM)

For example, if the input data is

    10 -2 8

then the output would look like this:

          10   -2   8   24

Observe that a WRITE statement, like a READ statement, may have any number of parameters. However, each parameter of WRITE may be an expression, not necessarily a simple variable, and it is the value of this expression which is written.

Example 4.3

Assuming that M and N are INTEGER variables and that values have been assigned to them, the following statement writes the values of M and N followed by their sum, difference and product:

    WRITE (M, N, M+N, M-N, M*N)

4.4 THE COMPLETE PROGRAM

To build a complete Pascal program, we must collect together all the necessary definitions, declarations and statements.

Example 4.4

Here is an example of a complete Pascal program which performs a simple tax calculation:

    PROGRAM COMPUTETAX (INPUT, OUTPUT) ;

    (* This program computes a taxpayer's tax payment
       for a year, given as input the taxpayer's annual
       income and number of children. It is assumed
       that tax is calculated at one-third of income
       less tax allowances, where the allowances consist
       of a personal allowance of $5000 plus a child
       allowance of $1000 per child.   *)

    CONST
       PERSONALALLOWANCE = 5000 ;
       CHILDALLOWANCE   = 1000 ;

    VAR
       NMROFCHILDREN   : INTEGER ;
       INCOME, TAXABLEINCOME, TAX : INTEGER ;

```
BEGIN
READ (INCOME, NMROFCHILDREN) ;
TAXABLEINCOME := INCOME - PERSONALALLOWANCE -
                 NMROFCHILDREN * CHILDALLOWANCE ;
     (* ... taxable income is income less allowances *)
TAX := TAXABLEINCOME DIV 3 ;
     (* ... tax is calculated as a whole number of $ *)
WRITE (INCOME, TAXABLEINCOME, TAX, INCOME - TAX)
END .
```

This program first reads the taxpayer's income (in $) and number
of children; then it computes the taxable income and tax; and finally
it writes the income, taxable income, tax and nett income after tax.
For example, if the input data is

11000 2

then the written output from the program would look like this:

    11000   4000   1333   9667

This example illustrates all the parts of a complete program.

(1) "PROGRAM COMPUTETAX" gives a name or identifier, COMPUTETAX, to the
    program.
(2) "(INPUT, OUTPUT)" specifies that this program performs both input
    and output. INPUT and OUTPUT are called program parameters. Until
    Chapter 17, where program parameters will be treated more fully,
    take it on trust that INPUT must be present if the program reads any
    input, and that OUTPUT must be present if the program writes any
    output.
(3) The program parameters are followed by the declaration part, which
    consists of a group of constant definitions headed by CONST,
    followed by a group of variable declarations headed by VAR.
(4) The words BEGIN and END enclose the program body. The program body
    consists of a sequence of statements, separated by semicolons, and
    these statements are obeyed one after another in exactly their order
    of occurrence. The period following END marks the end of the
    program text.

    Each piece of text enclosed between the special brackets "(*" and
"*)" is called a comment. Although part of the program text, these
comments are entirely ignored by the compiler, and are included only to
help explain the program to a human reader. A comment may be placed
anywhere within a Pascal program text, except (obviously!) in the middle
of a symbol such as a word or number.
    The order of the program parts is summarized by the syntax diagrams
of Figures 4.1 and 4.2. Notice that CONST would be omitted in the

absence of any constant definitions, and that VAR would be omitted in the absence of any variable declarations.

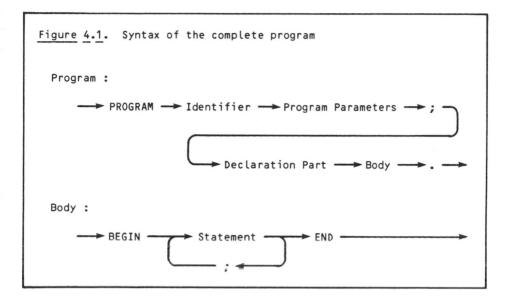

Figure 4.1. Syntax of the complete program

Program :

   ⟶ PROGRAM ⟶ Identifier ⟶ Program Parameters ⟶ ;

            ⟶ Declaration Part ⟶ Body ⟶ . ⟶

Body :

   ⟶ BEGIN ⟶ Statement ⟶ END ⟶
              ; ⟵

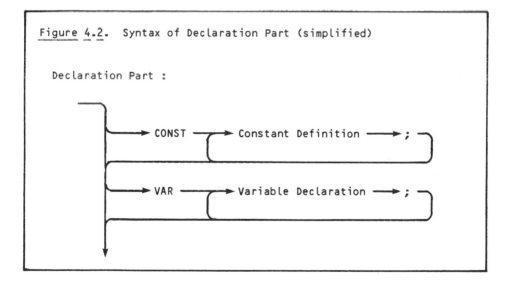

Figure 4.2. Syntax of Declaration Part (simplified)

Declaration Part :

   ⟶ CONST ⟶ Constant Definition ⟶ ;

   ⟶ VAR ⟶ Variable Declaration ⟶ ;

PROGRAM, CONST, VAR, BEGIN and END are all reserved words. They are so called because they look like identifiers but they must not be chosen as identifiers (for constants, variables or anything else). They have special, fixed, meanings in Pascal, implied by their occurrence in the

23

syntax diagrams. Pascal has thirty-five reserved words in all, which are listed in Appendix 2.1; they include the operators DIV and MOD introduced in Chapter 3 (but <u>not</u> READ and WRITE, which are ordinary identifiers).

4.5 PROGRAMMING STYLE

You probably found the first complete program, in Example 4.4, easy to understand. Partly this was because the program was very short, with only four statements. (By comparison, some programs have been written which contain more than 100000 statements!) Another reason was that the program was deliberately written in a style intended to make it readable.

Here are the main features of good programming style, as illustrated by Example 4.4.

(a) The layout of the program text has been designed for easy reading. Each constant definition, each variable declaration and each statement is on a separate line. The symbols within each line are well spaced out. The constant definitions and variable declaration are indented to make the words CONST and VAR stand out. The program text is "paragraphed" by blank lines separating the parts of the program.

(b) All the identifiers have been chosen to suggest the significance of the data they represent. For example, the variable NMROFCHILDREN is clearly intended to hold a value which is the number of children.

(c) Comments are used in the program text to summarize the function of the program and to explain how it performs its function.

It must be emphasized that these stylistic features are intended solely for the benefit of the human reader. The layout of the program text is of no concern to the compiler. (Consecutive words and numbers must, however, be spaced apart, just as in ordinary English: BEGIN N:=7 is interpreted very differently from BEGINN:=7.) Comments also are entirely ignored by the compiler. Finally, any significance suggested to the human reader by an identifier like NMROFCHILDREN is quite lost on the compiler (which understands no English); the compiler would "understand" the program just as well if the identifier N were used instead.

Example 4.5

As an illustration of <u>bad</u> programming style, let us rewrite the program of Example 4.4 without concern for layout, without comments, and with short meaningless identifiers.

```
PROGRAM COMPUTETAX(INPUT,OUTPUT);CONST PA=5000;CA=1000;VAR N:
INTEGER;I,TI,T:INTEGER;BEGIN READ(I,N);TI:=I-5000-N*1000;T:=
TI DIV 3;WRITE(I,TI,T,I-T)END.
```

This version of the program is certainly much more concise than the original version, and moreover it will produce exactly the same results as the original when run on a computer. Its only drawback, but a major one, is that it is difficult and unpleasant for human readers.

Throughout this book a reasonably consistent programming style has been adopted. We do not suggest that you should imitate this style slavishly; feel free to develop your own style. What is important is that all your programs should be written in a style which makes them easy to understand by yourself and by other people.

4.6 FURTHER INPUT AND OUTPUT

Examine the sample output from the program of Example 4.4:

    11000   4000   1333   9667

What would you make of this output if you had never seen the program which produced it? It is just a line of numbers with no indication of their significance.

Since computer output is intended ultimately to be read by ordinary people (i.e. non-programmers), it is essential that the output should be self-explanatory, with appropriate headings, captions, etc. For this purpose we need a means of writing text as well as numbers. In Pascal we can request a piece of text to be written by enclosing the desired text in apostrophes and supplying it as a parameter in a WRITE statement. This text is written out, without the apostrophes, when the WRITE statement is obeyed.

Example 4.6

The statement

    WRITE ('TAX DUE IS $', TAX)

would produce output like this:

TAX DUE IS $ 1333

The text enclosed in apostrophes is called a string. If the string itself is to contain an apostrophe, this apostrophe must be doubled to distinguish it from the apostrophe which ends the string. Thus the statement WRITE('THAT''S THE QUESTION') would write the following output:

THAT'S THE QUESTION

The output in Example 4.6 still looks rather peculiar, because of all the blank characters between the currency sign and the number. The reason for this is that each number is written in a <u>field</u> of a certain width, and if the number has too few digits then the field is filled with blank characters to the left of the number. We can control the layout by specifying explicitly what field width we require for any parameter in a WRITE statement. (If no field width is specified explicitly for an INTEGER parameter, a default field width will be assumed – typically 12, as above – but this default field width will vary from one compiler to another.)

Example <u>4.7</u>

If we know in advance that the value of TAX will not be greater than 9999, then we can modify the WRITE statement of Example 4.6 as follows:

```
WRITE ('TAX DUE IS  $', TAX:4)
```

The suffix ":4" of the parameter "TAX:4" specifies that the value of TAX is to be written in a field of 4 spaces. Now we can expect output like this:

```
TAX DUE IS  $1333
```

If we replace the WRITE statement of Example 4.4 by the following:

```
WRITE ('INCOME: $' , INCOME:5,
   '   TAXABLE: $', TAXABLEINCOME:4,
   '   TAX: $'    , TAX:4,
   '   NETT: $'   , (INCOME-TAX):5)
```

then we can expect output like this:

```
INCOME: $11000   TAXABLE: $4000   TAX: $1333   NETT: $ 9667
```


All data written by WRITE statements, whether numbers or strings or anything else, is written on a single line, as illustrated by Example 4.7. If we want to write output on <u>several</u> lines, we can use <u>WRITELN</u> instead of WRITE. WRITELN is analogous to WRITE in every respect but one: <u>after</u> a WRITELN statement has been obeyed, the current line of output is terminated and any subsequent output will be written on a new line.

Example <u>4.8</u>

If we replace the WRITE statement of Example 4.4 by the following statements:

```
WRITELN ('INCOME              $', INCOME:5) ;
WRITELN ;
WRITELN ('TAXABLE INCOME      $', TAXABLEINCOME:5) ;
WRITELN ('TAX DUE             $', TAX:5) ;
WRITELN ('NETT INCOME         $', (INCOME-TAX):5)
```

then we can expect output like this:

```
INCOME              $11000

TAXABLE INCOME      $ 4000
TAX DUE             $ 1333
NETT INCOME         $ 9667
```

Note the use of WRITELN without any parameters at all; its effect, when it immediately follows another WRITELN statement, is to write a single blank line.

We may also consider the input data to consist of a number of lines. (If the input data is punched on cards, then each card is considered to be a line of data.) This point is of no concern to the READ statement, which will automatically move on to a new line of input data if there is no more data on the current line. Thus program COMPUTETAX would happily accept its input data on two lines:

```
11000
2
```

For some purposes it is desirable to force the input data to be read a line at a time. For this purpose the READLN statement (which is otherwise analogous to the READ statement) is useful: after a READLN statement has been obeyed, the unread part of the current line of input data is skipped, and any subsequent input will be taken from the next line.

Example 4.9

Consider the statements

```
READLN (NMROFSHEEP) ;
READLN (NMROFGOATS)
```

where NMROFSHEEP and NMROFGOATS are INTEGER variables. If the input data is

```
10  SHEEP
 4  GOATS
```

27

then the values 10 and 4 respectively will be assigned to the two variables; the textual data on both lines will be ignored. If the READLN statements were replaced by READ statements, on the other hand, the second READ statement would fail, by attempting to interpret "SHEEP" as an integer number!

A last word about input and output. The input data is always read from left to right within each line, and from one line to the next. Once a data item has been read, it cannot subsequently be re-read. {By comparison, a person reading a book can go back and re-read any passage he wishes.} Likewise, output data is written from left to right within each line, and from one line to the next. Once data has been written, it is not (usually) possible to go back and erase it, nor to write some more data above it. {By comparison, a person writing on paper can erase any part of his previous work, or write from the bottom of the page to the top, if he wishes.} These restrictions, which reflect the properties of the common computer input and output devices, have an important influence on many programs, as we shall see in later examples.

EXERCISES 4

4.1. Show what output you would expect from program COMPUTETAX if the following input data were supplied:

    8000   6

4.2. Consider the following program:

```
PROGRAM BALANCEOFPAYMENTS ( INPUT, OUTPUT ) ;

(* This program computes a country's trading balance, given its
    import and export bills and its balance on "invisible" trade. *)

VAR
    IMPORTS, EXPORTS, VISIBLEBALANCE,
      INVISIBLEBALANCE, TOTALBALANCE : INTEGER ;

BEGIN
READ (IMPORTS, EXPORTS) ;
VISIBLEBALANCE := IMPORTS - EXPORTS ;
READ (INVISIBLEBALANCE) ;
TOTALBALANCE := VISIBLEBALANCE + INVISIBLEBALANCE ;
    (* ... positive for a surplus, negative for a deficit *)
WRITELN ('   IMPORTS   EXPORTS   VISIBLE INVISIBLE    TOTAL') ;
WRITELN ('      $M        $M        $M        $M       $M') ;
WRITELN ;
WRITELN (IMPORTS:10, EXPORTS:10,
        VISIBLEBALANCE:10, INVISIBLEBALANCE:10, TOTALBALANCE:10)
END .
```

Show exactly what output this program would write, if the following input data were supplied:

(a)
    9120 9670 750
(b)
    555   405
     -12

4.3. Write down some statements which write out your name and address in the form you would print them on an envelope.

4.4. Write a program which reads a number and which writes the number together with its square, cube and fourth power.

4.5. Write a program which reads three integers representing a date (day, month and year), and which writes the date neatly in the form "day/month/year" (writing only the last two digits of the year).

PROGRAMMING EXERCISES 4

4.6. Write a program which reads the number of seconds since midnight and writes the time in the form "hours:minutes:seconds", allowing two digits for each component of the time. Test your program by running it several times, with various numbers in the range 0 to 86399 as input data.

4.7. A business employs four grades of staff, of which grade A staff are paid monthly and grades B, C and D are paid weekly. Four lines of input data are supplied: the first line contains the number of grade A staff and their monthly pay; the remaining lines contain the number of staff and weekly pay in each of grades B, C and D. Write a program which reads this data and writes the total weekly pay bill, the total monthly pay bill and the total annual pay bill, with appropriate captions. Assume all money sums are in dollars (or whatever). Test your program by running it at least with the following input data:

     5   1500   A
    10   150   B
    20   200   C
    50   125   D

5 The data type BOOLEAN

5.1 CONDITIONS IN PROGRAMMING

Valuable results can certainly be obtained with the simple statements introduced in the previous chapters: the assignment, reading and writing of INTEGER values. However these limited means effectively restrict the computer to the role of a calculator. For most applications the program being obeyed by the computer must be able to vary the course of the calculation. It is sometimes necessary to select one of several alternative actions, depending on some stated conditions; at other times it is necessary to repeat an action over and over again, so long as some continuation condition is satisfied.

Take as an example a program which is processing a company's payroll file and printing each employee's payslip. The calculation of an employee's tax deduction illustrates the need for selective action, as the tax payable might depend on gross pay (with different rates of tax at different income levels), marital status, number of children, etc. To take account of these factors the program must be able to adapt its behaviour to the circumstances of the employee. Repetition is also needed: the program must be able to repeat the same calculation for every employee, stopping when all the payslips have been printed.

To make full use of the speed, reliability and flexibility of the computer in applications such as this we must have a way of expressing in the program conditions which the computer is to test.

Most of the conditions encountered in programming are very simple in nature: either they hold or they do not. If a condition holds it has the value TRUE. Otherwise it has the value FALSE. TRUE and FALSE are constant identifiers denoting the only two values of a new data type – the BOOLEAN type.

Like INTEGER values, BOOLEAN values are derived in the computer by following mechanical rules. To the same extent as INTEGER values they are imperfect models of the world.

The name BOOLEAN commemorates George Boole (1815-1864) who first placed the study of logic on a sound mathematical basis. His book "The Laws of Thought" described an algebra of logical values, now called Boolean Algebra, which underlies the manipulation of BOOLEAN values in the same way that the conventional algebra of arithmetic underlies the INTEGER type. To make progress in the study of programming a good understanding of the elements of Boolean Algebra is vital. Do not despair! As you will discover in the following sections, Boolean Algebra is largely a formal restatement of common sense.

5.2 COMPARISONS

The most familiar way of computing a BOOLEAN value is by a <u>comparison.</u>
In Pascal the values to be compared may be of any suitable type. It is
not generally possible to compare values of different types, nor would
it make any sense to do so. For the present, take it that any two
INTEGER values or any two BOOLEAN values can be compared.

The normal arithmetical rules for comparing signed numbers apply to
INTEGER values, so that the comparisons -1<6, 100>99 and -23<-20 all
have the value TRUE. Similarly, 7<3, -44>-37 and 13582<9 all have the
value FALSE. The result of comparisons such as X=Y and A+B<C will,
of course, depend on the values of the variables involved. Comparing
BOOLEAN values is an unusual operation, but it can sometimes provide a
very elegant formulation of a complicated condition. This is discussed
in Section 5.5.

A full range of comparison operators is available in Pascal.
Unfortunately several of the conventional mathematical symbols are
absent from the character sets of most computers. To meet this problem
the following notational conventions are used:

for	>	⩾	⩽	<	=	≠
use	>	>=	<=	<	=	<>

The expressions introduced in Chapter 3, and all expressions other
than comparisons, are more correctly called Simple Expressions. An
Expression is then either a Simple Expression or a Comparison. See
Figure 5.1. This syntax has two important consequences.

Firstly, comparison operators have the lowest priority of all
operators in Pascal. Thus the expressions:

    2*A <> B+C   and   (2*A) <> (B+C)

are entirely equivalent.

Secondly, the convenient notations X<Y<Z, A>B>C, and so on are not
allowed in Pascal. To compute an INTEGER value we can write expressions
like:

    MAXIMUM - MINIMUM + 1

but the following attempt at a BOOLEAN expression, although apparently
similar, is incorrect:

    FREEZING < TEMPERATURE < BOILING

We shall see in the next section how this can be expressed properly.

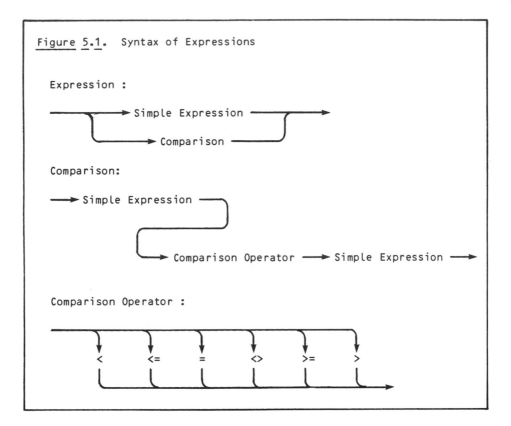

Figure 5.1. Syntax of Expressions

Expression :

Simple Expression

Comparison

Comparison:

Simple Expression

Comparison Operator → Simple Expression →

Comparison Operator :

<   <=   =   <>   >=   >

Finally we emphasize again that, in a program, a comparison makes the computer examine the values involved and produce a TRUE or FALSE result. When we write a comparison such as TEMPERATURE>BOILING we are not making a statement of fact. Rather, we are defining a condition which may or may not hold and which must be tested at that point in the program.

5.3 THE BOOLEAN OPERATORS

It is often necessary to be able to construct BOOLEAN expressions which involve more than a single comparison. The operators AND, OR and NOT allow us to express a condition of any complexity, along lines similar to the construction of INTEGER expressions. (AND, OR and NOT are all reserved words.)

The operator AND takes two BOOLEAN operands and yields a BOOLEAN result which has the value TRUE if and only if both operands are TRUE. Definitions of BOOLEAN operators are most easily given in the form of a "truth table" listing all possible operand values and the corresponding results. For the operator AND the truth table is:

```
x          y          x AND y

FALSE      FALSE      FALSE
FALSE      TRUE       FALSE
TRUE       FALSE      FALSE
TRUE       TRUE       TRUE
```

The word "or" has two meanings in English. In the inclusive sense we
have phrases such as "These clothes are suitable for summer or winter
wear". In the exclusive sense we have "Either the world is flat or it
is round". The inclusive meaning has been adopted in Boolean Algebra
and hence in Pascal. The operator OR takes two BOOLEAN operands and
yields a BOOLEAN result which has the value TRUE if at least one of the
operands is TRUE:

```
x          y          x OR y

FALSE      FALSE      FALSE
FALSE      TRUE       TRUE
TRUE       FALSE      TRUE
TRUE       TRUE       TRUE
```

The operator NOT takes a single BOOLEAN operand and yields a BOOLEAN
result which is the opposite of the operand. For NOT the truth table is
particularly simple:

```
x          NOT x

FALSE      TRUE
TRUE       FALSE
```

Using AND we can recast the troublesome condition of the previous
section in an acceptable form, as:

    (FREEZING < TEMPERATURE) AND (TEMPERATURE < BOILING)

Note that the parentheses are necessary here, the reason being that the
comparison operators are of lower priority than AND. Without
parentheses we would have:

    FREEZING < TEMPERATURE AND TEMPERATURE < BOILING

which is equivalent to:

    FREEZING < (TEMPERATURE AND TEMPERATURE) < BOILING

This is obviously meaningless. To avoid such errors, comparisons used
as operands of AND, OR and NOT must always be parenthesized in Pascal.

5.4 USING BOOLEAN DATA

BOOLEAN data may be used in all the ways previously described for INTEGER data. BOOLEAN constants may be defined; BOOLEAN variables may be declared; BOOLEAN expressions may be computed, assigned to BOOLEAN variables, and output by WRITE or WRITELN. The effect of writing a BOOLEAN value is, naturally enough, to write either 'TRUE' or 'FALSE'.

We rely on the internal consistency of Pascal to avoid much tedious reworking of these ideas in the new context. Unfortunately, there is one minor restriction in Standard Pascal: READ and READLN cannot be used to read BOOLEAN values. Although a nuisance, this does not create insuperable difficulties.

Refer to the collected syntax diagrams of Appendix 1.3 to see how BOOLEAN operators fit into the syntax of Expressions. The following are some of the most important consequences.

Firstly, AND has the same priority as "*", OR has the same priority as "+", and NOT has the highest priority of all operators in Pascal. Contrast the following arithmetic expression:

    - A * B + C   which is equivalent to (-(A*B)) + C

with the following BOOLEAN expression:

    NOT A AND B OR C   which is equivalent to ((NOT A) AND B) OR C

Secondly, parentheses may be included to override these priorities and to clarify complicated expressions.

Thirdly, any of the following may stand by itself as a BOOLEAN expression: a BOOLEAN constant, a BOOLEAN variable, or a BOOLEAN function.

A useful predeclared function is ODD, which takes an INTEGER parameter, delivering TRUE if the parameter is an odd number and FALSE otherwise. In fact ODD(x) is equivalent to (x MOD 2 <> 0).

Example 5.1

The following examples are, respectively, a BOOLEAN constant definition, a BOOLEAN variable declaration, a BOOLEAN assignment statement and a WRITE statement with a BOOLEAN parameter.

    FOREVER = FALSE

    VOTER, PEER, PRISONER, INSANE : BOOLEAN

    VOTER := (AGE>=18) AND NOT (PEER OR PRISONER OR INSANE)

    WRITE(VOTER)

5.5 THE RULES OF BOOLEAN ALGEBRA

{This section should be omitted at a first reading.}

There are many rules, or "laws", defining relationships between NOT, AND and OR which are of importance in formulating, simplifying and understanding BOOLEAN expressions. Several of these rules are closely analogous to rules in the algebra of arithmetic, which may be helpful in grasping their significance. Others have no helpful analogy.

The laws of Boolean Algebra are summarized below, the corresponding rules of arithmetic being given where possible. The symbol "=" means "is equivalent to". In the cases which seem strange, it is a good idea to construct truth tables and so demonstrate their validity.

Redundancy Laws

(R1) x AND FALSE $\equiv$ FALSE   {c.f. a * 0 $\equiv$ 0}

(R2) x AND TRUE $\equiv$ x   {c.f. a * 1 $\equiv$ a}

(R3) x OR FALSE $\equiv$ x   {c.f. a + 0 $\equiv$ a}

(R4) x OR TRUE $\equiv$ TRUE   {There is no analogy in arithmetic}

(R5) x AND x $\equiv$ x   {No analogy}

(R6) x OR x $\equiv$ x   {No analogy}

(R7) x AND NOT x $\equiv$ FALSE   {No analogy}

(R8) x OR NOT x $\equiv$ TRUE   {No analogy}

Commutative Laws

(C1) x AND y $\equiv$ y AND x   {c.f. a * b $\equiv$ b * a}

(C2) x OR y $\equiv$ y OR x   {c.f. a + b $\equiv$ b + a}

Associative Laws

(A1) (x AND y) AND z $\equiv$ x AND y AND z $\equiv$ x AND (y AND z)
      {c.f. (a * b) * c $\equiv$ a * b * c $\equiv$ a * (b * c) }

(A2) (x OR y) OR z $\equiv$ x OR y OR z $\equiv$ x OR (y OR z)
      {c.f. (a + b) + c $\equiv$ a + b + c $\equiv$ a + (b + c) }

Distributive Laws

(D1) (x AND y) OR (x AND z) $=$ x AND (y OR z)
     {c.f. (a * b) + (a * c) $=$ a * (b + c) }

E.g.   (MARRIED AND (SALARY<=LIMIT)) OR (MARRIED AND (CHILDREN>1))
  $=$ MARRIED AND ((SALARY<=LIMIT) OR (CHILDREN>1))

(D2) (x OR y) AND (x OR z) $=$ x OR (y AND z)
     {There is no analogy in arithmetic}

E.g.   (BRITISH OR SPEAKSGAELIC) AND (BRITISH OR SPEAKSIRISH)
  $=$ BRITISH OR (SPEAKSGAELIC AND SPEAKSIRISH)

Involution Law

(I) NOT (NOT x) $=$ x   {c.f. -(-a) $=$ a }

E.g. NOT (NOT MARRIED) $=$ MARRIED

De Morgan's Laws

{Neither of these laws has an analogy in arithmetic}

(DeM1) NOT (x AND y) $=$ NOT x OR NOT y

E.g.   NOT ((FREEZING<TEMPERATURE) AND (TEMPERATURE<BOILING))
  $=$ NOT(FREEZING<TEMPERATURE) OR NOT(TEMPERATURE<BOILING)
  $=$ (FREEZING>=TEMPERATURE) OR (TEMPERATURE>=BOILING)

(DeM2) NOT (x OR y) $=$ NOT x AND NOT y

E.g.   NOT ((SALARY<=LIMIT) OR (CHILDREN>1))
  $=$ NOT (SALARY<=LIMIT) AND NOT (CHILDREN>1)
  $=$ (SALARY>LIMIT) AND (CHILDREN<=1)

    When BOOLEAN values are compared by an operator implying relative magnitude (i.e. "<=", "<", ">=" or ">"), the result follows from the fact that, in Pascal, FALSE is considered to be less than TRUE. Since the results of such comparisons are themselves BOOLEAN values, they can be defined by truth tables and have corresponding BOOLEAN expressions. The table for "<=" follows as an example:

x	y	x <= y
FALSE	FALSE	TRUE
FALSE	TRUE	TRUE
TRUE	FALSE	FALSE
TRUE	TRUE	TRUE

From any truth table we can derive an equivalent expression in terms of AND, OR and NOT. Then, using the rules of Boolean Algebra, this can be converted to its simplest equivalent form. For the example of "<=" we work as follows; x<=y has the value TRUE if:

(a) x and y are both FALSE, i.e. (NOT x AND NOT y); or
(b) x is FALSE and y is TRUE, i.e. (NOT x AND y); or
(c) x and y are both TRUE, i.e. (x AND y).

Thus we can write:

x <= y $\equiv$ (NOT x AND NOT y) OR (NOT x AND y) OR (x AND y)

We can now simplify this expression:

x <= y	=	NOT x AND (NOT y OR y) OR (x AND y)	{D1}
	=	NOT x AND TRUE OR (x AND y)	{C2, R8}
	=	NOT x OR (x AND y)	{R2}
	=	(NOT x OR x) AND (NOT x OR y)	{D2}
	=	TRUE AND (NOT x OR y)	{C2, R8}
	=	NOT x OR y	{C1, R2}

The laws applied at each step are indicated on the right. More simply, we can use the single FALSE case: x<=y is FALSE only when x is TRUE and y is FALSE, i.e. only when (x AND NOT y). Thus we can write:

x <= y $\equiv$ NOT (x AND NOT y) $\equiv$ NOT x OR y   {DeM1, I}

   Manipulations of expressions more complicated than this are unlikely to occur in practice. Indeed, complicated BOOLEAN expressions may be symptomatic of flaws in the design of a program.

EXERCISES 5

5.1. Let NUMBER be an INTEGER variable, and let POSITIVE, ZERO and NEGATIVE be BOOLEAN variables. Write statements which will assign to POSITIVE, ZERO and NEGATIVE values which are TRUE if the value of NUMBER is, respectively, greater than zero, equal to zero, and less than zero.

5.2. Let LEFT be a BOOLEAN variable and let PAGENMR be an INTEGER variable. Write a statement which will assign to LEFT a BOOLEAN value meaning "the value of PAGENMR is even".

5.3. Let SCOT, IRISH and CELT be BOOLEAN variables, where SCOT means "speaks Gaelic" and IRISH means "speaks Erse". Write a statement which assigns to CELT a BOOLEAN value meaning "speaks Gaelic or Erse, but not both". Note that this is an example of the exclusive sense of the word "or", as mentioned in Section 5.3.

5.4. Write a program which reads two INTEGER numbers, then writes "TRUE" if the first is greater than the second, and "FALSE" otherwise.

5.5. Write a program which reads two integers representing a date (month and day-of-the-month), then writes "TRUE" if that is the date of Christmas Day, and "FALSE" otherwise.

5.6. Assuming that an INTEGER variable YEAR contains the number of a year, write a statement which assigns to a BOOLEAN variable LEAPYEAR a value meaning "the year is a leap year". (a) Assume that any year whose number is a multiple of 4 is a leap year. (b*) More accurately, take into account the fact that years whose numbers are multiples of 100, but not of 400, are not leap years. (Thus 2000 will be a leap year, but 1700, 1800 and 1900 were not.)

{The following exercises should not be attempted until Section 5.5 has been read.}

5.7. Construct BOOLEAN expressions for the other five Comparison Operators when applied to BOOLEAN operands, as was done in Section 5.5 for "<=".

5.8. Simplify the BOOLEAN expressions x=TRUE, x=FALSE, x<>TRUE, and x<>FALSE. What conclusions can be drawn about the advisability of writing such expressions in programs?

5.9. Simplify the following BOOLEAN expressions:

    (a) (a OR x) AND (b OR x) AND (c OR x)

    (b) b OR NOT (a AND b)

    (c*) a AND x OR b AND x OR c AND x OR
        a AND y OR b AND y OR c AND y OR
        a AND c OR b AND c OR c

6 The flow of control

6.1 CONTROL STRUCTURES

The programs which have appeared up to this point have all displayed the simplest possible structure. One action followed another in time in exactly the way indicated by the textual order of the statements which invoked them. Thus every statement is obeyed once and only once. However, we have seen that selective and repetitive execution are necessary for practical use of a computer, so we now turn to the language structures which will allow this.

Repetitive execution

Repetitive execution is specified by two things:
(a) the statement to be repeated; and
(b) the condition to be tested before each repetition.
The sequence of operations is as follows:

(1) Test the condition. If it is FALSE continue from step (4).
(2) Obey the statement, knowing the condition to be TRUE.
(3) Repeat from step (1).
(4) Knowing the condition to be FALSE, go on with the rest of the program.

Because of the link back from step (3) to step (1) repetitive program structures have come to be called loops. The repeated statement must eventually (i.e. on the last repetition) make the condition FALSE. Failure to do this results in an infinite loop which is obeyed indefinitely, wasting much computer time.

Selective execution

For selective execution we need the following three components:
(a) the condition to be tested;
(b) the statement to be obeyed if the condition is satisfied (statement A); and
(c) an alternative statement to be obeyed if the condition is not satisfied (statement B). (Often the alternative is to do nothing.)
The sequence of operations is:

(1) Test the condition. If it is TRUE, continue from step (2), otherwise continue from step (4).
(2) Obey statement A, knowing the condition to be TRUE.
(3) Continue from step (5).
(4) Obey statement B, knowing the condition to be FALSE.
(5) Go on with the rest of the program; nothing can be assumed about the value of the condition.

When the alternative statement is to do nothing, this simplifies to:

(1) Test the condition. If it is TRUE, perform step (2), otherwise perform step (3).
(2) Obey statement A, knowing the condition to be TRUE.
(3) Go on with the rest of the program; nothing can be assumed about the value of the condition.

Because control goes forward in either of two ways at step (1), selective program structures are also called branches.

In some programming languages, especially the earlier ones such as FORTRAN and BASIC, it is necessary to describe selective and repetitive control structures in terms of very primitive steps such as the above. More modern languages, among them Pascal, have been designed to make life easier. They have notations – the WHILE and IF statements – that correspond exactly with looping and branching program structures.

6.2 THE WHILE STATEMENT

The fundamental means of constructing loops in Pascal is the WHILE Statement. Its syntax is given in Figure 6.1. Note that WHILE and DO are both reserved words.

Figure 6.1. Syntax of the WHILE Statement

WHILE Statement :

⟶ WHILE ⟶ Boolean Expression ⟶ DO ⟶ Statement ⟶

The syntax of the WHILE Statement requires the repeated action to be a single statement, but we often want to repeat a group of statements. This requirement is met by the Compound Statement, whose only significance is to cause a sequence of statements to be treated as a single statement for syntactic purposes. This is done by bracketing the statement sequence between the reserved words BEGIN and END. See Figure

6.2.

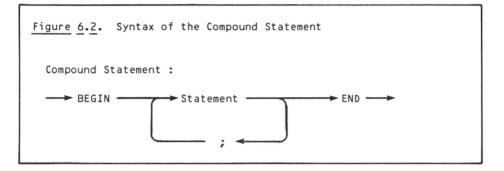

Figure 6.2. Syntax of the Compound Statement

Compound Statement :

⟶ BEGIN ⟶ Statement ⟶ END ⟶
      ;

Example 6.1

Pascal does not provide an operator to calculate powers of numbers. The following program fragment will calculate the B-th power of A for non-negative values of B (so that the result is an integer).

```
I := 0; APOWERB := 1;
WHILE I < B DO
   BEGIN
   APOWERB := APOWERB * A;
   I := I + 1
   END
```

We can check this solution by tracing through it with two test cases: B=0, and some B greater than 0, e.g. B=2. In either case I is initially set to 0 and APOWERB to 1. Suppose A contains 7.

If B is 0 the WHILE condition, I<B, already has the value FALSE, so that the body of the loop is not obeyed. Thus the final value of APOWERB is 1, which is correct.

If B is 2 the WHILE condition has the value TRUE and the body of the loop is obeyed. This sets APOWERB to 7 and I to 1. Again the condition is tested and found to be TRUE. The body of the loop then sets APOWERB to 49 and I to 2. On the third repetition the WHILE condition is found to be FALSE and the loop is left. The final value of APOWERB is 49, which is also correct.

Study the program fragment carefully and convince yourself that the loop will always terminate and deliver the correct result, for any non-negative value of B.

It is usually more convenient to set down the results of tracing in a tabular form. A column is used to represent the successive values of each variable, the current value being that written lowest-down in the column. Each row shows the outcome of obeying a statement or testing a

41

condition. The current statement or condition is shown in the first column, the second column being used for the value of the condition. If you feel it tedious to write and rewrite the same statements you may prefer to number them and record their numbers in the first column. Figure 6.3 repeats the checks on Example 6.1, in tabular form.

Figure 6.3. Checking Example 6.1

(a) A=7, B=0

Statement	Condition	I	APOWERB
I := 0		0	
APOWERB := 1			1
WHILE I<B	FALSE		

(b) A=7, B=2

Statement	Condition	I	APOWERB
I := 0		0	
APOWERB := 1			1
WHILE I<B	TRUE		
APOWERB := APOWERB*A			7
I := I+1		1	
WHILE I<B	TRUE		
APOWERB := APOWERB*A			49
I := I+1		2	
WHILE I<B	FALSE		

Example 6.2

The following program reads six integers, one per line of input, and writes their sum.

```
PROGRAM ADD6 ( INPUT, OUTPUT );
VAR
    SUM, DATUM, COUNT : INTEGER;
BEGIN
SUM := 0;
COUNT := 1;

WHILE COUNT <= 6 DO
    (* Read the next integer and add it to SUM *)
    BEGIN
    READLN ( DATUM );
    SUM := SUM + DATUM;
    COUNT := COUNT + 1
    END;

WRITELN ( 'SUM OF 6 INTEGERS READ IS ', SUM )
END.
```

Program ADD6 can easily be generalized to sum a list containing any number of integers. One approach is to supply the size of the list as the first item of data. A disadvantage is that someone has to count the data items. This is liable to error and may be impractical if the data items are numerous. Example 6.3 illustrates the idea.

Example 6.3

```
PROGRAM ADDN ( INPUT, OUTPUT );
VAR
    SUM, DATUM, COUNT, SIZE : INTEGER;
BEGIN
SUM := 0;
COUNT := 1;

READLN ( SIZE );
```

43

```
WHILE COUNT <= SIZE DO
    (* Read the next integer and add it to SUM *)
    BEGIN
    READLN ( DATUM );
    SUM := SUM + DATUM;
    COUNT := COUNT + 1
    END;

WRITELN ( 'SUM OF ', SIZE, ' INTEGERS READ IS ', SUM )
END.
```

An alternative approach is to mark the end of the list in some way the program can detect. The problem here is that it may be difficult to define a suitable endmarker. If all the data are known to be positive numbers, for example, a negative number could be used as an endmarker; however a typing error might result in a negative number being accidentally included in the data. Similar objections could be raised to other proposals.

Fortunately, Pascal provides a way to detect the end of the input data which is independent of the data itself. This is the predeclared BOOLEAN function EOF(INPUT) which has the value TRUE if and only if all the input data has been read. Its use is illustrated by Example 6.4. (Beware: when reading numbers the EOF test can be used in this way only when the most recent input operation was READLN, rather than READ. This restriction will be explained in Section 8.1.)

Example 6.4

```
PROGRAM ADDALL ( INPUT, OUTPUT );
VAR
    SUM, DATUM : INTEGER;
BEGIN
SUM := 0;

WHILE NOT EOF(INPUT) DO
    (* Read the next integer and add it to SUM *)
    BEGIN
    READLN ( DATUM );
    SUM := SUM + DATUM
    END;

WRITELN ( 'SUM OF INTEGERS READ IS ', SUM )
END.
```

Hand-test programs ADDN and ADDALL yourself, in the manner shown for

Example 6.1. In particular, verify that they are correct in the extreme case when the list of numbers to be read is empty.

These programs exemplify structures which appear in almost all programs. Despite their apparent simplicity they repay careful study.

6.3 THE IF STATEMENT

In Pascal, branching programs are constructed using the IF Statement, which has the syntax given in Figure 6.4. IF, THEN and ELSE are all reserved words. This syntax, like that of Figure 6.1, forces the alternative actions to be specified by single statements. If either alternative action is required to consist of a number of statements, the remedy is the same: use a Compound Statement to make a sequence of statements into a single statement.

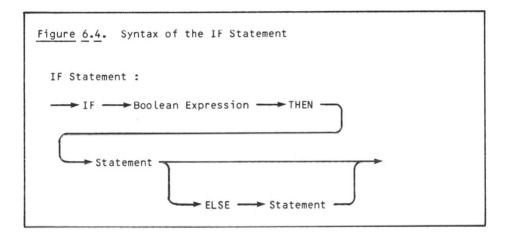

Figure 6.4. Syntax of the IF Statement

IF Statement :

IF ──► Boolean Expression ──► THEN

Statement

ELSE ──► Statement

Example 6.5

The following statement sets X to the larger of Y and Z:

```
IF Y>Z THEN
   X := Y
ELSE
   X := Z
```

Replacing "Z" by "X" throughout, we get a statement which sets X to the larger of Y and itself:

```
IF Y>X THEN
   X := Y
ELSE
   X := X
```

45

Since the ELSE part has no useful effect, it can be omitted without changing the meaning of the IF statement:

```
IF Y>X THEN
   X := Y
```

Example 6.6

The following statements write suitable messages according to the value of SCORE:

```
IF SCORE>70 THEN
   WRITE('EXCELLENT');
IF SCORE<30 THEN
   WRITE('DISMAL');
IF (SCORE<=70) AND (SCORE>=30) THEN
   WRITE('TYPICAL');
```

There is much redundancy in these statements. When SCORE exceeds 70 there is no point in making the two further tests of its value, both of which must give FALSE. Similarly, once SCORE is known to be less than 30 the test in the final IF statement is futile. This is an example of a very common situation: testing for one of several mutually exclusive conditions, with an appropriate action for each. It can be written more concisely using ELSE:

```
IF SCORE>70 THEN
   WRITE('EXCELLENT')
ELSE
IF SCORE<30 THEN
   WRITE('DISMAL')
ELSE
   WRITE('TYPICAL')
```

A common and quite subtle error is to try something along these lines:

```
IF (TALLY <> 0) AND (TOTAL DIV TALLY > THRESHOLD) THEN
   WRITE('ACCEPTABLE AVERAGE')
ELSE
   WRITE('UNACCEPTABLE AVERAGE')
```

The mistake is that, when TALLY is zero, TOTAL DIV TALLY causes an attempt to divide by zero (usually with disastrous results). In cases like this the two parts of the condition must be separated, as shown in Example 6.7.

Example 6.7

```
IF TALLY <> 0 THEN
    IF TOTAL DIV TALLY > THRESHOLD THEN
        WRITE('ACCEPTABLE AVERAGE')
    ELSE
        WRITE('UNACCEPTABLE AVERAGE')
```

An ambiguity lurking in the syntax of Figure 6.4 now comes to light! In a statement with the following structure:

IF ... THEN IF ... THEN ... ELSE ...

to which IF does the ELSE correspond? Pascal has the reasonable (though arbitrary) rule that in such a case the ELSE goes with the closest IF. We have already anticipated this in the indentation of Example 6.7. Compare that with Example 6.8.

Example 6.8

```
IF TALLY <> 0 THEN
    BEGIN
    IF TOTAL DIV TALLY > THRESHOLD THEN
        WRITE('ACCEPTABLE AVERAGE')
    END
ELSE
    WRITE('NOTHING TO FIND THE AVERAGE OF')
```

It is advisable, in all doubtful cases, to make the meaning perfectly clear by liberal use of the statement brackets BEGIN and END.

6.4 NESTED LOGIC

Very often a programming problem will demand both repetition and selection in its solution. There is no difficulty about this. Remember that the WHILE and IF constructs both contain statements and are themselves statements. Thus a WHILE can govern an IF or another WHILE and an IF can govern a WHILE or another IF (as we have already seen). Structures of any complexity can be built up in this way, each statement being nested within another. When it is necessary to govern a sequence of statements, rather than just one, the Compound Statement allows this to be done.

Example 6.9

Program DISPLAY is to read a sequence of integers, one per line of input. When a positive number is read, that many asterisks are to be written. Negative numbers and zeros are to be written-out numerically. No number will be greater than 99 in absolute value. {The effect is to display the data as a bar-chart, or histogram, thus making it easier for the user to assimilate.}

```
PROGRAM DISPLAY ( INPUT, OUTPUT );
VAR
    STARS, COUNT : INTEGER;
BEGIN
WHILE NOT EOF(INPUT) DO
   BEGIN
   (* read the next COUNT *)
   READLN(COUNT);
   IF COUNT <= 0 THEN
      (* Output COUNT in numerical form *)
      WRITE(COUNT:5)
   ELSE
      BEGIN (* Output a row of COUNT asterisks *)
      WRITE('    ');
      STARS := 0;
      WHILE STARS < COUNT DO
         BEGIN
         WRITE('*');
         STARS := STARS + 1
         END
      END;
   (* Start a new line of output *)
   WRITELN
   END
END .
```

Note the layout of program DISPLAY. Here, as in the preceding examples, the repeated statements in loops have been indented relative to the WHILE symbol. Similarly, the alternative statements in selections have been indented relative to the IF and ELSE symbols. This convention shows clearly how much of the text is actually included in each construct and makes the program much easier to read.

It is essential to adopt a methodical approach when writing relatively complicated programs like Example 6.9. Methodical programming is the topic of the following chapter.

6.1. Work systematically through program DISPLAY from Example 6.9, tracing the actions of the computer as it reads data, changes variables, tests conditions and writes output. Show exactly what output is produced if the input data is (on successive lines):

5, -73, 9, 6, 0, 1

6.2. Write a program fragment which computes the factorial of N, given that the value of N is a positive integer. (The factorial of N is the product 1*2*...*(N-1)*N.)

6.3. Given that the value of N is a positive integer, write a program fragment which determines how many decimal digits are needed to write down the value of N. (For example, 99 needs two digits, and 100 needs three digits.)

6.4. Write a program fragment which writes 'POSITIVE', 'NEGATIVE' or 'ZERO', depending on the value of N.

6.5. Write a program which reads three integers representing today's date (day, month and year), followed by three integers representing a person's birth-date, and which writes that person's age in years.

6.6. Write a program to read a list of positive integers and write out the largest of them: (a) when the size of the list is given as the first datum; and (b) when the list is terminated by a negative number.

PROGRAMMING EXERCISES 6

6.7. Modify your program of Exercise 4.5 to write the time in terms of the 12-hour clock rather than the 24-hour clock. (For example, write 10:50:30 P.M. rather than 22:50:30.)

6.8. Write a program which reads an integer N and produces a table of the squares of the integers from 1 to N inclusive.

6.9. Details taken from an invoice are supplied as input data. Each line of input contains the number of units of one item invoiced, followed by the unit price (in $) of that item. Write a program which will read this data, write the data in tabular form, and finally write the total amount invoiced. {Hint: you can use a statement like READLN (NMROFUNITS, UNITPRICE) to read each line of input data, and use EOF(INPUT) to detect the end of the input data.}

7 Programming methodically

{This is a very important chapter. Read it carefully before going on to the rest of the book, and review it after reading Chapter 20.}

7.1 PROGRAMMING BY STEPWISE REFINEMENT

The objective of computer programming is the creation of correct, efficient and easily-modified programs. Correct, because a program that gives the wrong results will not be used. Efficient, because an inefficient program may be too costly to run, or fail to give timely results. Easily-modified, because a program may be changed very often during its life. Correctness is the primary criterion of a good program. Efficiency and modifiability, though important, are secondary. In certain circumstances it may be necessary to sacrifice efficiency for flexibility, or ease of modification for lower cost. We are not prepared to sacrifice correctness in any circumstances.

These may seem to be modest aims, but all the experience of the past indicates that good programming is very difficult. Correctness has been achieved so seldom that efficiency and ease of modification have seemed like unattainable luxuries. Why is this so? The basic reason is probably the diversity of the skills a programmer must possess, and the complexity of their inter-relationships. The ideal programmer is versatile, creative, logical and persistent. He is capable of meticulous attention to detail, yet never loses sight of the overall picture.

Since most of us fall short of these requirements it seems a good idea to avoid unnecessary difficulties and adopt a methodical habit of work. The particular method chosen matters less than its consistent application, but we advocate in this book a method which is both simple and effective: stepwise refinement.

The basic idea of stepwise refinement is this: given a complex problem, such as designing a program, split it up into several, more or less independent, sub-problems. If we can assume that these sub-problems are solvable we have an outline solution to the original problem. Call this the Level 1 description of the solution. Now turn to the sub-problems and solve these separately. If a sub-problem is trivial, write down its final solution directly. If not, solve the sub-problem by applying stepwise refinement to it. This generates a set of sub-sub-problems. Assuming that these are solvable they constitute a second, more detailed, solution of the original problem. This is the

Level 2 description of the solution. Go on in this way until all the remaining sub-problems are trivial. Combining all the final solutions of the sub-problems gives the final solution of the original problem, in the most convenient form: a complete design! Splitting up a problem into sub-problems is a refinement step; the successively more detailed descriptions are the levels of refinement.

We now bring this rather abstract idea to life with an example. The DISPLAY program from Example 6.9 was developed along the following lines. The program is to read and process a sequence of numbers and this at once suggests a loop, in fact the sort of loop used in Example 6.4. Each repetition of the loop reads a number, let us call it COUNT (remembering it will have to be declared as an INTEGER variable). If COUNT is negative or zero it is just written in numerical form. If it is positive that number of asterisks are written. To give the correct format each number should be represented on a separate line. These considerations lead to the following sketch of the program.

Level 1 of program DISPLAY

```
declarations;
BEGIN
WHILE not end of data DO
   BEGIN
   read the next COUNT;
   IF COUNT<=0 THEN
      output COUNT in numerical form
   ELSE
      output a row of COUNT asterisks;
   start a new line of output
   END
END .
```

This is intended to be a self-explanatory description of the program. Material in upper case is already formalized in terms of the programming language. Material in lower case is informally descriptive of some action to be performed or some expression to be evaluated, the context should make clear which. For example, "not end of data" must represent a BOOLEAN expression which we are to interpret in terms of the end-of-data condition. At the moment it does not matter how the condition is to be detected: any valid implementation will result in a correct program. In the same way, "output a row of COUNT asterisks" represents a statement which, we are to assume, will write out one row of the histogram. The whole program can now be checked before any further refinements are made. This is done by tracing through it with sample data, just as we would do with the final program. Only when satisfied that the description is correct do we continue with the refinement. Check Level 1 now, using the data given in Exercise 6.1.

Refinements from Level 1

The data for this program consists of a sequence of numbers, one on each line of input, so we can use READLN and EOF. A number can be output in numerical form by either WRITE or WRITELN. In this case WRITE is correct, because there is separate provision in the program to start a new line. The latter can be done with WRITELN. Since the data item is always less than 100 in magnitude it can be represented in at most two decimal digits. Allowing for two initial blanks and a minus sign a number can be output numerically in five columns. Following these ideas we now write:

Refinement 1.1: not end of data

   NOT EOF(INPUT)

Refinement 1.2: read the next COUNT

   READLN(COUNT)

Refinement 1.3: output COUNT in numerical form

   WRITE(COUNT:5)

Refinement 1.4: start a new line of output

   WRITELN

These four refinements are complete: they take us to the level of Pascal code and need no more development.

Refinement 1.5: output a row of COUNT asterisks

A single asterisk is easily output by the statement WRITE('*'); to output several we will have to include this in a count-controlled loop (c.f. Example 6.3). This will require more than one statement, so it will all have to be enclosed in BEGIN and END brackets:

```
BEGIN
prepare to output the row;
WHILE COUNT asterisks have not yet been written DO
   output another asterisk
END
```

Replacing each of these components in the Level 1 description by its refinement we get a more detailed description of the program at Level 2. To show how it was derived we include appropriate comments.

```
   declarations;
   BEGIN
   WHILE NOT EOF(INPUT) DO
      BEGIN
      (* Read the next COUNT *)
      READLN(COUNT);
      IF COUNT <= 0 THEN
         (* Output COUNT in numerical form *)
         WRITE(COUNT:5)
      ELSE
         BEGIN (* Output a row of COUNT asterisks *)
         prepare to output the row;
         WHILE COUNT asterisks have not yet been written DO
            output another asterisk
         END;
      (* Start a new line of output *)
      WRITELN
      END
   END .
```

This must be checked before continuing the refinement. The check can now be much more complete than was possible with the Level 1 description, as more detail of the implementation is available. Again, try this yourself using the data given in Exercise 6.1.

Refinements from Level 2

To record the number of asterisks that have been output by the inner WHILE loop the program must keep a tally of them in a suitable variable. Thus we introduce the INTEGER variable STARS (remembering that it will have to be declared). Each time a row of asterisks is begun STARS will start off at zero; each time an asterisk is output it will be incremented by one. Thus the value of STARS represents the number of asterisks already output in the current row. We now write:

Refinement 2.1: COUNT asterisks have not yet been written

```
   STARS < COUNT
```

Refinement 2.2: output another asterisk

```
   BEGIN
   WRITE('*');
   STARS := STARS + 1
   END
```

The preparation for each row must include zeroizing STARS. Another point: non-positive numbers are output in a field of five columns. To preserve the format of the bar-chart five blanks should be output before each row of asterisks. Thus:

<u>Refinement 2.3</u>: prepare to output the row

```
WRITE('    ');
STARS := 0
```

The whole program has now been converted to Pascal code, with the exception of the declarations. Since we know all the variables needed we can finally write:

<u>Refinement 2.4</u>: declarations

```
VAR
    STARS, COUNT : INTEGER
```

This completes the stepwise refinement of program DISPLAY. The checking of the complete program has been already been set as Exercise 6.1.

It is important to use a consistent notation for stepwise refinement and to be thorough about writing down design decisions. In this way the written record of the design process acts as an extension of our limited memory and allows more factors to be taken into account than would otherwise be possible without confusion.

A program description at a given level is written in terms of a set of actions and expressions whose implementation has not yet been determined. These actions and expressions should be given precisely descriptive names that will suggest exactly what the program is doing, even to a casual reader of the description. Accuracy is much more important than conciseness, because a misleading or vague name is both a symptom and a cause of sloppy thinking. The aim in writing a program description should be to make it so clear that it reads "like a book". In the search for such clarity it is often tempting to name part of a program in terms of one possible implementation. Guard against this, for it biases all your later ideas and may blind you to alternative, and better, implementations.

The notation for refinement steps has been chosen with two aspects in mind. Firstly, a refinement expands an expression or action from the program description at the level above and it should be made clear how it fits into that context. For this reason the refinements are numbered systematically. Secondly, a refinement introduces a new set of expressions and actions. These will form part of the program description at the next level down and it should be made clear what they are implementing. For this reason each refinement is headed by its own descriptive name, in full. By reading just the refinement step it is possible to see WHAT is being done, HOW it is being done, and WHERE it belongs in the overall structure. Omitting either the name or the number destroys this self-explanatory quality of the notation.

Using the numbers of the refinement steps we can draw a diagram which shows the structure of the complete program in a vivid way. The structure diagram of the program DISPLAY, developed in the last section, is shown in Figure 7.1.

Each level of a program description contains all the refinements of the previous level, as well as all the unrefined material, which is simply carried forward. Also, every refinement lies on a path down through the structure diagram, starting at Level 1. If no such path can be found for a refinement, then something is missing.

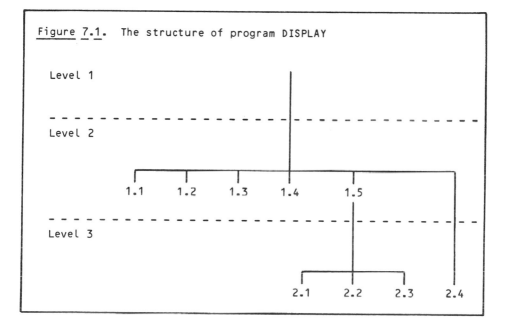

Figure 7.1. The structure of program DISPLAY

7.2 MAKING REFINEMENTS

How do we choose a refinement? Part of the answer is that, like most things, it gets easier with practice. Many problems lead to similar program structures. The skilled programmer soon recognizes these structures in the specification, enabling him to write down suitable refinements very quickly. However there is a trap here. Quite small differences of specification can cause large differences of program structure and parrotting a stock refinement then leads to difficulties. Habit is never a substitute for thought.

A more adequate answer is that _every_ action can be refined either as a sequence of actions, or as a loop, or as a selection. Anything which can be programmed, in any way at all, can be programmed using just these fundamental constructions. This is reassuring: we only have to choose one alternative from three. Although it is usually obvious which choice to make, the following points are worth noting.

Apparently the simplest kind of refinement is to split an action into several parts which are then performed in sequence, but experience shows that many structural errors come from doing this wrongly, or when it is not appropriate. In particular, be sure that it is indeed possible to perform the component actions in sequence, and that they are obeyed in the correct order. For example, the sequence:

```
read all data;
calculate;
write all results
```

implies that the data can be stored until the calculation phase and that the results can be stored until they are written. Often, however, it is necessary to incorporate data items into a calculation as they are read and to write results as soon as they are calculated.

Another common sequence is of the form:

```
preparation;
main calculation;
finalization
```

where the "preparation" or the "finalization" may be absent. Here the "main calculation" does most of the work, but it may need to be started-off properly and there may be some final tidying-up to do. This pattern is especially evident when the "main calculation" is refined as a loop:

```
preparation;
WHILE continuation condition DO
    repeated action;
finalization
```

When refining a loop it is a good idea to tackle the "continuation condition" first: this is usually easy. Then attack the "repeated action", ensuring that it contains a statement which will eventually make the "continuation condition" FALSE. If any "finalization" is required refine that next. Finally do the "preparation". It may seem strange to leave this to the end, but in stepwise refinement a good maxim is "the first shall be last". Until you know WHAT you must prepare for, you cannot know HOW to prepare it. Similarly, declarations cannot be written until all the variables have been introduced and this is not known until all the statements have been fully refined.

Whatever its form, a good refinement usually has the following desirable properties:

(a) Modularity. A program is said to be <u>modular</u> if its various components are relatively independent of each other. Choose refinements whose components interact as little as possible. This reduces the complexity of the refinements to be made at the next level down.

(b) Localization. A program displays good <u>localization</u> when logically-related components are written close to each other in the text. This reduces the need to scan back and forth through a program to see how things connect together, improving readability.

(c) Consistency of detail. Choose refinements whose components are expressed in roughly comparable detail. This tends to reduce the distracting effect of minutiae.

(d) Delayed decisions. Choose refinements which incorporate only those design decisions that <u>must</u> be made. This avoids committing the design prematurely to specific implementation ideas and increases the ease with which modifications can subsequently be made.

(e) Simplicity. The human mind cannot easily handle large numbers of facts or complex inter-relationships. Avoid overloading yourself by choosing refinements with at most four or five components (two or three would be preferable). This reduces the likelihood of error.

From time to time every programmer finds that ideas stop flowing and a difficult problem blocks all further progress. When this happens, suspect a design error at a higher level which has set an impossible task. However if the design seems to be sound there are a few things worth trying. First of all, look for a solution by someone else. This may be found in the literature of the subject, or there may be a ready-made program in the computer centre's software library. If no solution of exactly the current problem turns up you may still be able to find solutions to closely related problems. These are a fertile source of ideas. Failing that, try to simplify the problem, solve the simpler problem and then work back to the original.

If you find yourself staring blankly at the title of a refinement, the same useless ideas whirling around in your mind, that is the time to put the thing aside. Relax, or work on something quite different. Unconscious mental processes will continue to grind away at the problem, free from conscious preconceptions. More often than not a solution will come to mind when you least expect it. Reading Robert Pirsig's novel "Zen and the Art of Motorcycle Maintenance" (Bodley Head, London, 1974) would be a profitable way to spend your time while you wait for inspiration. Besides being a good story this book contains many insights into problem solving, most of which are directly relevant to programming by stepwise refinement.

7.3 TESTING AND CORRECTING

Newcomers to programming are usually surprised by how often they make mistakes. Many are reluctant to believe that the mistakes are their own fault and blame the computer at every opportunity: such people seldom become good programmers. The only realistic attitude to this problem is a humble one: accept that mistakes will be made and try to minimize their effects.

Errors in the use of a programming language are "trivial". This may not be evident while you are struggling to master such a new and alien way of expressing yourself. However the remark is supported by the fact that the detection of these errors can safely be left to the computer. Of course it is desirable to avoid them, so the syntax and semantics of the language should be learned thoroughly, and the language manual should be kept at hand for easy reference. If in doubt, look it up!

More serious are those errors of structure or logic which cause a program to fail when it is run. Some failures may be detected by the computer system, which should respond by supplying detailed and useful diagnostic information to help you trace the cause (although many systems are very unhelpful in this respect). Other failures only manifest themselves in erroneous output. Sometimes the failure is very obvious. Everyone has heard tales about computers terrorizing old ladies with demands for the immediate payment of astronomical electricity bills. Regrettably, these things do happen. Even more worrying is the thought that less extreme failures may completely escape attention. In fact the computer user has only two alternatives: either to trust a program, or not to use it. This places on the programmer the onus of convincing others that his program is trustworthy.

Testing a program is a process which begins as soon as a Level 1 description has been written and continues throughout the implementation and maintenance phases. We have already seen how, by working through a program or a program description with suitable data, its correct operation can be checked. The same technique will show up errors in processing that data, if such are present. Testing by hand can only be done on a small scale: more comprehensive tests are made by running the program on a computer with larger sets of data. This is indispensible, because people make as many mistakes during hand testing as they do when programming. The question is, how do we choose the test data?

A good starting point is to consider all the control structures and select data to ensure that they are well exercised. A necessary condition for proper testing is that every statement in a program be obeyed at least once during the run. But this is not sufficient. A fragment of the form:

```
statement 1;
IF condition THEN
   statement 2;
statement 3
```

gives rise to two different paths through the program. If the "condition" is TRUE we get the path "statement 1 - statement 2 - statement 3", but if it is FALSE the path followed is "statement 1 - statement 3". Both possibilities must be tested. In other words, we also have to test the effect of not executing a statement. Similar remarks apply to WHILE loops.

The other aspect to consider is testing the expressions, to be sure that they represent the correct formulas. In arithmetic expressions large, small, positive, zero and negative data should be tried, as appropriate. A BOOLEAN expression must be tested with every combination of TRUE and FALSE operands. If the expression is at all complicated this will require an enormous amount of test data, so here is another reason for keeping things simple.

Take the example of program DISPLAY. The outermost control structure is a WHILE loop with condition NOT EOF(INPUT). There are two cases: (a) when the body of the loop is not obeyed at all (no data supplied), and (b) the normal case in which the body is repeated once for each number read. These cases will require separate test runs. The next control structure to consider is the IF statement. Again there are two cases: COUNT<=0 and COUNT>0. A thorough test will have to try out paths in which these cases alternate and paths in which one case occurs several times in succession. When COUNT<=0 a WRITE statement is obeyed which is supposed to allow for numbers in the range -99 to 0. This range must be checked. When COUNT>0 an inner WHILE loop is reached, but the body of this loop is obeyed at least once. Again, the range from +1 to +99 asterisks must be checked. Thus suitable test data sets for DISPLAY would be the following:

(a) no data at all; and

(b) 13, 55, -1, 6, 0, -2, -99, 27, 1, 72, 99.

Any errors revealed in this way must be corrected as methodically as the program was originally constructed. Never make random changes in your program in the hope that the error will go away. You may succeed in masking the symptoms, but you will not cure the disease. Instead, work back through the development of the program, starting at Level 1, until you find the refinement where the error was introduced. Correct that refinement and carry the correction down to the Pascal coding, retesting each level as you go. Only then should you modify the program text. This approach ensures that the consequences of a change on other parts of the program are reviewed and keeps the program description accurate.

When can a program be assumed to be correct? Unfortunately the answer is: never! Like scientific theories, programs can never be proved correct by testing (although they can be proved to be incorrect). A program which has always behaved perfectly may fail outright on the next set of data. Nonetheless, thorough testing is vital. If a program has performed according to specification on a variety of carefully-chosen and realistic test data, confidence in it is justifiably increased.

7.4 DOCUMENTATION

The documentation of a program consists of those supporting specifications and descriptions which are needed by the user and by the maintenance programmer. It is of the utmost importance to document a program well. The user of a program is entirely dependent on the documentation for his information about it and nothing is more annoying than discrepancies between the documentation and what the program does in practice. The maintenance programmer can have his work greatly expedited by good documentation. Bad documentation is probably worse than useless. His inclination may be to scrap a poorly documented program and write a well documented replacement, as this would certainly be easier to maintain.

A "User Guide" might contain some or all of the following sections.

(1) A brief description of the program. This is equivalent to the abstract of an article and its purpose is the same - to let the reader find out quickly whether the program is relevant to his needs.

(2) A detailed description of the program. This section should contain

subsections for each facility, giving complete descriptions of input and output formats.

(3) Theoretical background. If the program is based on any mathematical or scientific theory, a brief summary should be given. In the case of work which has been published a reference is adequate.

(4) Resources used. The amount of store and time needed to run the program are described. Where possible an approximate formula should be given, relating these factors to the input values. If this is not practical, the resources needed to run a "typical" job should be stated.

(5) Operational description. The instructions for the computer operator and/or the operating system control program are given, including the actions to be taken on the various kinds of failure.

The maintenance programmer relies on an "Implementation Description". This might contain the following items.

(1) A complete program description and refinement history, with discussion of the reason for each design decision.

(2) A program structure diagram (e.g. Figure 7.1).

(3) The program text. Only the text of a program can lay claim to being a fully authoritative description. To assist the maintainer, programs should be written with a view to readability. Consistent indentation, "paragraphing" by use of additional blank lines, truly meaningful identifiers, careful use of comments - all these help the reader to digest the content of the program.

Whatever its nature, documentation should be clearly-written, complete, unambiguous, accurate, timely and up-to-date. Writing documentation to this standard is just as difficult as programming and should be undertaken with an equal amount of care. It is worth noting that many of the ideas that lead to readable programs help in writing readable English. The principles of modularity, localization, consistency, and simplicity are particularly relevant.

7.5 CASE STUDY I: THE TRAFFIC SURVEY PROBLEM

Problem specification

A traffic survey is conducted automatically by placing a vehicle detector at the roadside, connected by data links to a computer. Whenever a vehicle passes the detector it transmits a signal consisting of the number 1. A clock in the detector is started at the beginning of a survey, and at one-second intervals thereafter it transmits a timing signal consisting of the number 2. At the end of a survey the detector transmits a 0. Each signal is received by the computer as a number on a line by itself. Write a program which reads such a set of signals and outputs the following:

    (a) the length of the survey period,
    (b) the number of vehicles recorded, and
    (c) the length of the longest interval between vehicles.

Solution

These results cannot be known until all the signals have been read. Hence the Level 1 description can safely be written as follows.

Level 1 of program TRAFFIC

```
declarations;
BEGIN
prepare to process signals;
WHILE not end of data DO
    act on the current signal;
output results
END.
```

As the other components seem to be quite simple, we tackle "act on the current signal" first. Again, the approach is based on an understanding of the data. The simplest point of view is that it consists of a jumble of vehicle signals and timing signals in random order. This suggests that the refinement should be in terms of an IF, with "process a timing signal" and "process a vehicle signal" as its component statements.

Refinement 1.1a: act on the current signal (first version)

```
BEGIN
IF it is a vehicle signal THEN
    process a vehicle signal
ELSE
IF it is a timing signal THEN
    process a timing signal;
read the next signal
END
```

Level 2a is derived by substituting this in Level 1.
Another way of looking at the data is that it consists of a sequence of "runs", each run being several consecutive signals of the same kind. A typical set of data might contain the signals:

1, 2, 2, 2, 1, 1, 2, 1, 2, 2, 1, 2, 2, 0

This interpretation is a natural one, because we want to measure time intervals and each interval is defined by the start and end of a run of timing signals. A sequence of signals of the same kind suggests a loop. These ideas lead to the following alternative refinement for "act on the current signal".

Refinement 1.1b: act on the current signal (second version)

```
BEGIN
WHILE it is a vehicle signal DO
   handle a vehicle signal;
start timing an interval;
WHILE it is a timing signal DO
   handle a timing signal;
finish timing an interval
END
```

Level 2b is obtained by substituting this in Level 1. If these inner WHILE loops are to terminate, "handle a vehicle signal" and "handle a timing signal" must read the next item of data. From this it follows that the last signal read on each execution of "act on the current signal" may be neither a vehicle signal nor a timing signal. Looking back at Level 1 we can see that this is catered for by the condition in the outer WHILE.

Refinement 1.1b seems to be more complex than Refinement 1.1a, so we will try to expand the latter first. Remembering that one objective is to measure vehicle-free intervals, we see that "process a vehicle signal" and "process a timing signal" must interact in such a way that the start and end of each interval can be recognized. Define the current interval to be that which has elapsed since the most recent vehicle signal and let INTERVAL be an INTEGER variable whose value is the length in seconds of the current interval. It follows that "process a vehicle signal" must set INTERVAL to zero and "process a timing signal" must increment it by one (as the timing signals come once a second). To count the vehicles and note the total elapsed time we need two more INTEGER variables, VEHICLES and SECONDS.

Refinements from Level 2a

Refinement 2.1a: process a timing signal

```
BEGIN
SECONDS := SECONDS + 1;
INTERVAL := INTERVAL + 1
END
```

Refinement 2.2a: process a vehicle signal

In addition to counting the vehicles and starting a new interval it is necessary to update a record of the longest interval so far. This requires another INTEGER variable, LONGEST.

```
BEGIN
VEHICLES := VEHICLES + 1;
IF INTERVAL>LONGEST THEN
   LONGEST := INTERVAL;
INTERVAL := 0
END
```

We have already reached the level of Pascal code, and all the remaining components of Level 2 are easily refined. To hold the current data item we introduce an INTEGER variable, SIGNAL. This gives us:

Refinement 2.3a: it is a vehicle signal

    SIGNAL=1

Refinement 2.4a: it is a timing signal

    SIGNAL=2

Refinement 2.5a: not end of data

    SIGNAL<>0

Refinement 2.6a: read the next signal

    READLN(SIGNAL)

Refinement 2.7a: output results

The details depend entirely on the layout required, but this has not been specified. One possibility is shown in the complete program, following.

Refinement 2.8a: prepare to process signals

    VEHICLES := 0;
    SECONDS := 0;
    LONGEST := 0;
    INTERVAL := 0;
    READLN(SIGNAL)

Refinement 2.9a: declarations

    VEHICLES, SECONDS, LONGEST, INTERVAL, SIGNAL : INTEGER

    Putting all of this together, we get a complete Pascal program.

Level 3a

    PROGRAM TRAFFICA(INPUT, OUTPUT);
    VAR
        VEHICLES, SECONDS, LONGEST, INTERVAL, SIGNAL : INTEGER;

```
BEGIN
(* Prepare to process signals *)
VEHICLES := 0;  SECONDS := 0;  LONGEST := 0;
INTERVAL := 0;
READLN(SIGNAL);

WHILE SIGNAL<>0 DO
   BEGIN (* Process the next signal *)
   IF SIGNAL=1 THEN
      BEGIN (* Process a vehicle signal *)
      VEHICLES := VEHICLES + 1;
      IF INTERVAL>LONGEST THEN
         LONGEST := INTERVAL;
      INTERVAL := 0
      END
   ELSE
   IF SIGNAL=2 THEN
      BEGIN (* Process a timing signal *)
      SECONDS := SECONDS + 1;
      INTERVAL := INTERVAL + 1
      END;

   (* Read the next signal *)
   READLN(SIGNAL)
   END;

(* Output results *)
WRITE(VEHICLES, '  VEHICLES PASSED IN', SECONDS, '  SECONDS; ');
WRITELN('THE LONGEST GAP WAS', LONGEST, '  SECONDS.')
END .
```

We now return to Refinement 1.1b. Two of its components, the loop conditions, have already been expanded as Refinements 2.3a and 2.4a, so we begin by looking at the loop bodies: "handle a vehicle signal" and "handle a timing signal". There is explicit provision in this version of the program for timing intervals, so dealing with a signal involves no more than incrementing the appropriate tally and reading the next signal. As before we use INTEGER variables, VEHICLES and SECONDS. To "start timing an interval" simply note the current value of SECONDS in the INTEGER variable STARTTIME. To "finish timing an interval", compute the difference between the updated value of SECONDS and the old value held in STARTTIME. This can then be compared with LONGEST, as before.

Refinements from Level 2b

Refinement 2.1b: handle a vehicle signal

```
BEGIN
VEHICLES := VEHICLES + 1;
read the next signal
END
```

Refinement 2.2b: handle a timing signal

```
BEGIN
SECONDS := SECONDS + 1;
read the next signal
END
```

Refinement 2.3b: start timing an interval

```
STARTTIME := SECONDS
```

Refinement 2.4b: finish timing an interval

```
IF SECONDS-STARTTIME > LONGEST THEN
   LONGEST := SECONDS - STARTTIME
```

The final Pascal program can now be constructed, using refinements 2.5a, 2.6a and 2.7a directly, along with slightly modified versions of 2.8a and 2.9a.

Level 3b

```
PROGRAM TRAFFICB(INPUT, OUTPUT);
VAR
   VEHICLES, SECONDS, STARTTIME, LONGEST, SIGNAL : INTEGER;

BEGIN
(* Prepare to process signals *)
VEHICLES := 0;  SECONDS := 0;  LONGEST := 0;
READLN(SIGNAL);

WHILE SIGNAL<>0 DO
   BEGIN (* Process the next signal *)
   WHILE SIGNAL=1 DO
      BEGIN (* Handle a vehicle signal *)
      VEHICLES := VEHICLES + 1;
      READLN(SIGNAL)
      END;

   (* Start timing an interval *)
   STARTTIME := SECONDS;

   WHILE SIGNAL=2 DO
      BEGIN (* Handle a timing signal *)
      SECONDS := SECONDS + 1;
      READLN(SIGNAL)
      END;
```

```
        (* Finish timing an interval *)
        IF SECONDS-STARTTIME > LONGEST THEN
           LONGEST := SECONDS - STARTTIME

        END;

     (* Output results *)
     WRITE(VEHICLES, '  VEHICLES PASSED IN', SECONDS, '  SECONDS; ');
     WRITELN('THE LONGEST GAP WAS', LONGEST, '  SECONDS.')
     END .
```

Let us now compare our two programs, according to the criteria
discussed in Section 7.2. Which is the more modular? There cannot be
any great difference between two such short programs, but the answer is
surely TRAFFICB: the routines to handle signals are quite independent of
each other and of the interval timing. This is not the case with
TRAFFICA. Which is the more localized? Again, marginally, TRAFFICB.
Which is the simpler? Refinements 1.1a and 1.1b are broadly comparable,
with 1.1a perhaps slightly simpler, but the subsequent development of
TRAFFICB is certainly simpler than that of TRAFFICA.

It is noteworthy that the improved version, TRAFFICB, was obtained by
adopting a better view of the data and that this is directly reflected
in a better program structure. This sort of correspondence between data
structure and program structure is very common and can often be used as
a guide to choosing a refinement.

7.6 THE SOFTWARE DEVELOPMENT CYCLE

Programming is not conducted in a vacuum. On the one hand, a program is
written with some purpose in mind, whether serious or frivolous; and for
some user or group of users, even if only for the programmer himself.
On the other hand is the computer: powerful but primitive. Reconciling
these disparate elements is a complex process, the software development
cycle. It is generally thought to consist of the following six stages.
(1) First comes the job of discovering exactly what the user would like
    the computer to do. This may involve interviews, market surveys, or
    simple introspection (if you are your own user).
(2) The user requirement may need to be tempered with practicality, as
    there is no point in trying to provide a facility which is beyond
    the capacities of the computer system.
(3) The modified requirement is submitted to the user for approval. If
    this is not forthcoming, steps (1) to (3) will have to be repeated
    until a final and practical statement of the requirement is agreed
    upon, or until it is recognized that agreement cannot be reached.
(4) The user requirement is stated in the user's terms and must now be
    expressed in terms of computer operations. In general a suite of
    programs will be needed, interacting with several sets of data.
    Usually the data is the heart of the matter. Once it is determined
    what data is initially available, and what must be generated by the
    system, each program can be specified by detailing its inputs and

outputs. Such a specification is no more than a first refinement step, on a much larger scale than the refinements made <u>within</u> programs, but no different in principle.

(5) Given these specifications, each program is designed, coded in a programming language, and tested.

(6) Since the user requirement is always subject to change, the programs must be modified and improved accordingly. When it seems that further modifications are necessary, but impractical, the whole cycle begins again from step (1).

Steps (1) through (3) are known as systems analysis, step (4) is system design, step (5) is implementation and step (6)`is maintenance. Taken together steps (5) and (6) constitute what we call <u>programming</u> (in the strict sense of the word; some people apply the term to the whole software development cycle). This book is almost exclusively concerned with programming. Systems analysis and design are neglected not because they are unimportant – quite the contrary – but because they depend on a mature understanding of the problems and possibilities of programming. A much longer book than this is required to do them justice.

EXERCISES 7

7.1. Which version of the traffic survey program is more efficient, in the sense of doing less work for the same result?

7.2. What does each version do when there is no timing signal in the data (i.e. the survey period is less than one second)? Is this behaviour reasonable?

7.3. What does each version do when there is no vehicle signal in the data? Is this behaviour reasonable? If not, suggest a change to improve it. {The treatment of such "degenerate" cases was not set out in the specification. This is an example of the sort of problem a programmer has to discuss with the systems analyst/designer.}

7.4. What does each version do when there are errors in the data (i.e. signals >2 or <0)? Is this behaviour reasonable?

7.5. Write a User Guide and an Implementation Description for program TRAFFICB.

PROGRAMMING EXERCISES 7

7.6. Revise both versions of the traffic survey program in a systematic manner so that (a) errors are detected and counted and (b) an error invalidates any interval in which it occurs.

7.7. Write a program which reads students' examination marks, one per line of input data, and writes the number of passes (marks of 50 or over) and the number of failures (marks of under 50).

7.8*. Write a program which reads details of transactions on a bank account and writes a bank statement summarizing these transactions. The first line of the input data contains the initial balance (in $) of the bank account; the remaining lines of input data each contain a positive or negative number, a positive number indicating the amount (in $) of a credit transaction (deposit) and a negative number indicating the amount (in $) of a debit transaction (withdrawal). The bank statement should consist of the credits and debits, written in separate columns, followed by the initial and final balances of the account. An overdrawn (negative) balance should be indicated by writing the amount of the overdraft followed by the word 'OVERDRAWN'. For example, given the input data

```
1000
+200
-500
+100
-1000
-100
```

your program should write a bank statement like this:

```
CREDITS ($)       DEBITS ($)

   200
                     500
   100
                    1000
                     100

INITIAL BALANCE ($)    1000
FINAL    BALANCE ($)    300 OVERDRAWN
```

7.9*. The takings from each turnstile of a stadium are available as data in the following form:
(a) the identification number of the turnstile;
(b) a series of positive integers, representing the income from the sale of tickets at that turnstile;
(c) a negative integer as terminator.
Write a program to read several such sets of data, calculate and write the total income for each turnstile separately, calculate and write the total income for the stadium, and report the number of the turnstile with the largest taking.

II More data types

8 Ordinal types and type definitions

8.1 THE DATA TYPE CHAR

As already stated, in Chapter 2, characters are the most common means of communication between people and computers: a program written in Pascal (or any other programming language), the input data read by a program, and the output written by a program, are all expressed in characters.

For technical reasons, computer character sets are restricted in size, and unfortunately not all computers use the same character set. The two most common are the ASCII (or ISO) character set, which consists of 128 characters, and the EBCDIC character set, which consists of 256 characters. Both ASCII and EBCDIC include upper- and lower-case letters, digits, blanks, punctuation marks and some mathematical symbols. They are listed in full in Appendix 5.

In order to write programs which manipulate characters, we need constants and variables whose values are characters, and for this purpose Pascal provides the data type CHAR. A variable declared with type CHAR can take values which are characters in our own computer's character set. A character constant in a program is denoted by enclosing the character between apostrophes, such as 'A' or '7' or '+' or ' ', the last of which denotes the blank character. An exceptional case is the apostrophe character itself, which is denoted by ''''.

Example 8.1

The following constant definitions make BLANK a synonym for the blank character and QUERY a synonym for the character '?':

    BLANK = ' ' ; QUERY = '?'

The following variable declaration declares CH and INITIAL to be variables of type CHAR:

    CH, INITIAL : CHAR

We can now assign character values to these variables, e.g.:

    CH := BLANK ; INITIAL := 'W'

after which the variables have the following values:

CH $\boxed{\text{' '}}$ INITIAL $\boxed{\text{'W'}}$

It is important to distinguish the latter assignment statement from

    INITIAL := W

in which W is an identifier, denoting perhaps a constant or a variable, not the character 'W'.

As well as assignment, character values can be transmitted by reading and writing. The statement READ(CH), where CH is a CHAR variable, reads a single character from the input data and stores that character in CH. The statement WRITE(CH) writes the character stored in CH. READLN and WRITELN can also be used to transmit characters.

Example 8.2

The following program fragment reads a person's forename and surname (assuming that each name is followed by one or more blanks, and allowing for blanks preceding the forename as well) and writes the person's surname followed by initial (separated by a single blank). It presumes the definition of BLANK and the declaration of CH and INITIAL as in Example 8.1.

```
READ (CH) ;
(* skip any blanks preceding the forename *)
    WHILE CH = BLANK DO
        READ (CH) ;
(* note the initial *)
    INITIAL := CH ;
(* skip the rest of the forename *)
    WHILE CH <> BLANK DO
        READ (CH) ;
(* skip the blanks between the forename and the surname *)
    WHILE CH = BLANK DO
        READ (CH) ;
(* read and write the surname *)
    WHILE CH <> BLANK DO
        BEGIN
        WRITE (CH) ;
        READ (CH)
        END ;
(* write the initial *)
    WRITE (BLANK, INITIAL, '.')
```

For example, if the input contains

EDSGER DIJKSTRA

then the output would be

DIJKSTRA E.

Check this by working through the program fragment by hand.

As illustrated by Example 8.2, character values may be compared using
"=" or "<>". Other operations on character values are introduced in
Section 8.4.

What happens if we obey READ(CH) when all the characters in the
current line of input have already been read? The answer is that a
blank character is stored in CH, and the next character read will be the
first character of the following line. You can think of it as an
imaginary blank character appended automatically to every line of input.

Sometimes we wish to know when we have reached the end of the current
line of input, and for this purpose Pascal provides the BOOLEAN
predeclared function EOLN(INPUT), which is TRUE when the last (genuine)
character of a line has just been read (just as EOF(INPUT) becomes TRUE
when the very last character of the input data has been read).

Example 8.3

Assuming the variable declarations

```
CH          : CHAR ;
NMROFSTARS : INTEGER
```

the following program fragment reads a complete line of input and
counts the asterisks on that line.

```
NMROFSTARS := 0 ;
WHILE NOT EOLN(INPUT) DO    (* more characters on this line *)
   BEGIN
   READ (CH) ;
   IF CH = '*' THEN
      NMROFSTARS := NMROFSTARS+1
   END
```


You must understand clearly that when you write down "7" or "365",
what you are writing is not itself a number, but a representation of a
number by a sequence of characters. There is nothing inherently
meaningful about this representation. We could choose to represent
numbers in many ways, such as "7" (using decimal notation), or "111"
(using binary notation), or "VII" (using a Roman numeral), for the
number seven. Decimal notation has been adopted as the standard

representation for numbers read and written by computers, but this was an arbitrary choice, and there is nothing to prevent anyone from writing a program which reads and/or writes Roman numerals, for example.

Numbers and other data require a representation inside the computer too, and this internal representation may well be different from the external representation. In particular, a binary representation is usually adopted for numbers inside the computer, since this is more efficient for computer arithmetic than a decimal representation. Thus whenever a number is read it must be converted from character form into its internal representation; and whenever a number is written it must be converted from its internal representation into characters. These conversions are automatically performed by READ, READLN, WRITE and WRITELN.

It is appropriate now to describe precisely the effect of a statement like READ(D), where D is an INTEGER variable. A <u>sequence</u> of characters is read, namely the digits which comprise the representation of a number, preceded by any number of blanks. Given the following line of input data, for example:

    DATE   17/2/78

if the last character read was the 'E', then the effect of READ(D) is to skip several blanks, read the characters '1' and '7', and assign to D the value 17 represented by this sequence of characters.

If, instead, we obey the statement READ(D,S1,M,S2,Y), where D, M and Y are INTEGER variables and S1 and S2 are CHAR variables, then we reach the following situation:

D [17]   M [2]   Y [78]   S1 ['/']   S2 ['/']

Now suppose that '8' is the very last character in this line and that the line is the very last line of the input data. EOLN(INPUT) is TRUE, but it is still possible to read one more character, the imaginary end-of-line blank character, as explained above. Therefore, EOF(INPUT) is still FALSE. If instead we had used READLN(D,S1,M,S2,Y), however, EOF(INPUT) would now be TRUE, since READLN always reads the entire remainder of the current line of input, including the imaginary end-of-line blank character. This is the explanation of the point made in Section 6.2 about the interaction between READLN and EOF.

8.2 ENUMERATION TYPES

So far we have met three data types provided by Pascal: INTEGER, whose values are positive and negative integers; BOOLEAN, whose values are FALSE and TRUE; and CHAR, whose values are the characters of some character set. Sometimes we need a wider choice than this; for example we might need a data type whose values are days-of-the-week, or a data type whose values are months, or a data type whose values are primary colours. We could extend this list of possibly useful data types indefinitely, and it would be unreasonable to expect Pascal to anticipate all possible needs. Instead Pascal provides a means for us to specify our own data types.

Suppose, for example, we wish to declare variables TODAY and TOMMORROW whose values are days-of-the-week. We could declare them as INTEGER variables, and write down statements like TODAY := 4, where it is understood that 0 represents Sunday, 1 represents Monday, 2 represents Tuesday, etc. This is rather artificial, and we must make an effort to remember which integers represent which days. An improvement is to introduce the constant definitions

    SUNDAY = 0 ; MONDAY = 1 ; TUESDAY = 2 ; WEDNESDAY = 3 ;
    THURSDAY = 4 ; FRIDAY = 5 ; SATURDAY = 6

which allows us to replace the statement above by the more natural TODAY := THURSDAY. Even now we can get into trouble; if TODAY=6 and we carelessly obey the statement TOMORROW := TODAY+1, what interpretation will be placed on the new value of TOMORROW?

In fact, nearly all programming languages allow no alternative to declaring TODAY and TOMORROW as INTEGER variables. Pascal is richer than most in that it allows us explicitly to declare variables whose values will be days-of-the-week, as follows:

    TODAY, TOMORROW :
        (SUNDAY,MONDAY,TUESDAY,WEDNESDAY,THURSDAY,FRIDAY,SATURDAY)

This declaration has three effects:
(a) it introduces a new data type (SUNDAY,MONDAY,TUESDAY,....);
(b) it implicitly defines SUNDAY, MONDAY, etc. to be constant identifiers which denote the values of this new data type (just as FALSE and TRUE denote the two values of the data type BOOLEAN);
(c) it declares TODAY and TOMORROW to be variables of this new data type.

The new data type is an example of an enumerated type, so called because it is specified by enumeration of its values.

Having declared these variables, we can write statements such as TODAY := THURSDAY, after which we can picture the contents of TODAY as follows:

TODAY [THURSDAY]

We cannot now write statements like TODAY := 4, since 4 is not a value of the new data type; nor TOMORROW := TODAY+1, since the value of TODAY is not a number and therefore cannot be added to anything.

We could declare variables of the other data types mentioned in the opening paragraph as follows:

    MONTH : (JAN,FEB,MAR,APR,MAY,JUN,JUL,AUG,SEP,OCT,NOV,DEC) ;
    COLOUR : (RED,YELLOW,BLUE)

The syntax of enumerated types is summarized in Figure 8.1.

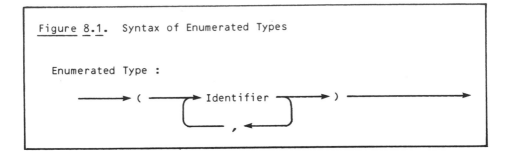

Figure 8.1. Syntax of Enumerated Types

Enumerated Type :

Example 8.4

Assume the variable declaration

```
DAY : (SUNDAY,MONDAY,TUESDAY,WEDNESDAY,THURSDAY,FRIDAY,SATURDAY)
```

In Standard Pascal the value SUNDAY is unrelated to the string 'SUNDAY'. To emphasize this, Standard Pascal does not allow statements like WRITE(DAY), whose effect might be expected to be to write one of the words 'SUNDAY', 'MONDAY', 'TUESDAY', ..., depending on the value of DAY. If we wish to achieve this effect, therefore, we must program it explicitly:

```
IF      DAY = SUNDAY    THEN WRITE ('SUNDAY   ')
ELSE IF DAY = MONDAY    THEN WRITE ('MONDAY   ')
ELSE IF DAY = TUESDAY   THEN WRITE ('TUESDAY  ')
ELSE IF DAY = WEDNESDAY THEN WRITE ('WEDNESDAY')
ELSE IF DAY = THURSDAY  THEN WRITE ('THURSDAY ')
ELSE IF DAY = FRIDAY    THEN WRITE ('FRIDAY   ')
ELSE                         WRITE ('SATURDAY ')
```

(We shall, however, find a better way to do the same thing in Section 11.2.)

The following program fragment reads a day-of-the-week represented in the input data by 'S', 'M', 'T', 'W', 't', 'F' or 's', assuming that CH is a CHAR variable:

```
READ (CH) ;
IF      CH = 'S' THEN DAY := SUNDAY
ELSE IF CH = 'M' THEN DAY := MONDAY
ELSE IF CH = 'T' THEN DAY := TUESDAY
ELSE IF CH = 'W' THEN DAY := WEDNESDAY
ELSE IF CH = 't' THEN DAY := THURSDAY
ELSE IF CH = 'F' THEN DAY := FRIDAY
ELSE IF CH = 's' THEN DAY := SATURDAY
ELSE
    WRITELN ('INVALID DAY-OF-THE-WEEK REPRESENTATION: ', CH)
```

As illustrated by Example 8.4, values of a given enumerated type may be compared with one another. More operations applicable to enumerated types will be introduced in Section 8.4.

8.3 SUBRANGE TYPES

Suppose we wish to declare a variable NMROFDAYSINMONTH whose value will be the number of days in some month. We could declare NMROFDAYSINMONTH to be an INTEGER variable, but the trouble with this idea is that NMROFDAYSINMONTH can now be assigned nonsensical values like 32 or -9999. In fact we know in advance that this variable can legitimately take only the values 28 to 31 inclusive. Pascal allows us to incorporate this foreknowledge into the variable's type, as follows:

    NMROFDAYSINMONTH : 28 .. 31

28..31 is an example of a subrange type, specifically the subrange of INTEGER values from 28 to 31 inclusive. Now NMROFDAYSINMONTH can be used just like an ordinary INTEGER variable, with this exception: if inadvertently an out-of-range value such as 32 or -9999 is assigned to NMROFDAYSINMONTH, it can be detected automatically and a suitable error message issued by the computer. This error message will draw attention to a logical error in the program which might have remained undetected if NMROFDAYSINMONTH were an INTEGER variable.

We are not restricted to subranges of INTEGER; we can specify subranges also of CHAR or of any enumerated type, e.g.:

    DIGIT   : '0' .. '9' ;
    WEEKDAY   : MONDAY .. FRIDAY ;
    SUMMERMONTH : JUN .. AUG

The second and third declarations assume prior occurrences of the enumerated types (SUNDAY,MONDAY,TUESDAY,....) and (JAN,FEB,MAR,.....) respectively. Now DIGIT can be used just like an ordinary CHAR variable, WEEKDAY just like an ordinary variable of type (SUNDAY,MONDAY,TUESDAY,....), and so on, except that any attempt to assign an out-of-range value to one of these variables, for example by the statement WEEKDAY := SUNDAY, can be detected automatically.

Example 8.5

The following program will, given as input the number of rainy days in each of the years 1900 to 1977, write these numbers followed by a total for the whole period.

```
PROGRAM RAINYDAYS ( INPUT, OUTPUT ) ;
CONST
   FIRSTYEAR     = 1900 ;
   LASTYEARPLUS1 = 1978 ;
VAR
   YEAR            : FIRSTYEAR .. LASTYEARPLUS1 ;
   NMROFRAINYDAYS : 0 .. 366 ;
   TOTALRAINYDAYS : INTEGER ;
BEGIN
TOTALRAINYDAYS := 0 ;
YEAR := FIRSTYEAR ;
WHILE YEAR < LASTYEARPLUS1 DO
   BEGIN
   READ (NMROFRAINYDAYS) ;
   WRITELN (YEAR:5, NMROFRAINYDAYS:8) ;
   TOTALRAINYDAYS := TOTALRAINYDAYS + NMROFRAINYDAYS ;
   YEAR := YEAR+1
   END ;
WRITELN ('TOTAL', TOTALRAINYDAYS:8)
END .
```

Observe that the variable YEAR is incremented at the end of each
iteration of the loop, and on the last iteration it will be
incremented to 1978. That is why its declared type must be
1900..1978, not just 1900..1977.

The syntax of subrange types is summarized in Figure 8.2. Note that
each bound may be specified by any constant, but the bounds must have
the same type and the lower bound must not exceed the upper bound.

Figure 8.2. Syntax of Subrange Types

Subrange Type :

        ─────────► Lower Bound ──────► .. ──────► Upper Bound ─────────►

Lower Bound :

        ─────────────────► Constant ─────────────────────────────►

Upper Bound :

        ─────────────────► Constant ─────────────────────────────►

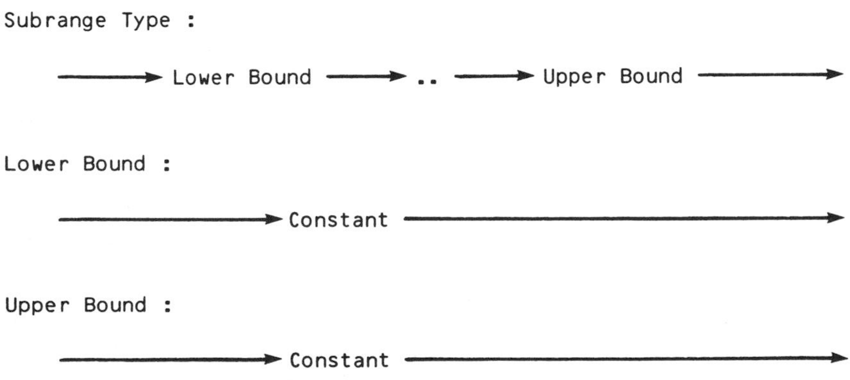

All the data types we have met so far — INTEGER, BOOLEAN, CHAR, enumerated types, and subranges thereof — are collectively called ordinal types. The ordinal types have certain properties in common which are not all shared by the other data types of Pascal. (We shall meet data types which are not ordinal in the rest of Part II and in Part V.)

Each value of an ordinal type (with certain exceptions) has an unique predecessor and an unique successor. For example:

(a) the predecessor and successor of the INTEGER value 10 are 9 and 11 respectively;

(b) the predecessor and successor of the CHAR value 'E' are 'D' and 'F' respectively (at least in the ASCII and EBCDIC character sets);

(c) in the enumerated type (SUNDAY,MONDAY,TUESDAY,....), the predecessor and successor of MONDAY are SUNDAY and TUESDAY respectively, since these are the constant identifiers which immediately precede and succeed MONDAY in the enumeration.

Pascal provides two predeclared functions, PRED and SUCC, which take a single parameter of any ordinal type and return the predecessor and successor, respectively, of its value. Thus PRED(MONDAY) = SUNDAY and SUCC(MONDAY) = TUESDAY. If N is of type INTEGER, then clearly PRED(N) is equivalent to N-1 and SUCC(N) to N+1.

Example 8.6

The following program fragment determines what day TOMORROW is:

```
IF TODAY = SATURDAY THEN
    TOMORROW := SUNDAY
ELSE
    TOMORROW := SUCC(TODAY)
```

Note that it would be an error to attempt to evaluate SUCC(TODAY) when TODAY=SATURDAY, since SATURDAY has no successor. Likewise, it be would erroneous to attempt to evaluate PRED(SUNDAY).

The existence of predecessors and successors implies an ordering on the values of each ordinal type. We have already seen, in Chapter 5, that we can compare two INTEGER values (or two BOOLEAN values) using any of the comparison operators "=", "<>", "<", "<=", ">=" or ">". The same applies to all ordinal types.

In the case of enumerated types, the ordering of the values is specified by their order of enumeration. Thus, for example, the expression TODAY < TUESDAY evaluates to TRUE if and only if the current value of the variable TODAY is SUNDAY or MONDAY.

In the case of CHAR values, you will be familiar with the alphabetic ordering, whereby 'A'<'B', 'B'<'C', etc. The alphabetic ordering can be generalized to the lexicographic ordering of a complete character set.

Unfortunately, computer character sets are inconsistent in their lexicographic ordering, as you can see by comparing the ASCII and EBCDIC character sets in Appendix 5. Nevertheless, all computer character sets respect the alphabetic ordering and also the obvious ordering for digits: '0'<'1', '1'<'2', etc.

Example 8.7

The following program counts the number of letters and digits in the input data.

```
PROGRAM CHARACTERCOUNT ( INPUT, OUTPUT ) ;
VAR
   LETTERCOUNT, DIGITCOUNT : INTEGER ;
   CH                      : CHAR ;
BEGIN
LETTERCOUNT := 0 ;
DIGITCOUNT  := 0 ;
WHILE NOT EOF(INPUT) DO
   BEGIN
   READ (CH) ;
   IF ('A' <= CH) AND (CH <= 'Z') OR
      ('a' <= CH) AND (CH <= 'z') THEN
      LETTERCOUNT := LETTERCOUNT+1
   ELSE IF ('0' <= CH) AND (CH <= '9') THEN
      DIGITCOUNT := DIGITCOUNT+1
   END ;
WRITELN (LETTERCOUNT, ' LETTERS, ',
         DIGITCOUNT,  ' DIGITS.')
END .
```

This program assumes that, in the lexicographic ordering, every character between 'A' and 'Z' inclusive is an upper-case letter, and every character between 'a' and 'z' inclusive is a lower-case letter. This assumption is valid in most character sets including ASCII, but it is not strictly valid in the EBCDIC character set where certain "control characters" occur among the letters (see Appendix 5.2). These control characters are unlikely to occur in normal data, however, so the assumption is not a bad one. We shall continue to make this assumption in the examples, using declarations like

```
LETTER : 'A' .. 'Z'
```

for variables whose values will be upper-case letters.

The program also assumes that every character between '0' and '9' inclusive is a digit. This assumption is in fact valid in every character set.

To every value of a given ordinal type there corresponds a unique

INTEGER value, called its ordinal number. (This is why ordinal types are so called.) It is these ordinal numbers which underlie the PRED and SUCC functions and the ordering of the values of each ordinal type. The predeclared function ORD accepts a parameter of any ordinal type and returns its ordinal number. In the case of the enumerated type (SUNDAY,MONDAY,TUESDAY,....), for example, ORD(SUNDAY) = 0, ORD(MONDAY) = 1, ORD(TUESDAY) = 2, etc. In the case of the type CHAR, the ordinal numbers depend on the particular character set in use; see Appendix 5.

Example 8.8

The statement READ(NUMBER), where NUMBER is an INTEGER variable, reads an integer number in the conventional decimal notation. The following program fragment could be used to read an unsigned integer number represented in octal (base 8) notation. The number may be preceded by any number of blanks.

```
READ (CH) ;
(* skip any blanks preceding the number *)
   WHILE CH = ' ' DO
       READ (CH) ;
NUMBER := 0 ;
WHILE ('0' <= CH) AND (CH <- '7') DO
   BEGIN
   NUMBER := 8*NUMBER + (ORD(CH) - ORD('0')) ;
   READ (CH)
   END
```

The following variable declarations have been assumed:

```
NUMBER : INTEGER ;
CH      : CHAR
```

The expression ('0'<=CH) AND (CH<='7') is used to test whether the character stored in CH is an octal digit. Now to compute the value of the octal number, we must determine the value represented by each octal digit. This value is not given simply by ORD(CH), since, for example, ORD('0') = 48 and ORD('7') = 55 in ASCII. However, in every character set the digits have consecutive ordinal numbers, so the value represented by any digit CH is given by the expression (ORD(CH)-ORD('0')), as used above.

For the type CHAR only, the inverse of ORD is also provided by Pascal. This is the predeclared function CHR, which accepts a single INTEGER parameter and returns the corresponding CHAR value (if such a CHAR value exists). Thus if the character set in use has consecutive ordinal numbers for its letters, then the expression CHR (ORD('A')+I-1) yields the I-th letter of the alphabet.

8.5 TYPE DEFINITIONS

We have already seen that constant definitions can help to make programs easier to write and to read. By giving a suitable name (identifier) to a constant, as in the constant definition

    NMROFELEMENTS = 104

we can concentrate on the significance of the constant rather than its specific value. Should it be necessary to change this constant's value, it would be necessary to change only the constant definition, rather than hunt through the program for all occurrences of the constant 104.

   For similar reasons, Pascal provides the type definition, which is a means of giving a name (identifier) to a type.

Example 8.9

   The following are examples of type definitions:

    DAYSOFWEEK =
       (SUNDAY,MONDAY,TUESDAY,WEDNESDAY,THURSDAY,FRIDAY,SATURDAY) ;
    MONTHS = (JAN,FEB,MAR,APR,MAY,JUN,JUL,AUG,SEP,OCT,NOV,DEC) ;
    WEEKDAYS   = MONDAY .. FRIDAY ;
    COLOURS   = (RED,YELLOW,BLUE) ;
    LETTERS   = 'A' .. 'Z' ;
    YEARSOFTHISCENTURY = 1900 .. 1999

MONTHS, DAYSOFWEEK, etc. are thus defined to be type identifiers. We can now use these type identifiers in variable declarations like

    MONTH   : MONTHS ;
    TODAY   : DAYSOFWEEK ;
    WORKDAY : WEEKDAYS ;
    COLOUR : COLOURS ;
    INITIAL : LETTERS ;
    YEAR   : YEARSOFTHISCENTURY

The above declaration of WORKDAY, for example, is equivalent to the declaration

    WORKDAY : MONDAY .. FRIDAY

but is more concise and probably clearer.

   It may now be seen that INTEGER, BOOLEAN and CHAR are just predefined type identifiers. In fact, we can consider the definition of BOOLEAN to be

    BOOLEAN = (FALSE,TRUE)

The syntax of type definitions is summarized in Figure 8.3. In a program type definitions are grouped together and preceded by the reserved word TYPE (just as constant definitions are grouped together and preceded by CONST). Type definitions must follow any constant definitions and precede any variable declarations.

Figure 8.3. Syntax of Type Definitions

Type Definition :

────────▶ Identifier ────────▶ = ────────▶Type ─────────────────▶

More examples of the use of type definitions can be found in later chapters, e.g. Examples 10.9, 12.2, 12.3, 13.1, 13.3, 13.5, 13.6.

EXERCISES 8

8.1. Write a program fragment which reads a character followed by an integer N, and which writes that character N times.

8.2. Write a program fragment which reads a single line of characters and writes them out, replacing every sequence of consecutive blanks by a single blank.

8.3. A University has faculties of Science, Medicine, Law and Arts. (a) Write a declaration of a variable FACULTY which can be used to indicate in which faculty a student is studying. (b) Write a program fragment to read a value for this variable, represented in the input data by 'S', 'M', 'L' or 'A'. (c) Write a program fragment which writes, in full, the name of this faculty.

8.4. Assuming that today's date has been stored in the variables

DAY : 1..31 ; MONTH : MONTHS ; YEAR : 0..9999

(see Example 8.9 for the definition of MONTHS), write a program fragment which writes today's date, writing 1 for January, 2 for February, etc.

8.5*. Continuing from the previous exercise, write a program fragment which updates the variables to tomorrow's date.

8.6. One of the earliest uses of computers was in cryptography. The simplest method of encoding a message is to encode each character by a unique integer (such as its ordinal number). This kind of code is broken rather easily, however, by an analysis based on the known relative frequencies of the characters. A better method is to encode the first character of the message by its ordinal number, and each subsequent character by the sum, modulo 1000 (say), of that character's ordinal number and the previous character's encoding. (Thus if the first few characters have ordinal numbers 100, 600, 400, ..., then they would be encoded as 100, 700, 100, ...; the second code being 600+100 modulo 1000, and the third code being 400+700 modulo 1000.)

(a) Write a program which, given a message as input data, uses this method to encode the message as a sequence of integers.

(b) Devise a method of <u>decoding</u> a message encoded as above. Write a program to perform this decoding, and test it with the output from your encoding program. Make sure that your decoding program successfully reconstructs the original message!

8.7*. Write a program which reads natural-language text (consisting of words separated by blanks and punctuation), and which computes and writes the average number of letters per word and the average number of words per sentence in the text. The program should also write the sum of these averages, which is quite a good measure of the obscurity of a written text! For the purposes of this exercise, assume that a "word" is a sequence of consecutive letters, and that every period ('.') marks the end of a sentence. (Note: you will not need to use the EOLN function in this program.) Test your program with a substantial piece of text from a book.

9 The data type REAL

REAL NUMBERS AND REAL ARITHMETIC

So far we have concerned ourselves only with integer arithmetic, i.e. the arithmetic of whole numbers. These numbers are useful for purposes of counting, but they are inadequate when we wish to deal in measurements of physical quantities, such as distances, time intervals, weights, etc. For example, the distance between two points might be expressed as 14.65 metres, and the time interval between two events might be expressed as 9.2 seconds. Such numbers we call real numbers. {Mathematicians call them real numbers to distinguish them from complex numbers rather than from integer numbers.}

Just as with integer numbers, there is a limit to the number of digits of a real number which can be stored in a digital computer. As a consequence:

(a) there is a limit on the magnitude of real numbers which can be stored in the computer (typically about a million million million million million!); and

(b) there is a limit to the precision with which real numbers can be represented in the computer (this limit varies from 6 to 17 decimal digits on different computers).

The magnitude limit is indeed enormous, and the precision may seem excellent, but nevertheless these are limitations which must be taken into account in programming. The limited precision in particular gives rise to subtle programming problems.

In order to exploit the available precision fully, only the significant digits of a real number are stored in a digital computer. For example, in a computer capable of storing a real number to 6 decimal digits:

```
0.0099       would be stored as  0.00|990000 |
9.9            "    "    "    "       |9.90000  |
9900.0         "    "    "    "       |9900.00  |
99000000.0     "    "    "    "       | 990000  |00.0
8.7654321      "    "    "    "       |8.76543  |
1234.56789     "    "    "    "       |1234.57  |
```

(Only the digits between the lines are stored; the zeros outside are non-significant.) This is the floating-point representation, so called because the number of significant digits is fixed and the point "floats" relative to the significant digits. The computer automatically keeps track of the position of the point and takes this into account when performing arithmetic.

The limited precision of the floating-point representation forces numbers with too many significant digits to be rounded, as illustrated above. This can give surprising results.

Example 9.1

If we divide 1.0 by 3.0 and then multiply by 3.0, we might expect the result to be 1.0. The mathematical result of the division is 0.3333333333...., but in our 6-digit computer this result must be rounded to 0.333333. Then when we multiply by 3.0, we end up with 0.999999!

Example 9.2

If we subtract 10000.0 from 10000.1 and then add 0.04, we expect the result to be 0.14, and in our 6-digit computer this will indeed be so. If we perform the calculation in a different order, however, we may get a different result. If we first add 0.04 to 10000.1, the mathematical result, 10000.14, is rounded to 10000.1; now when we subtract 10000.0, the result is 0.1!

In some computers, results of arithmetic operations are truncated rather than rounded, i.e. the result 0.66666666666.... would be truncated to 0.666666 rather than rounded to 0.666667. Evidently, truncation causes even more inaccuracy than rounding.

In nearly every digital computer, numbers are stored in a binary base rather than a decimal base. Nevertheless, the problems illustrated by these examples remain. The use of the binary base does, however, create an additional problem for us, accustomed as we are to expressing numbers in the conventional decimal base. Many rational numbers, such as 1/3, cannot be expressed exactly as decimal fractions. Similarly, there are many numbers, such as 0.9, which can be expressed exactly as decimal fractions but cannot be expressed exactly as binary fractions. Thus when we use a constant like "0.9" in a program, or in a set of data, we should be aware that the number actually stored in the computer will only be an approximation to 0.9.

Let us summarize the errors inherent in the use of real arithmetic on digital computers.

(a) Real numbers obtained by physical measurement will have only limited accuracy, which depends on the device used to measure them. This is called observational error. We cannot expect a calculation to yield results which are more accurate than the original input data. For example, quoting the distance to the moon as "240000 miles, or 386473 kilometres" is just silly, since the original figure was accurate only to 2 significant digits.

(b) Most real numbers cannot be represented exactly in a given computer. This applies to all irrational numbers, to rational numbers which have no exact binary representation, and to numbers with too many significant digits. This phenomenon is called representational error, and it forces numbers input to the computer, and those resulting from arithmetic operations, to be rounded or truncated.

(c) Arithmetic operations tend to compound any errors in their operands. For example, if we subtract 4.999996 (represented by 5.00000) from 6.000004 (represented by 6.00000), we get the result 1.00000, in spite of the fact that the mathematical result, 1.000008, rounded to 6 significant digits yields 1.00001. This phenomenon is called computational error.

Normally representational and computational errors will be smaller than observational errors; computer users should make sure of this by presenting their real data to a computer which can store more significant digits than their data actually possesses. We shall see, however, that computational errors can accumulate, especially in highly iterative programs, so it is unsafe to neglect them altogether.

9.2 REAL ARITHMETIC IN PASCAL

Real numbers, within the limitations of magnitude and precision discussed in the previous section, are values of the Pascal data type REAL. We may declare variables whose type is REAL, and we may assign REAL values to such variables.

In Pascal, real numbers may be expressed either in the conventional notation for decimal fractions, or alternatively in the scientific notation, which is convenient for expressing very large and very small numbers, e.g.:

```
55E15      is equivalent to   55000000000000000.0;
-3.8E3        "        "       "   -3800.0;
1E-4          "        "       "   0.0001;
1.23E-20      "        "       "   0.0000000000000000000123.
```

Here E should be read as "times ten to the power of". The syntax of real numbers is summarized in Appendix 1.7.

REAL expressions may be composed in a similar manner to INTEGER expressions. The following operators may be used in REAL expressions:

    +   -   *   /

The operator "/" denotes REAL division: the result of applying "/" to any two numbers is a REAL number as close as possible to the exact quotient of these numbers. Thus 7/3 yields the REAL result 2.33333 on a 6-digit computer. (Compare the expression 7 DIV 3, which yields the INTEGER result 2.) The operator "/" has the same priority as "*".

A REAL value may be assigned to a REAL variable by an assignment statement with a REAL (or INTEGER) expression to the right of ":=".

Placing a REAL variable in a READ (or READLN) statement results in a real (or integer) number being read from the input data. Including a REAL expression in a WRITE (or WRITELN) statement results in a real number being written.

Example 9.3

The following constant definition defines PI to be a REAL constant:

    PI = 3.14159265

The following variable declaration declares several REAL variables:

    RADIUS, CIRCUMFERENCE, AREA : REAL

The following program fragment reads the radius of a circle, computes its circumference and area, and writes all three values:

    READ (RADIUS) ;
    CIRCUMFERENCE := 2 * PI * RADIUS ;
    AREA := PI * SQR(RADIUS) ;
    WRITELN (RADIUS, CIRCUMFERENCE, AREA)

Given the input data

    3.0

the output would look like this:

        3.00000E+00   1.88500E+01   2.82743E+01

i.e. REAL values are normally written in scientific notation.
    We can control the layout by specifying field widths, as in Section 4.6:

    WRITELN (RADIUS:14, CIRCUMFERENCE:20, AREA:20)

    We can also request ordinary fractional notation, as opposed to scientific notation, by specifying the required number of digits after the decimal point, in addition to the field width:

    WRITELN (RADIUS:8:1, CIRCUMFERENCE:12:1, AREA:12:1)

would make the output look like this:

        3.0   18.9   28.3

Because there is a real number equivalent to every integer number, a

REAL expression may contain INTEGER operands, as illustrated by the expression from Example 9.3:

    2 * PI * RADIUS

Likewise it is legitimate to assign an INTEGER value to a REAL variable:

    RADIUS := 3   has the same effect as   RADIUS := 3.0

On the other hand, REAL operands may not be used in INTEGER expressions, nor may a REAL value be assigned to an INTEGER variable. If N is an INTEGER variable, for example, the statement

    N := 3.14159

would be meaningless as N may take only INTEGER values and there is no INTEGER value equal to 3.14159.

Example 9.3 also illustrates a use of the predeclared function SQR in a REAL expression. Pascal provides a variety of predeclared functions for performing common, and sometimes complicated, computations. Each of the following predeclared functions accepts a single INTEGER or REAL parameter, and returns a result of the same type:

    ABS(x)   computes the absolute value (magnitude) of x.
    SQR(x)   "   " square of x.

Each of the following predeclared functions accepts a single REAL parameter and returns a REAL result:

    SIN(x)   computes the sine of x.
    COS(x)   "   " cosine of x.
    ARCTAN(x)   "   " arctangent of x.
    EXP(x)   "   " value of e raised to the power of x.
    LN(x)   "   " logarithm of x to the base e.
    SQRT(x)   "   " square root of x.

(The parameters of SIN and COS, and the result of ARCTAN, are angles expressed in radians.) Each of the following predeclared functions accepts a single REAL parameter and returns an INTEGER result:

    ROUND(x)   computes x rounded to the nearest integer.
    TRUNC(x)   "   x truncated to its integral part.

Thus ROUND(2.6) = 3, but TRUNC(2.6) = 2.

Finally, REAL expressions may be compared using any of the comparison operators "=", "<>", "<", "<=", ">=" or ">".

Example 9.4

    Given a rectangle with sides SIDE1 and SIDE2, and a circle with radius RADIUS, where SIDE1, SIDE2 and RADIUS are all REAL variables, the following program fragment determines which figure has the longer perimeter:

```
IF SIDE1 + SIDE2 > PI * RADIUS THEN
    WRITE ('RECTANGLE')
ELSE
    WRITE ('CIRCLE') ;
WRITELN (' HAS LONGER PERIMETER')
```

9.3 PROGRAMMING WITH REAL DATA

Section 9.1 illustrated the approximate nature of REAL arithmetic on digital computers. Thus "obvious" equalities like

$$X / Y * Y = X$$

$$X + Y - Z = X - Z + Y$$

do not exactly hold in REAL arithmetic. When writing programs which manipulate REAL data, we must always take arithmetic errors into account, as the following examples illustrate.

Example 9.5

Let us write a program fragment which determines whether a triangle is right-angled, given that the lengths of the sides of the triangle have been stored in REAL variables A, B and C, and assuming that side A is the longest.

Using a BOOLEAN variable RIGHTANGLED, we might be tempted to write down simply

```
RIGHTANGLED := SQR(A) = SQR(B) + SQR(C)
```

which is a direct transcription of Pythagoras' law.

Unfortunately, exact equality between two computed REAL values is extremely unlikely on a digital computer: representational and computational errors make it likely that the values being compared will be slightly different even when they would be expected to be equal.

The test is better expressed like this:

```
RIGHTANGLED := ABS( (SQR(B)+SQR(C))/SQR(A) - 1 ) < 0.0001
```

This version checks whether SQR(A) and SQR(B)+SQR(C) are equal to within 4 significant figures. (Observational and computational errors should be taken into account in selecting the tolerance figure 0.0001.)

Example 9.6

Let us write a program which writes a table of square roots of numbers from 1.0 to 1.1 in steps of 0.001.
We might be tempted to write down the following simple program:

```
PROGRAM SQUAREROOTS1 ( OUTPUT ) ;
CONST
   FIRSTX   = 1.0 ;
   LASTX    = 1.1 ;
   INTERVAL = 0.001 ;
VAR
   X : REAL ;
BEGIN
WRITELN ('    NUMBER      SQUARE ROOT') ;
WRITELN ;
X := FIRSTX ;
WHILE X <= LASTX DO
   BEGIN
   WRITELN (X:12:6, SQRT(X):12:6) ;
   X := X + INTERVAL
   END
END .
```

Here are the last few lines of output from this program, obtained by running it on a computer capable of about 7 decimal digits precision:

```
......       ......
......       ......
1.094993     1.046419
1.095993     1.046896
1.096992     1.047374
1.097992     1.047851
1.098992     1.048328
1.099992     1.048805
```

The stored value of INTERVAL is only an approximation to 0.001, and it is this approximate value which is repeatedly added to X. The output shows that the value of X drifts further and further from its expected value.
More accurate results are obtained from the following program:

```
PROGRAM SQUAREROOTS2 ( OUTPUT ) ;
CONST
   NMROFLINES = 101 ;
   FIRSTX     = 1.0 ;
   INTERVAL   = 0.001 ;
VAR
   LINECOUNT : INTEGER ;
   X         : REAL ;
```

```
BEGIN
WRITELN ('    NUMBER        SQUARE ROOT') ;
WRITELN ;
LINECOUNT := 0 ;
WHILE LINECOUNT < NMROFLINES DO
   BEGIN
   X := FIRSTX + LINECOUNT*INTERVAL ;
   WRITELN (X:12:6, SQRT(X):12:6) ;
   LINECOUNT := LINECOUNT + 1
   END
END .
```

The last few lines of output in this case were:

```
......      ......
......      ......
1.096999    1.047377
1.097999    1.047854
1.098999    1.048331
1.099999    1.048808
```

The reason for this improvement is that program SQUAREROOTS2 uses the INTEGER variable LINECOUNT for counting, and computes X afresh in each iteration. This avoids the cumulative computational error observed with program SQUAREROOTS1, which uses the REAL variable X for counting.

Example 9.7

Write a program fragment which computes and writes the roots of the quadratic equation

A*x*x + B*x + C = 0

given the REAL coefficients A, B and C. Assume that the roots are real.
   The two roots are given by the formulas

   (-B+S) / (2*A)   and   (-B-S) / (2*A)

where S is the square root of (B*B-4*A*C). We could transcribe these formulas directly:

```
S := SQRT(SQR(B)-4*A*C) ;
WRITELN ('ROOTS ARE: ', (-B+S)/(2*A), (-B-S)/(2*A))
```

But consider the case A=C=0.001, B=1.0; this gives S=0.999998 correct to 6 significant digits. Thus the first root will be computed as (-1.00000+0.999998)/0.002, i.e. -0.001 correct to only 1 significant digit. The problem here is cancellation of significant digits,

90

caused by subtracting two nearly equal numbers 1.00000 and 0.999998. In general, addition and subtraction yield results which are accurate only to the same number of decimal places (not to the same number of significant digits) as their operands.

We can achieve greater accuracy by first computing the larger root (in magnitude), and then computing the other root using the fact that the product of the roots is C/A:

```
S := SQRT(SQR(B)-4*A*C) ;
IF B > 0 THEN
   LARGERROOT := (-B-S)/(2*A)
ELSE
   LARGERROOT := (-B+S)/(2*A) ;
WRITELN ('ROOTS ARE: ', C/A/LARGERROOT, LARGERROOT)
```

The following output was obtained by running each of the program fragments (on the same computer as in Example 9.6):

(1)
ROOTS ARE: -1.043081E-03   -9.999989E+02

(2)
ROOTS ARE: -1.000000E-03   -9.999989E+02

As you can see, the smaller root is very inaccurate in the first case.

EXERCISES 9

9.1. Express the following numbers in scientific notation, in such a way that each number's mantissa (the part to the left of 'E') lies between 0.1 and 1.0:

0.00000000001234   0.009   0.254   3.14159265   981.0   250000.0

9.2. Express the following numbers in ordinary fractional notation:

45.67E-10   981E-2   3.00E0   1.885E+1   2.82743E+3   93E6

9.3. Evaluate the following REAL expressions, working to three significant decimal digits:

A+B+C   B+C+A   X*Y/Y   Z+Z+Z+Z+Z+Z+Z+Z+Z+Z   10*Z

assuming that A=0.004, B=1.00, C=-1.00, X=3.88, Y=3.88 and Z=0.333. Comment on the results.

9.4. Write down expressions which will compute the following: (a) the volume of a sphere whose radius is R; (b) the surface area of a rectangular block whose sides have lengths A, B and C; (c) the polar

coordinates of a point whose rectangular coordinates are X and Y; and
(d) the power dissipated in an electrical component whose resistance is
R and whose rated voltage is V.

9.5. Given the lengths A, B and C of the sides of a triangle, write a
program fragment which writes the area of the triangle. (The area is
equal to the square root, if it exists, of $S*(S-A)*(S-B)*(S-C)$, where S
is half the perimeter of the triangle.)

9.6. Assume that income tax in Ruritania is computed as 30% of taxable
income, plus 10% of taxable income in excess of 10000.00 groats.
Taxable income is income less allowances, or zero if the allowances
exceed the income. Write a program fragment which reads a Ruritanian
taxpayer's income and allowances, and which writes these followed by
his/her taxable income and tax payment.

PROGRAMMING EXERCISES 9

9.7. Write a program which reads real numbers AMOUNT and RATE, and an
integer N, and which writes out a table showing the simple interest and
the compound interest which will have accrued after 1, 2, ..., N years
to the sum of money AMOUNT at the annual rate of interest RATE. Sums of
money should be written in the conventional format for your national
currency. (Simple interest is calculated on AMOUNT only. Compound
interest is calculated each year on AMOUNT plus all the interest
accumulated in previous years.)

9.8. A rough graph of a suitable function can be plotted on a line-
printer, like this:

GRAPH OF X*X*X - 6*X*X + 11*X   SCALE FACTOR = 2.0

```
0.0 *
0.5 |      *
1.0 |         *
1.5 |          *
2.0 |         *
2.5 |       *
3.0 |       *
3.5 |          *
4.0 |              *
4.5 |                    *
5.0 |                                        *
```

The position of the plotted point in each line is obtained by
multiplying the function value by a suitable scale factor (2.0 above)
and then rounding to the nearest integer. Write a program which plots
SIN(X) for values of X from 0 to 180 degrees, in intervals of 5 degrees.
Use a scale factor of 50.0. Then modify the program to handle negative
function values, and extend the plot of SIN(X) to 360 degrees.

92

10 Arrays

10.1 THE NEED FOR ARRAYS

So far we have met only simple variables, as they are called. These are variables whose values are single numbers, Boolean values, characters, or such like. Much of programming, however, is concerned with collections of data, such as arrays, which we now introduce by means of an example.

Example 10.1

Consider an election contested by four candidates; let us write a program fragment to read the ballots and count the votes cast for each candidate. Assume that the candidates are numbered 1 to 4, and that each ballot is presented as a line of input containing one of these numbers.

The following is a skeleton solution:

```
initialize all vote-counts to 0 ;
WHILE not all ballots have been read DO
    BEGIN
    read a ballot ;
    add 1 to the chosen candidate's vote-count
    END ;
write the vote-counts
```

To hold the vote-counts, we could use four INTEGER variables COUNT1, COUNT2, COUNT3, and COUNT4. Then we could refine as follows:

```
(* read a ballot *)
    READLN (CANDIDATE) ;
(* add 1 to the chosen candidate's vote-count *)
    IF CANDIDATE = 1 THEN
        add 1 to COUNT1
    ELSE IF CANDIDATE = 2 THEN
        add 1 to COUNT2
    ELSE IF CANDIDATE = 3 THEN
        add 1 to COUNT3
    ELSE IF CANDIDATE = 4 THEN
        add 1 to COUNT4
```

You might feel that this solution is rather clumsy. Imagine how much worse it would be if the program were modified to handle ten or fifty candidates!

If we observe that the variables COUNT1, COUNT2, COUNT3 and COUNT4 are used in exactly the same way, however, we have a clue to a better solution. Let us rename the variables COUNT[1], COUNT[2], COUNT[3], and COUNT[4]. The variables now form an array, with a single identifier COUNT. We distinguish the variables from one another by writing a subscript between square brackets after COUNT. {This terminology is borrowed from mathematics, since subscripts in programming are in many respects similar to subscripts in mathematics. In conventional mathematical notation the subscripts are written below the line without brackets; Pascal uses brackets because of the limitations of most computer input devices.} COUNT[2] is one element of the array COUNT, namely the element whose subscript is 2.

We have made no real progress if we can use only constants as subscripts. The power of the subscript notation, however, is such that we can use COUNT[CANDIDATE] to refer to the element of COUNT whose subscript is the value of CANDIDATE. Thus we can recast our refinement as follows:

```
(* add 1 to the chosen candidate's vote-count *)
    add 1 to COUNT[CANDIDATE]
```

This is much more elegant and, moreover, requires no modification if the number of candidates is changed.

Arrays occur in daily life, where they are called tables. For example:
(a) A table of train departure times is an array. If we call the array DEP, we can denote the departure time of the I-th train by DEP[I].
(b) A table of the number of days in each month is an array. If we call the array DAYSINMONTH, we can denote by DAYSINMONTH[MAY] the number of days in May.

10.2 ARRAYS IN PASCAL

In Pascal an array is declared just like any other variable, but its type will be an array type which specifies:
(a) the range of subscripts of the array, and
(b) the type of its elements.
It is an important property of an array that every element has the same type.

Example 10.1 (continued)

The array COUNT would be declared in Pascal as follows:

```
COUNT : ARRAY [1..4] OF INTEGER
```

This declaration specifies that the type of the variable COUNT is an array

(a) whose <u>subscript type</u> is 1..4, i.e. the possible subscripts of the array are 1, 2, 3 and 4; and

(b) whose <u>element type</u> is INTEGER, i.e. each element of the array is INTEGER.

We can picture COUNT as a row of "boxes", or storage locations, one for each subscript value:

```
          1    2    3    4
COUNT [  27 | 36 |  0 |  9  ]
```

here showing the current values of the array elements to be COUNT[1]=27, COUNT[2]=36, COUNT[3]=0, and COUNT[4]=9.

COUNT[CANDIDATE] is an example of a <u>subscripted variable</u>. The element of COUNT for which it stands depends on the <u>current</u> value of CANDIDATE. It is most important that this value is indeed a value of the subscript type, here 1..4. Suppose that one of the numbers read by our program is 0, so that the value of CANDIDATE becomes 0. Then COUNT[CANDIDATE] in this case refers to COUNT[0], which does not exist. This is a common and serious programming error (<u>subscript out of range</u>) which must always be avoided, since it will cause the program to fail.

In this example, it is quite possible that one of the numbers read may be outside the range 1 to 4, and our program, as it stands, will indeed fail. We might reasonably treat a number outside the range 1 to 4 as a "spoilt ballot", and ignore it. Here is a complete program for the election problem which does this:

```
PROGRAM ELECTION ( INPUT, OUTPUT ) ;

CONST
   NMROFCANDIDATES = 4 ;
VAR
   CANDIDATE : INTEGER ;
   COUNT     : ARRAY [1..NMROFCANDIDATES] OF INTEGER ;

BEGIN
(* initialize all vote-counts to 0 *)
   CANDIDATE := 1 ;
   WHILE CANDIDATE <= NMROFCANDIDATES DO
      BEGIN
      COUNT[CANDIDATE] := 0 ;
      CANDIDATE := SUCC(CANDIDATE)
      END ;
```

```
WHILE (* not all ballots have been read *) NOT EOF(INPUT) DO
   BEGIN
   (* read a ballot *)
      READLN (CANDIDATE) ;
   (* add 1 to the chosen candidate's vote-count,
                    unless the ballot was spoilt *)
      IF (CANDIDATE >= 1) AND
         (CANDIDATE <= NMROFCANDIDATES) THEN
         COUNT[CANDIDATE] := COUNT[CANDIDATE] + 1
   END ;
(* write the vote-counts *)
   CANDIDATE := 1 ;
   WHILE CANDIDATE <= NMROFCANDIDATES DO
      BEGIN
      WRITELN ('CANDIDATE ', CANDIDATE:2, ' OBTAINED ',
              COUNT[CANDIDATE]:3, ' VOTES') ;
      CANDIDATE := SUCC(CANDIDATE)
      END
END .
```

Note that the refinement of "initialize all vote-counts to 0" is a
loop which assigns 0 to each element of COUNT in turn; and that the
refinement of "write the vote-counts" is a loop which writes the
value of each element in turn.
   Note also the use of the constant NMROFCANDIDATES, which makes the
program more flexible: if the program had to be modified to handle
more candidates, then only the constant definition need be altered.

Example 10.2

Given some suitable definitions of the constant identifier
NMROFTRAINS and the type identifier TIME, a table of train departure
times might be declared as follows:

    DEP : ARRAY [1..NMROFTRAINS] OF TIME

Example 10.3

Assuming the type definition

    MONTHS = (JAN,FEB,MAR,APR,MAY,JUN,JUL,AUG,SEP,OCT,NOV,DEC)

a table of days per month could be declared as follows:

    DAYSINMONTH : ARRAY [MONTHS] OF 28..31

and it would look like this:

	JAN	FEB	MAR	APR	MAY	JUN	JUL	AUG	SEP	OCT	NOV	DEC
DAYSINMONTH	31	28	31	30	31	30	31	31	30	31	30	31

The syntax of array types is summarized in Figure 10.1. ARRAY and OF are both reserved words. Array types may be used, like other types, in type definitions as well as in variable declarations.

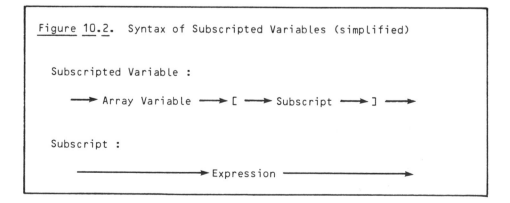

Figure 10.1. Syntax of Array Types (simplified)

Array Type :

⟶ ARRAY ⟶ [⟶ Subscript Type ⟶]

⟶ OF ⟶ Element Type ⟶

Subscript Type :

⟶ Ordinal Type ⟶

Element Type :

⟶ Type ⟶

Figure 10.2. Syntax of Subscripted Variables (simplified)

Subscripted Variable :

⟶ Array Variable ⟶ [⟶ Subscript ⟶] ⟶

Subscript :

⟶ Expression ⟶

97

The syntax of subscripted variables is summarized in Figure 10.2. Note that any expression can be used as a subscript, i.e. we are not restricted to constants or simple variables. In every case, however, the subscript must yield a value of the array's subscript type.

A subscripted variable may be used anywhere a simple variable can, for example in an assignment statement:

```
COUNT[CANDIDATE] := COUNT[CANDIDATE] + 1
```

10.3 ELEMENTWISE PROCESSING OF ARRAYS

The most common manipulation of arrays is elementwise processing, whereby we perform similar operations on some or all elements of the array, one at a time. We have already met some simple examples of elementwise processing: the initialization of the vote-counts, and the writing of the vote-counts, in Example 10.1.

Since several elements are to to be processed, elementwise processing is performed by a loop. We need a variable to subscript the array; we initialize this variable to be the subscript of the first element to be processed, and inside the loop we update the variable to be the subscript of the next element to be processed. We make iteration continue until the variable has passed the subscript of the last element to be processed.

Example 10.4

Assuming the type identifier MONTHS is defined as in Example 10.3, and given a table of monthly rainfall readings stored in the array

```
RAINFALL : ARRAY [MONTHS] OF REAL
```

let us write a program fragment to determine the total rainfall from April to September.

We declare the following variables:

```
MONTH : MONTHS ;
TOTAL : REAL
```

and we use MONTH as the subscripting variable. Then the solution is:

```
(* determine total rainfall from April to September *)
    TOTAL := 0 ;
    MONTH := APR ;
    WHILE MONTH <= SEP DO
        BEGIN
        TOTAL := TOTAL + RAINFALL[MONTH] ;
        MONTH := SUCC(MONTH)
        END
```

Verify this solution by hand-testing. Note that the order of the two statements inside the loop is important; what happens if these statements are interchanged?

Finally, a warning: we can directly modify this piece of program to total the rainfall for any other continuous period, except a period ending in December! If we modified the WHILE clause to WHILE MONTH <= DEC DO, then in the last iteration we would attempt to evaluate SUCC(DEC), which does not exist. We shall see how to avoid this difficulty when we meet FOR statements in Chapter 11. This problem did not arise in Example 10.1 because the subscripting variable, CANDIDATE, was declared INTEGER, and so it could legitimately take values outside the subscript range 1..NMROFCANDIDATES of the array.

Example 10.5

Continuing Example 10.4, let us write a program fragment to determine the maximum rainfall in any one month between April and September.

This problem amounts to finding the value of the maximum of RAINFALL[APR], ..., RAINFALL[SEP]. We add the variable declaration

    MAXRAINFALL : REAL

Then the following is a solution:

```
(* determine maximum monthly rainfall from April to September *)
   (* initially assume April was the wettest *)
      MAXRAINFALL := RAINFALL[APR] ;
   MONTH := MAY ;
   WHILE MONTH <= SEP DO
      BEGIN
      IF RAINFALL[MONTH] > MAXRAINFALL THEN
         (* revise the previous assumption *)
            MAXRAINFALL := RAINFALL[MONTH] ;
      MONTH := SUCC(MONTH)
      END
```


Example 10.6

We return to the election problem (Example 10.1). Let us write a program fragment to determine the winner of the election, i.e. the candidate with the greatest number of votes (neglecting the possibility of a tie).

This amounts to finding the subscript of the maximum element of the array COUNT. Note the difference from Example 10.5, where the problem was to find the value of the maximum element.

We insert the variable declaration

```
       WINNER : 1..NMROFCANDIDATES

Then a solution is:

   (* determine the election winner, neglecting ties *)
      (* initially assume candidate 1 is the winner *)
         WINNER := 1 ;
      CANDIDATE := 2 ;
      WHILE CANDIDATE <= NMROFCANDIDATES DO
         BEGIN
         IF COUNT[CANDIDATE] > COUNT[WINNER] THEN
            (* revise the previous assumption *)
               WINNER := CANDIDATE ;
         CANDIDATE := SUCC(CANDIDATE)
         END
```

Another common theme is <u>linear search</u>, whereby the elements of an array are examined one by one to find which element, if any, satisfies some specified condition.

Example <u>10.7</u>

Returning once more to the election problem, let us write a program fragment to determine which candidate, if any, received a clear majority of the votes cast.
   We insert the variable declarations

```
   VOTES, MAJORITY : INTEGER ;
   SEARCHING       : BOOLEAN
```

First we must modify program ELECTION to accumulate, in VOTES, the total number of unspoilt ballots. (Do this as an exercise!) Then we add the following:

```
   MAJORITY := VOTES DIV 2 + 1 ;
   (* determine which candidate, if any,
                   received at least MAJORITY votes *)
      CANDIDATE := 1 ;
      SEARCHING := TRUE ;
      WHILE SEARCHING AND (CANDIDATE <= NMROFCANDIDATES) DO
         IF COUNT[CANDIDATE] >= MAJORITY THEN
            SEARCHING := FALSE
         ELSE
            CANDIDATE := SUCC(CANDIDATE) ;
   IF SEARCHING THEN
      WRITELN ('NO CLEAR MAJORITY')
   ELSE
      WRITELN ('CLEAR MAJORITY FOR CANDIDATE ', CANDIDATE)
```

This example illustrates the general method of programming a linear search. As before, we use a variable for subscripting the array (CANDIDATE in the example). We also use a BOOLEAN variable to control the search (SEARCHING in the example); this variable is initialized to TRUE, and is reset to FALSE if and when an element is found which satisfies the specified condition (COUNT[CANDIDATE] >= MAJORITY in the example). Iteration is terminated when the BOOLEAN variable becomes FALSE or the elements are exhausted, whichever comes sooner. After termination, the BOOLEAN variable can be tested (as in the example) to see whether the search was successful or not.

It is important to understand why both parts of the loop condition were necessary in Example 10.7.

(a) If the WHILE-clause were simply WHILE SEARCHING DO then, in the case where no candidate has a clear majority, the program would eventually fail by trying to examine COUNT[NMROFCANDIDATES+1].

(b) If the WHILE-clause were simply WHILE CANDIDATE <= NMROFCANDIDATES DO then, in the case where one candidate does have a clear majority, the program would get stuck in the loop forever.

Verify both these effects by hand-testing! Convince yourself also that the two parts of the loop condition will never both be FALSE at the same time.

10.4 TYPES OF SUBSCRIPTS AND ELEMENTS

Within reason, any ordinal type may be chosen as the subscript type of an array: BOOLEAN, CHAR, any enumeration type, or any subrange type.

Example 10.8

Given the type definition of MONTHS in Example 10.3, the following are legitimate array variable declarations:

```
CHARCOUNT        : ARRAY [CHAR] OF INTEGER ;
LETTERCOUNT      : ARRAY ['A'..'Z'] OF INTEGER ;
MONTHLYRAINFALL  : ARRAY [MONTHS] OF REAL ;
SUMMERRAINFALL   : ARRAY [JUN..AUG] OF REAL ;
YEARLYRAINFALL   : ARRAY [1900..1999] OF REAL
```

The subscript type determines the number of elements of an array; for example, YEARLYRAINFALL above will have 100 elements, and MONTHLYRAINFALL will have 12.

Bear in mind that, although some computers have very large stores, they are not unlimited, and you are very unlikely to be able to use "ARRAY [1..100000] OF ....." or "ARRAY [INTEGER] OF ....."! Most programming problems, certainly those you will meet in this book, can be solved without using very large arrays; if you find yourself declaring an array with thousands of elements, ask yourself whether you have missed a more economical solution.

There is no restriction at all on the element type of an array.

Example 10.9

The following is a legitimate array type definition:

    LINES = ARRAY [1..120] OF CHAR

The following are legitimate array variable declarations:

    WETTESTMONTH : ARRAY [1900..1999] OF MONTHS ;
    DAYSINMONTH : ARRAY [MONTHS] OF 28..31 ;
    PRIME   : ARRAY [1..N] OF BOOLEAN ;
    PAGEIMAGE   : ARRAY [1..64] OF LINES

Arrays of characters are of special interest since they can be used for storing and manipulating legible data, i.e. words and text. For example, given the declaration

    WORD : ARRAY [1..8] OF CHAR

we can store in WORD words of up to eight characters:

WORD `'C' 'O' 'M' 'P' 'U' 'T' 'E' 'R'`

    or

WORD `'P' 'A' 'S' 'C' 'A' 'L' ' ' ' '`

In the second diagram, WORD contains a word of fewer than eight characters; blank characters have been stored in the vacant elements. This common convention is known as padding out or filling out with blanks. Notice also that the word itself has been stored in the "leftmost" elements of the array, leaving the "rightmost" elements to be filled with blanks. We say that the word has been stored left-justified. Analogously, the word could be stored right-justified in the array, but left-justification is the more usual convention for words and text.

These conventions apply to the storage not only of single words but also of groups of words, as Example 10.10 illustrates.

Example 10.10

Assume that a title has been stored, left-justified, in the array

    TITLE : ARRAY [1..12] OF CHAR

102

e.g.:

TITLE | 'C' | 'A' | 'T' | 'C' | 'H' | ' ' | '2' | '2' | ' ' | ' ' | ' ' | ' ' |

Let us write a program fragment to write the title centralized on the page, assuming for this purpose that the page width is 60 spaces.

This can be done quite simply once we know the actual length of the title, i.e. excluding padding blanks:

    determine the length, LENGTH, of the title ;
    write the title, preceded by ((60-LENGTH) DIV 2) blanks

We can determine the length of the title by searching <u>backwards</u>, i.e. from right to left, to find the rightmost non-blank character. This is just an example of linear search, similar to Example 10.7. We define the constant

    BLANK = ' '

and declare the variables

    LENGTH : 0..12 ;
    PADDING : BOOLEAN

We can now refine the program fragment thus:

```
(* determine the length of the title *)
   LENGTH := 12 ;
   PADDING := TRUE ;
   WHILE PADDING AND (LENGTH > 0) DO
      IF TITLE[LENGTH] <> BLANK THEN
         PADDING := FALSE
      ELSE
         LENGTH := LENGTH-1
(* write the title preceded by necessary blanks *)
   WRITELN (BLANK:((60-LENGTH) DIV 2), TITLE)
```

As this example illustrates, an entire character array can be used as a parameter to WRITE (or WRITELN). The effect, as you might expect, is to write the entire contents of the character array, so the output in the case above would be:

                    CATCH 22

Now you may see why it is usual to pad out with <u>blanks</u>: when written they are invisible!

10.5 MULTI-DIMENSIONAL ARRAYS

As we have seen, the elements of an array may be of any type we choose. In particular, the elements may themselves be arrays.

An array whose elements are single numbers, Boolean values, or such like, is called a one-dimensional array; all the arrays used in previous examples have been one-dimensional. An array whose elements are themselves one-dimensional arrays is called a two-dimensional array. Likewise, we can define three-dimensional arrays, and so on.

{A vector in mathematics can be represented by a one-dimensional array, and a matrix by a two-dimensional array.}

Example 10.11

Consider a table containing the marks scored by a class of students in each of several papers of an examination. The marks of one student could be stored in a one-dimensional array of type

```
ARRAY [1..NMROFPAPERS] OF 0..100
```

The whole marks table could be stored in an array of such arrays, i.e. a two-dimensional array:

```
MARK : ARRAY [1..NMROFSTUDENTS] OF
            ARRAY [1..NMROFPAPERS] OF 0..100
```

Assuming the variable declarations

```
STUDENT : 1..NMROFSTUDENTS ;
PAPER   : 1..NMROFPAPERS
```

the subscripted variable MARK[STUDENT] selects one element of the array MARK. This element is itself an array with NMROFPAPERS elements; in fact it is an array containing all the marks of the student numbered STUDENT. Thus MARK[STUDENT][PAPER] is the mark obtained by the same student in paper PAPER.

Multi-dimensional arrays are so common that Pascal allows abbreviations both to the array type:

```
MARK : ARRAY [1..NMROFSTUDENTS,1..NMROFPAPERS] OF 0..100
```

and to the subscripted variable:

```
MARK[STUDENT,PAPER]
```

We can think of a two-dimensional array as having rows and columns. The array MARK would have one row for each student and one column for each paper. Assuming NMROFSTUDENTS=10 and NMROFPAPERS=4, it would look like this:

MARK

33	51	27	20
83	90	66	85
100	88	82	75
44	32	0	21
32	50	49	52
65	49	62	56
29	46	52	39
77	68	80	63
55	52	65	60
72	49	66	54

{Compare the mathematical notation for matrices.} Then MARK[2], the set of marks scored by student 2, is row 2 of MARK:

83	90	66	85

Finally, MARK[2,4], the mark scored by student 2 in paper 4, is element 4 of row 2, i.e. here MARK[2,4]=85.

The simplest examples of manipulation of multi-dimensional arrays are row and column processing.

Example 10.12

Given the array MARK of Example 10.11, let us write a program fragment to write the total mark of each student.

The best way to attack this problem is to consider it as an example of elementwise processing of MARK, forgetting for the moment that the elements of MARK are themselves arrays. We declare

```
STUDENT : INTEGER
```

and write

```
STUDENT := 1 ;
WHILE STUDENT <= NMROFSTUDENTS DO
   BEGIN
   calculate the total mark of student STUDENT ;
   write the total mark ;
   STUDENT := SUCC(STUDENT)
   END
```

Now the refinement of "calculate the total mark of student STUDENT" will itself be an example of elementwise processing, this time of the array MARK[STUDENT]. We further declare

```
PAPER : INTEGER ;
TOTAL : INTEGER
```

Then the final version is:

```
    STUDENT := 1 ;
    WHILE STUDENT <= NMROFSTUDENTS DO
       BEGIN
       (* calculate the total mark of student STUDENT *)
          TOTAL := 0 ;
          PAPER := 1 ;
          WHILE PAPER <= NMROFPAPERS DO
             BEGIN
             TOTAL := TOTAL + MARK[STUDENT,PAPER] ;
             PAPER := SUCC(PAPER)
             END ;
       (* write the total mark *)
          WRITELN (STUDENT, TOTAL) ;
       STUDENT := SUCC(STUDENT)
       END
```

This example illustrates a typical situation: a two-dimensional array being processed by two nested loops, using two subscripting variables.

EXERCISES 10

10.1. Assume the number of rooms in a hotel is given by a constant NMROFROOMS. (a) Write a declaration of an array variable suitable for keeping track of which rooms are free. (b) Write a program fragment which counts how many hotel rooms are free, given that appropriate values have been stored in the array.

10.2. Modify the program fragment of Example 10.10 so that it "underlines" the title, as well as centralizing it:

CATCH 22
----- --

10.3. Write a program fragment which reverses the order of the characters in an array TEXT of type ARRAY [LOW..HIGH] OF CHAR.

10.4. Write a program fragment which determines the range of the elements, i.e. the maximum difference between any two elements, of the array YEARLYRAINFALL of Example 10.8.

10.5. Assume that some text has been stored, but not left-justified, in the array TITLE of Example 10.10. Write a program fragment which will left-justify this text.

10.6*. Given a square matrix

MATRIX : ARRAY [1..N, 1..N] OF INTEGER

write program fragments which determine: (a) whether MATRIX is symmetrical about the main diagonal; and (b) whether MATRIX is triangular, i.e. every element below the main diagonal is zero. (The main diagonal is the one which runs from MATRIX[1,1] TO MATRIX[N,N].)

PROGRAMMING EXERCISES 10

10.7. Write a program which reads its input data a line at a time, and which writes each line back to front. Assume that no line is longer than (say) 80 characters.

10.8. Write a program which accumulates the frequency of occurrence of each of the letters of the alphabet in its input data, and which writes the frequency of each letter as a percentage of the total number of letters read. Run the program with some text from a book as input data.

10.9. The heights of a group of people are provided as input, one per line. Write a program which computes and writes the mean and standard deviation of these measurements, the number of measurements which are within one standard deviation of the mean, the number which are between one and two standard deviations from the mean, and the number outside this range. Note that it will be necessary to store all the measurements; you may assume that there are not more than (say) 100 of them.

The standard deviation of a group of N measurements is given by the formula SQRT(SUMOFSQUARES/N-SQR(MEAN)), where MEAN is their mean and SUMOFSQUARES is the sum of their squares.

III **More control structures**
11 More about flow of control

11.1 WHAT FURTHER CONTROL STRUCTURES DO WE NEED?

By now you should be thoroughly familiar with the two basic control structures, the IF statement, which is used for selection, and the WHILE statement, which is used for repetition. In theory we can write programs to do anything we want using just these basic control structures (plus the subprograms introduced in Part IV). So the short answer to the question posed above is "strictly speaking, none!".

Nevertheless, situations do arise in programming where certain specialized control structures are much more convenient than the basic ones. Pascal provides three such specialized control structures: the CASE statement, which is a selective control structure, and the FOR statement and the REPEAT statement, which are repetitive control structures. The CASE statement and the FOR statement are exceedingly useful, and you will find them turning up frequently in examples in this book. The REPEAT statement, on the other hand, is only occasionally useful, so you may wish to skip it on a first reading.

In certain rather exceptional circumstances we find that the desired flow of control becomes too irregular to be naturally expressed entirely in terms of nested selective and repetitive control structures. Pascal provides the GOTO statement which makes possible (almost) unrestricted jumps and can be used as a last resort in such circumstances. GOTO statements are notoriously difficult to use properly, so you should certainly skip this topic on a first reading.

11.2 MULTI-WAY SELECTION: THE CASE STATEMENT

The IF...THEN...ELSE... construct allows a program to select one of two alternative courses of action - either the statement following THEN or the statement following ELSE - depending on the value of the BOOLEAN expression following IF. Frequently, however, we wish the program to select one of several different courses of action, as the following examples illustrate.

Example 11.1

Recall the first program fragment of Example 8.4, where we wished to select one of seven courses of action, depending on the value of DAY:

```
IF       DAY = SUNDAY     THEN WRITE ('SUNDAY   ')
ELSE IF DAY = MONDAY     THEN WRITE ('MONDAY   ')
ELSE IF DAY = TUESDAY    THEN WRITE ('TUESDAY  ')
ELSE IF DAY = WEDNESDAY THEN WRITE ('WEDNESDAY')
ELSE IF DAY = THURSDAY   THEN WRITE ('THURSDAY ')
ELSE IF DAY = FRIDAY     THEN WRITE ('FRIDAY   ')
ELSE                              WRITE ('SATURDAY ')
```

This cascade of IF statements is certainly clumsy. It may be less
apparent that it is also rather inefficient, since the value of DAY
could be inspected as many as six times. When there are more than
seven courses of action, this style of programming is even less
satisfactory.

What we need is a new construct in which the desired course of
action is selected immediately after only one inspection of the value
of DAY. For such a purpose Pascal provides the CASE statement:

```
CASE DAY OF
    SUNDAY:     WRITE ('SUNDAY   ') ;
    MONDAY:     WRITE ('MONDAY   ') ;
    TUESDAY:    WRITE ('TUESDAY  ') ;
    WEDNESDAY: WRITE ('WEDNESDAY') ;
    THURSDAY:   WRITE ('THURSDAY ') ;
    FRIDAY:     WRITE ('FRIDAY   ') ;
    SATURDAY:   WRITE ('SATURDAY ')
END
```

Here DAY is the selector of the CASE statement. The constants
SUNDAY, MONDAY, TUESDAY, etc., which are the potential values of the
selector, are used as case labels; each case label is placed in front
of a component statement and separated from it by a colon.

The effect of a CASE statement is as follows. The selector is
evaluated, then one component statement is obeyed, namely that component
statement which is labelled by the selector value.

In Example 11.1, if the value of DAY is MONDAY, then the component
statement WRITE ('MONDAY   ') is obeyed (and no other).

The syntax of CASE statements is summarized in Figure 11.1. CASE, OF
and END are all reserved words. Note that the selector may be any
expression, but its type must be ordinal, and the case labels must have
the same type. Notice also that several case labels may be placed in
front of the same component statement; this is useful when the same
action is to be taken for several different selector values.

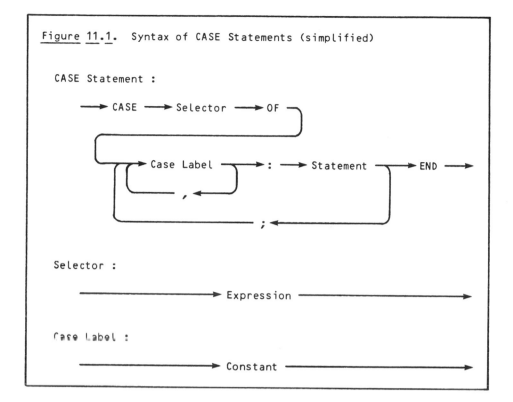

Figure 11.1. Syntax of CASE Statements (simplified)

CASE Statement :

CASE → Selector → OF

Case Label → : → Statement → END →

,

;

Selector :

Expression

Case Label :

Constant

Example 11.2

"Soundex" is a method of encoding names in such a way that slight
spelling variations are unlikely to affect the code. The basis of
the encoding is the following phonetic grouping of characters:

    group 0: A, E, I, O, U, H, W, Y,
              all non-alphabetic characters;
    group 1: B, F, P, V;
    group 2: C, G, J, K, Q, S, X, Z;
    group 3: D, T;
    group 4: L;
    group 5: M, N;
    group 6: R.

{The characters of the name are first encoded as digits according
to the grouping: thus SMITH becomes 25030, and SCHMIDT becomes
2205033. Then consecutive similar digits are replaced by a single
digit, and finally all zeros are removed: thus both SMITH and SCHMIDT
become 253.}
    Given the variables

```
CH     : CHAR ;
GROUP : '0'..'6'
```

let us write a program fragment to store, in GROUP, the group into which CH falls.

We can solve this problem using a CASE statement with CH as the selector; the case labels will be character constants.

```
IF (CH<'A') OR (CH>'Z') THEN     (* CH is non-alphabetic *)
   GROUP := '0'
ELSE
   CASE CH OF
      'A','E','I','O','U','H','W','Y': GROUP := '0' ;
      'B','F','P','V':                 GROUP := '1' ;
      'C','G','J','K','Q','S','X','Z': GROUP := '2' ;
      'D','T':                         GROUP := '3' ;
      'L':                             GROUP := '4' ;
      'M','N':                         GROUP := '5' ;
      'R':                             GROUP := '6'
   END
```

It is essential for every potential value of the selector to occur exactly once as a case label in a CASE statement. If the selector turns out to yield a value which is not present as a case label, the program will fail. In Example 11.2 only the letters were used as case labels, whereas CH could have any character value; hence the prior check which ensures that the CASE statement is obeyed only if CH is indeed a letter (assuming, however, that the letters are consecutive CHAR values).

Example 11.3

The following program fragment updates the score in a table-tennis game. It assumes the variables

```
SERVERSCORE, OTHERSCORE : INTEGER ;
FINISHED                : BOOLEAN ;
EVENT                   : (SERVERSPOINT,OTHERSPOINT,LET)
```

and that the result of the latest play has been recorded in the variable EVENT.

```
CASE EVENT OF
   SERVERSPOINT:
      BEGIN
      SERVERSCORE := SERVERSCORE+1 ;
      IF (SERVERSCORE>=21) AND (SERVERSCORE-OTHERSCORE>=2) THEN
         FINISHED := TRUE
      END ;
   OTHERSPOINT:
      BEGIN
      OTHERSCORE := OTHERSCORE+1 ;
      IF (OTHERSCORE>=21) AND (OTHERSCORE-SERVERSCORE>=2) THEN
         FINISHED := TRUE
      END ;
   LET:
END (* CASE *)
```

Example 11.3 illustrates nesting of compound statements and IF statements within a CASE statement. It also illustrates how we can arrange to do nothing at all when the case selector has a particular value (LET in the example): we use a dummy statement as the relevant component statement. A dummy statement consists of no symbols at all, and one can be "seen" between "LET:" and "END" in the example.

11.3 COUNT-CONTROLLED LOOPS: THE FOR STATEMENT

Refer back to Examples 6.3 and 6.4. There is a significant difference between the loops in these examples. In Example 6.4, the number of iterations of the loop cannot be predicted, since it depends on the data read by the loop itself. In Example 6.3, on the other hand, the number of iterations is in fact known in advance of entering the loop: it is the value of SIZE.

Loops with a predetermined number of iterations are very common, and they all have the same characteristic feature: they use a control variable (COUNT in Example 6.3) to count the iterations. The control variable is first given an initial value (1 in the example); inside the loop it is incremented (or decremented); and the loop is terminated when the control variable has passed its final value (SIZE in the example).

Such loops occur so frequently that Pascal provides a special construct, the FOR statement, to simplify writing them.

Example 11.4

We can recast the solution of Example 6.3, using a FOR statement, as follows:

```
          PROGRAM ADDN ( INPUT, OUTPUT ) ;
          VAR
             SUM, DATUM, COUNT, SIZE : INTEGER ;
          BEGIN
          SUM := 0 ;
          READLN (SIZE) ;
          FOR COUNT := 1 TO SIZE DO
             BEGIN
             READLN (DATUM) ;
             SUM := SUM + DATUM
             END ;
          WRITELN ('SUM OF ', SIZE, ' INTEGERS READ IS ', SUM)
          END .
```

The FOR clause FOR COUNT := 1 TO SIZE DO means "Repeatedly execute the following statement with the control variable COUNT taking consecutive values from 1 up to SIZE inclusive". Thus the FOR clause replaces the WHILE clause WHILE COUNT <= SIZE DO, and the statements COUNT := 1 and COUNT := COUNT+1, in Example 6.3.

In Example 11.4 the control variable was used solely for counting. There is nothing to prevent the control variable's value being used by statements inside the loop. For example, we could insert the statement

WRITELN ('DATUM ', COUNT, ' WAS ', DATUM)

inside the loop of Example 11.4. However, the statements inside a FOR-statement may not attempt to alter the control variable, for example by assigning a value to it. The FOR statement has the exclusive right to update the control variable, which it does "behind the scenes" on every iteration.

There is one, rather subtle, difference between the programs of Examples 6.3 and 11.4. When we leave the WHILE statement in Example 6.3, the value of COUNT is clearly one more than the value of SIZE, e.g.:

COUNT [9   ]   SIZE [8   ]

After leaving the FOR statement in Example 11.4, on the other hand, the value of the control variable COUNT would depend on the exact manner in which it is updated "behind the scenes" by the FOR statement, and this manner might vary from one compiler to another. We must assume that the control variable's value is undefined after leaving the FOR statement:

COUNT [?   ]   SIZE [8   ]

FOR statements are particularly useful for manipulating arrays, using the control variables as subscripts. Many of the examples in Chapter 10 could be programmed more neatly using FOR statements.

Example 11.5

The solution of Example 10.4 may be recast using a FOR statement:

```
(* determine total rainfall from April to September *)
   TOTAL := 0 ;
   FOR MONTH := APR TO SEP DO
      TOTAL := TOTAL + RAINFALL[MONTH]
```

We could, if we wished, total the rainfall for the whole year simply by making the FOR clause FOR MONTH := JAN TO DEC DO. The difficulty mentioned in Example 10.4 is avoided here, simply because we no longer attempt to evaluate SUCC(DEC).

By constrast, the loop in Example 10.7 cannot be recast as a FOR statement, since in linear search (by definition!) it is impossible to predict the number of iterations.

Example 11.6

We can recast the refinement of "write the vote-counts" in Example 10.1 using a FOR statement:

```
(* write the vote-counts *)
   FOR CANDIDATE := 1 TO NMROFCANDIDATES DO
      WRITELN ('CANDIDATE ', CANDIDATE:2, ' OBTAINED ',
               COUNT[CANDIDATE]:3, ' VOTES')
```

The output from this program fragment would look like this:

```
CANDIDATE  1 OBTAINED  27 VOTES
CANDIDATE  2 OBTAINED  36 VOTES
CANDIDATE  3 OBTAINED   0 VOTES
CANDIDATE  4 OBTAINED   9 VOTES
```

Let us modify the program fragment to present these results in a visually more attractive form, using a histogram like this:

```
CANDIDATE  1     ***************************
CANDIDATE  2     ************************************
CANDIDATE  3
CANDIDATE  4     *********
```

If we assume that the line is long enough, we can simply let one asterisk represent one vote. It is easy to write the appropriate number of asterisks using a FOR statement:

```
(* write the vote-counts in the form of a histogram *)
   FOR CANDIDATE := 1 TO NMROFCANDIDATES DO
      BEGIN
      WRITE ('CANDIDATE ', CANDIDATE:2, '        ') ;
      FOR VOTE := 1 TO COUNT[CANDIDATE] DO
         WRITE ('*') ;
      WRITELN
      END
```

In this we have assumed the declaration

```
VOTE : INTEGER
```

An important point to notice is that the inner FOR statement does exactly what we want when COUNT[CANDIDATE]=0. In this case the control variable's initial value, 1, is already greater than its final value, 0. In such circumstances, the number of iterations is zero.

If the line is not long enough for one asterisk to represent one vote, we could perform some sort of scaling. (See Exercises 11.)

Occasionally we need to write a FOR statement in which the control variable takes <u>decreasing</u> values. For this purpose we use DOWNTO instead of TO. In Example 11.5, the control variable successively takes the values APR, MAY, JUN, JUL, AUG, SEP. If we change the FOR clause to FOR MONTH := SEP DOWNTO APR DO, MONTH will successively take the values SEP, AUG, JUL, JUN, MAY, APR. In that particular example, of course, such replacement would make no difference at all. But there are some circumstances in which DOWNTO must be used.

Example <u>11.7</u>

<u>Pascal's triangle</u> is the following pattern:

```
                1
              1   1
            1   2   1
          1   3   3   1
        1   4   6   4   1
      1   5  10  10   5   1
    1   6  15  20  15   6   1
```

etc.

in which each integer inside the triangle is the sum of the two integers above it. {Mathematicians should recognize that the integers in Pascal's triangle are the binomial coefficients. Both the triangle and the programming language are named after the great Frenchman Blaise Pascal (1623-1662).}

116

Let us write a program to generate the first ten rows of Pascal's triangle.

Here is an outline solution:

```
PROGRAM PASCALTRIANGLE ( OUTPUT ) ;
CONST
   LASTROW = 10 ;
VAR
   ROW : 2..LASTROW ;
BEGIN
generate row 1 ;
write row 1 ;
FOR ROW := 2 TO LASTROW DO
   BEGIN
   generate row ROW from row (ROW-1) ;
   write row ROW
   END
END .
```

We could store the integers in a two-dimensional array, using the elements of each row to compute the elements of the next. If we write each row as soon as it is generated, however, each row need be preserved only long enough to generate the next row; it turns out that we need store only one row at a time, for which we can use a one-dimensional array.

If we insert the variable declarations

```
PASCAL : ARRAY [1..LASTROW] OF INTEGER ;
COL    : 2..LASTROW
```

then row ROW can be stored in the array elements PASCAL[1], ..., PASCAL[ROW]. Observe that the first and last integer in each row, i.e. PASCAL[1] and PASCAL[ROW], must always be 1. The generation of a new row is achieved by adding, to each element, its neighbour to the left, e.g.:

Before: PASCAL	1	3	3	1	?	?	?	?	?	?	?	ROW	4

After: PASCAL	1	4	6	4	1	?	?	?	?	?	?	ROW	5

You should see that we can generate the new row in situ, provided that we compute the new elements from right to left:

```
(* generate row ROW from row (ROW-1) *)
   PASCAL[ROW] := 1 ;
   FOR COL := ROW-1 DOWNTO 2 DO
       PASCAL[COL] := PASCAL[COL] + PASCAL[COL-1]

(* generate row 1 *)
   PASCAL[1] := 1
```

Verify these refinements by hand-testing. What happens if we use FOR COL := 2 TO ROW-1 DO? Complete the program yourself (see Exercises 11).

The syntax of FOR statements is summarized in Figure 11.2. FOR, TO, DOWNTO and DO are all reserved words. The control variable must be declared just like any other variable, and its type must be <u>ordinal</u>. The initial and final values of the control variable may be given by any expressions of the same type as the control variable; these expressions are evaluated just once, before entry to the loop.

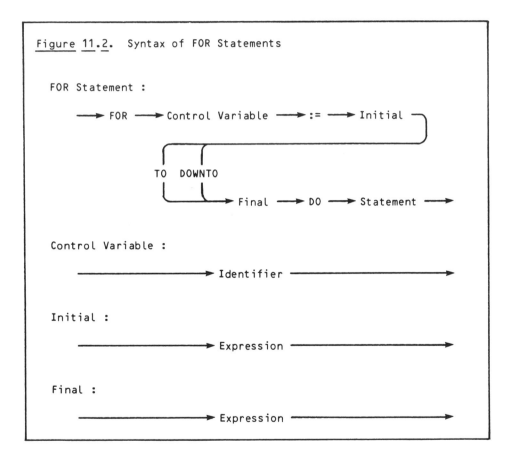

Figure 11.2. Syntax of FOR Statements

FOR Statement :

Control Variable :

Initial :

Final :

11.4 LOOPS WITH AT LEAST ONE ITERATION: THE REPEAT STATEMENT

{This section may be omitted on a first reading.}

We have already seen that with the WHILE construct it is possible for the number of iterations to be zero. For example, in

118

```
WHILE R >= N DO
   R := R-N
```

the statement R := R-N will not be executed at all if the condition
R>=N is initially FALSE.
   Occasionally (very occasionally!) we need a repetitive construct
which guarantees at least one iteration.

Example 11.8

   If NUMBER is an INTEGER variable, the statement WRITE(NUMBER)
   writes the value of NUMBER in decimal (base 10) notation. For some
   purposes we might want to write a number in a different base. Let us
   write a program fragment to convert the value of NUMBER to octal
   (base 8) notation, with leading zeros suppressed, and write it in a
   field of 12 spaces. (Assume that NUMBER>=0.) For example, if
   NUMBER=249, we want the output

        371

   We can generate the octal digits in reverse order if we repeatedly
divide NUMBER by 8, noting the remainder at each step, until we are
left with 0. For example:
        dividing 249 by 8 gives 31, remainder 1;
           "   31 " "   "   3,   "   7;
           "   3 " "   "   0,   "   3.
   Unfortunately, we cannot write the digits as they are generated,
since WRITE does not work from right to left! So we must store all
the digits before writing; we can use an array of 12 characters.
   Let us make our program more flexible by introducing the constant
definitions

   RADIX = 8 ;
   WIDTH = 12

Using the array variable declaration

   DIGITS : ARRAY [1..WIDTH] OF CHAR

our program skeleton will be:

   generate digits by repeated division of NUMBER by RADIX,
      storing them in DIGITS[WIDTH], DIGITS[WIDTH-1], ... ;
   IF overflow THEN
      write warning message
   ELSE
      BEGIN
      fill remaining elements of DIGITS with blanks ;
      WRITE (DIGITS)
      END
```
```

Let us concentrate on the refinement of "generate digits by repeated division .....". If we declare the variables

```
POSITION  : 0..WIDTH ;
QUOTIENT  : 0..MAXINT ;
REMAINDER : 0..RADIX
```

we can try:

```
(* generate digits by repeated division ..... *)
   POSITION := WIDTH ;
   QUOTIENT := NUMBER ;
   WHILE (QUOTIENT <> 0) AND (POSITION >= 1) DO
      BEGIN
      REMAINDER := QUOTIENT MOD RADIX ;
      QUOTIENT  := QUOTIENT DIV RADIX ;
      DIGITS[POSITION] := CHR (REMAINDER + ORD('0')) ;
      POSITION := POSITION-1
      END
   (* now QUOTIENT<>0 implies overflow *)
```

There is only one flaw in this coding: if NUMBER=0, no digits at all will be generated! When we use the term "suppress leading zeros", we do not mean to suppress a zero in the units position! If we can guarantee at least one iteration of the loop, however, then we can be sure that at least one digit will be generated. We can ensure this, by using a REPEAT statement instead of a WHILE statement:

```
(* generate digits by repeated division ..... *)
   POSITION := WIDTH ;
   QUOTIENT := NUMBER ;
   REPEAT
      REMAINDER := QUOTIENT MOD RADIX ;
      QUOTIENT  := QUOTIENT DIV RADIX ;
      DIGITS[POSITION] := CHR (REMAINDER + ORD('0')) ;
      POSITION := POSITION-1
   UNTIL (QUOTIENT = 0) OR (POSITION < 1)
   (* now QUOTIENT<>0 implies overflow *)
```

The effect of a REPEAT statement may be summarized by the following sequence of operations.

(1) Obey the statement(s) between REPEAT and UNTIL.
(2) Test the condition following UNTIL. If the condition is FALSE, then repeat from step (1).
(3) Knowing the condition to be TRUE, go on with the rest of the program.

Compare this sequence of operations with that of the WHILE statement (see Section 6.1). The principal difference is this: in the WHILE statement, the loop condition is tested <u>before</u> each iteration of the loop; in the REPEAT statement, the loop condition is tested <u>after</u> each iteration of the loop. This distinction is emphasized by the position of the WHILE clause at the beginning of the WHILE statement and the position of the UNTIL clause at the end of the REPEAT statement.

The syntax of REPEAT statements is summarized in Figure 11.3. Note that several statements may be placed inside the loop, without BEGIN...END brackets, since REPEAT and UNTIL themselves act as statement brackets. REPEAT and UNTIL are both reserved words.

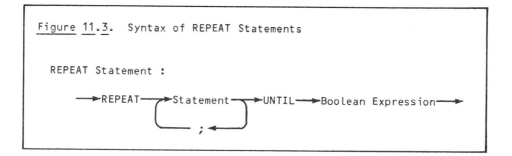

Figure <u>11.3</u>. Syntax of REPEAT Statements

REPEAT Statement :

11.5 EXCEPTIONAL FLOW OF CONTROL: THE GOTO STATEMENT

{This section should be omitted on a first reading.}

The great majority of programming problems — certainly those which you are likely to encounter at this stage — can be solved satisfactorily without resorting to control structures other than the ones you have met already, namely selection, repetition and subprograms. (You should be familiar with subprograms before you read this section.)

Nevertheless, we occasionally meet programming problems which are rather awkward to solve using only these control structures. A typical example of such a problem is a program whose input data is quite complex in its organization. A good-quality program will check its data as it reads it, so that appropriate warning messages can be issued if it detects any errors; this assists the user of the program to correct any such errors before running the program again. The problem is, how should the program continue after detecting an error and writing a message? Some errors are so severe that the program's only recourse is to abandon the task which it is currently performing, perhaps even to halt completely. The cleanest solution in such circumstances might be a direct jump out of the piece of program which detects the error. For such purposes Pascal (and nearly every programming language) provides the <u>GOTO</u> statement.

Example 11.9

The following procedure reads a matrix of non-negative integers and stores it in an array of type

    MATRICES = ARRAY [1..XSIZE, 1..YSIZE] OF NONNEGINTEGER

where XSIZE and YSIZE are appropriately defined constants and NONNEGINTEGER is an appropriately defined type. To guard against the possibility of the input data being incomplete (or there being too much input data), the matrix elements are assumed to be followed by a negative endmarker. The procedure checks every datum and, if it detects the endmarker prematurely, it writes a warning message and stops immediately.

```
PROCEDURE READMATRIX ( VAR MATRIX : MATRICES ;
                       VAR VALID  : BOOLEAN   ) ;
    LABEL 99 ;
    VAR
       DATUM : INTEGER ;
       X     : 1..XSIZE ;
       Y     : 1..YSIZE ;
    BEGIN
    VALID := FALSE ;    (* being pessimistic! *)
    FOR X := 1 TO XSIZE DO
       FOR Y := 1 TO YSIZE DO
          BEGIN
          READ (DATUM) ;
          IF DATUM >= 0 THEN
             MATRIX[X,Y] := DATUM
          ELSE     (* the endmarker has been read *)
             BEGIN
             WRITELN ('DATA INCOMPLETE') ;
             GOTO 99    (* leave the procedure immediately *)
             END
          END ;
    READ (DATUM) ;     (* ... this should be the endmarker *)
    IF DATUM >= 0 THEN
       WRITELN ('TOO MUCH DATA')
    ELSE
       VALID := TRUE ;
    99:
    END (* READMATRIX *)
```

There are three aspects to the use of a GOTO statement.

(a) A label declaration like LABEL 99 declares that 99 is to be used as a statement label, attached to some statement within the same block. (The statement label 99 has nothing to do with the integer constant

99, despite all appearances to the contrary!). The label declaration must be placed before any constant definitions.
(b) The occurrence of "99:" in front of a statement (in the example, a dummy statement preceding the final END of the procedure body) attaches the statement label 99 to that particular statement. Each statement label must be attached to exactly one statement within the block.
(c) The effect of the GOTO statement GOTO 99 is to pass control directly to the statement whose statement label is 99, thereby abandoning whatever was being done before the GOTO statement was obeyed. In the example, the nett effect of GOTO 99 is to jump out of the loop to the end of the procedure body (and thence return to the statement which invoked the procedure).

It cannot be emphasized too stongly that GOTO statements should never be used indiscriminately, for too many GOTO statements make a program difficult to understand. Just compare the following program fragments:

```
    IF M > N THEN GOTO 1 ;      IF M <= N THEN
    MAX := N ;                      MAX := N
    GOTO 2 ;                    ELSE
1:  MAX := M ;                      MAX := M ;
2:  WRITE (MAX)                 WRITE (MAX)
```

```
1:  IF R < N THEN GOTO 2 ;      WHILE R >= N DO
    R := R-N ;                      R := R-N ;
    GOTO 1 ;                    WRITE (R)
2:  WRITE (R)
```

Each program fragment has the same effect as the one beside it. But which are the easier to understand?
All the selective and repetitive control structures can be mimicked using only IF statements and GOTO statements. That fact is of little interest, however, since the selective and repetitive control structures are much more convenient to use and much easier for someone else to read. The reason for this is that their appearance alone tells the reader what he wants to know about the flow of control. Thus the word IF (or CASE) signals a selective control structure, and the word WHILE (or FOR or REPEAT) signals a repetitive control structure. By way of comparison, consider the statements GOTO 1 used in two of the program fragments above. It is impossible to deduce, from their appearance alone, the effect of these statements on the flow of control. It is necessary, first of all, to find the location of the statement label 1 in each program fragment. (If that seems easy in these short program fragments, imagine what it would be like in a program extending over several pages!) It turns out that the two statements have markedly different effects, one being a jump <u>forwards</u>, which causes statement(s) to be skipped, the other being a jump <u>backwards</u>, which causes statement(s) to be repeated.
Now, the procedure of Example 11.9 <u>could</u> be re-written without using

any GOTO statement, using nested WHILE statements rather than FOR statements, but it turns out to be rather awkward to write it this way, and the resulting procedure is not really any easier to understand. (Try it yourself as an exercise.)

The overriding criterion in this and all matters of programming style is whether a program can easily be understood by its author and by other readers. Nearly always this means that GOTO statements should be avoided, but in exceptional circumstances they are acceptable in order to avoid awkwardness of expression.

The syntax of GOTO statements, statement labels and label declarations can be found in Appendix 1.2 and 1.5. LABEL and GOTO are both reserved words.

EXERCISES 11

11.1. Recast your solution to Exercise 8.3(c) using a CASE statement.

11.2. Assume that the charge for sending a parcel overseas is calculated as follows. First, its weight is rounded up to the nearest multiple of 15 grams. Then the charge is taken from the table:

Weight (grams)	Charge (pence)
15	12
30	22
45	31
60	36, plus 2 per complete 1000 km
75 and over	40, plus 3 per complete 1000 km

Given that its weight in grams and the distance in kilometres have been stored in the INTEGER variables WEIGHT and DISTANCE respectively, write a program fragment which assigns the charge in pence to the INTEGER variable CHARGE. Use a CASE statement.

11.3. Recast the solutions of Examples 10.5, 10.6 and 10.12 using FOR statements.

11.4. Recast your solutions to Exercises 10 using FOR statements where appropriate.

11.5. Complete program PASCALTRIANGLE (Example 11.7).

11.6. Rewrite the program fragment of Example 11.6 so that each asterisk represents N votes, where N is chosen such that the histogram will fit into lines of (say) 60 characters.

11.7. Assume that every line of the input data contains a colon. Write a program which reads the input data and writes only the part of each line to the right of the colon.

11.8. Write a program which reads and writes a table MARK (declared as in Example 10.11). Assume that the table elements are supplied paper by paper in the input data. The table is to be written with one row for each student and one column for each paper. On the right of each row write that student's total mark. At the foot of each column write the average mark (rounded to the nearest integer) for that paper. Also write the average total mark at the foot of the totals column.

11.9. Write a program which reads a representation of a bridge hand of 13 cards, and which writes (a) the contents of the hand, with the cards arranged in descending order by rank within each suit, and (b) the points value of the hand (counting 4 for an Ace, 3 for a King, 2 for a Queen and 1 for a Jack), e.g.:

```
CLUBS       K 10  9
DIAMONDS    J  9  4  3
HEARTS      A  Q 10  8  2
SPADES      7

POINTS VALUE = 10
```

On input, each card is to be represented by a pair of integers, the first representing its suit (1 for Clubs, 2 for Diamonds, 3 for Hearts, 4 for Spades), and the second representing its rank (14 for Ace, 13 for King, 12 for Queen, 11 for Jack, 2-10 for other ranks). The cards are supplied in random order. (Hint: use a two-dimensional BOOLEAN array, with one element for every card of the pack.)

IV Subprograms
12 Functions

12.1 THE NEED FOR FUNCTIONS

Suppose we are writing a program in which we want to determine whether the INTEGER variables CHECK and PARITY have odd values. We could include in our program expressions such as (CHECK MOD 2 <> 0) and (PARITY MOD 2 <> 0). A better way to achieve the same effect, however, would be to use the predeclared function ODD. The program would then contain the expressions ODD(CHECK) and ODD(PARITY). These expressions are more readable, partly because they are shorter, but more importantly because the name "ODD" concentrates attention on the meaning of the expressions rather than the way they are computed. They are also more pleasant to write. The tedium of reworking similar expressions many times is avoided, and with it the risk of making a mistake.

When we consider functions such as SIN and EXP which are defined by complicated algorithms containing many statements, these advantages are strongly emphasized.

Although programming languages like Pascal provide a fair selection of such predeclared functions, this selection is necessarily limited. We are unlikely to find predeclared functions, for example, to compute the tangent of a given angle, to determine whether a given number is prime, or to determine whether a given character is a letter, although such functions might sometimes be just as useful as ODD, SIN and EXP. Since we cannot expect a programming language to anticipate every conceivable need for a function, we need a facility by which we ourselves can provide functions to our own specification. In Pascal this facility is called the function declaration.

12.2 FUNCTIONS IN PASCAL

A function declaration must provide the following information:
(a) the name of the function;
(b) the type(s) of the parameter(s) of the function;
(c) the type of the result to be computed;
(d) the body of the function, containing the statements which compute
    the value of the result from the values of the parameters.

A function may be invoked from several different places, possibly with different parameters. For example, if we declare a function TAN to compute the tangent of an angle, we might wish in different places to evaluate TAN(A) or TAN(B-C). This implies that the body of the function cannot refer directly to the actual parameter. The problem is solved by introducing into the declaration of TAN a name, say X, which will stand for the value of the actual parameter (i.e. X will stand for the value of A during the computation of TAN(A), and it will stand for the value of B-C during the computation of TAN(B-C).) We call X a formal parameter, and it is available for use within the function body only. Thus the following information must also be included in a function declaration:

(e) the name(s) of the formal parameter(s).

TAN(A) and TAN(B-C) are examples of function designators, and in these examples A and B-C are called actual parameters.

Example 12.1

We might declare the tangent function as follows:

```
FUNCTION TAN ( X : REAL ) : REAL ;
   BEGIN
   TAN := SIN(X) / COS(X)
   END
```

This example illustrates the features of a function declaration.
(a) "FUNCTION TAN" defines the name of the function to be TAN.
(b) "(X : REAL)" is the formal-parameter part. It says that the function has a single formal parameter, whose identifier is X and whose type is REAL.
(c) ": REAL" following the formal-parameter part defines the function's result type to be REAL.
(d) "BEGIN ..... END" is the body of the function.
(e) Within the body, the special assignment statement "TAN := ....." assigns a value to the function name itself. It is this value which is returned when the function is invoked.

Since TAN has a single REAL formal parameter, it may be invoked by a function designator containing a single REAL actual parameter. This function designator is a REAL operand (since the result type of TAN is REAL), and as such it may be used in expressions just like any other REAL operand, e.g.:

HEIGHT := RANGE * TAN(ELEVATION)

WRITE (TAN(DEGREES*PI/180))

In the first of these statements, the function designator TAN(ELEVATION) is evaluated as follows: first the current value of the actual parameter ELEVATION is used to initialize the formal parameter X of TAN; then the body of TAN is executed, and the value finally assigned to TAN becomes the value of the function designator. In the second statement, the function designator TAN(DEGREES*PI/180) is evaluated similarly, except that X is initialized to the value of the actual parameter DEGREES*PI/180.

The following complete program, incorporating the function TAN, writes a table of tangents of angles 0, 10, 20, ..., 360 degrees. Note that the function declaration is inserted between the variable declarations and the program body.

```
PROGRAM TABLEOFTANS ( OUTPUT ) ;

CONST
   PI = 3.1415926536 ;
VAR
   DEGREES : INTEGER ;

FUNCTION TAN ( X : REAL ) : REAL ;
   BEGIN
   TAN := SIN(X)/COS(X)
   END (* TAN *) ;

BEGIN (* TABLEOFTANS *)
DEGREES := 0 ;
WHILE DEGREES <= 360 DO
   BEGIN
   WRITE (DEGREES) ;
   IF DEGREES MOD 180 = 90 THEN
      WRITELN ('     INFINITY')
   ELSE
      WRITELN (TAN(DEGREES*PI/180)) ;
   DEGREES := DEGREES + 10
   END
END (* TABLEOFTANS *) .
```

Example 12.2

Given the type definitions

```
MONTHS = (JAN,FEB,MAR,APR,MAY,JUN,JUL,AUG,SEP,OCT,NOV,DEC) ;
YEARS  = 1500..9999
```

the following function determines whether a given year is a leap year:

```
FUNCTION ISLEAP ( YEAR : YEARS ) : BOOLEAN ;
   BEGIN
   ISLEAP := (YEAR MOD 4 = 0) AND (YEAR MOD 100 <> 0)
             OR (YEAR MOD 400 = 0)
   END (* ISLEAP *)
```

and the following function invokes ISLEAP to determine the number of days in a given month and year:

129

```
FUNCTION NMROFDAYSIN ( MONTH : MONTHS ;
                       YEAR  : YEARS   ) : INTEGER ;
BEGIN
CASE MONTH OF
   JAN, MAR, MAY, JUL, AUG, OCT, DEC:
      NMROFDAYSIN := 31 ;
   APR, JUN, SEP, NOV:
      NMROFDAYSIN := 30;
   FEB:
      IF ISLEAP(YEAR) THEN
         NMROFDAYSIN := 29
      ELSE
         NMROFDAYSIN := 28
END
END (* NMROFDAYSIN *)
```

ISLEAP has one formal parameter, of type YEARS, and its result type is BOOLEAN. NMROFDAYSIN has two formal parameters, the first of type MONTHS, the second of type YEARS, and its result type is INTEGER.

An example of a function designator invoking the latter procedure would be NMROFDAYSIN(FEB,1984), which would yield the value 29.

The syntax of function designators is summarized in Figure 12.1.

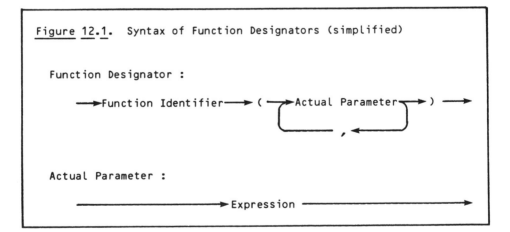

Figure 12.1. Syntax of Function Designators (simplified)

Function Designator :

Function Identifier ⟶ (⟶ Actual Parameter ⟶) ⟶

Actual Parameter :

⟶ Expression ⟶

A function designator must supply one actual parameter for each formal parameter of the function it invokes. Each actual parameter is used to initialize the corresponding formal parameter, as illustrated below. It follows that the types of the actual parameter and formal parameter must be compatible.

130

TAN (DEGREES*PI/180)

FUNCTION TAN (X : REAL) : REAL

NMROFDAYSIN (FEB , 1984)

FUNCTION NMROFDAYSIN (MONTH : MONTHS ; YEAR : YEARS) : INTEGER

Function declarations are constructed according to the syntax summarized in Figures 12.2 and 12.3. FUNCTION is a reserved word. Note that the result type of a function, and the types of its formal parameters, must all be specified by type identifiers (which may be predefined, such as INTEGER or BOOLEAN, or defined outside the function, such as MONTHS or YEARS). Every function must yield a result which is a simple value, so the result type must be ordinal or REAL, but not an array. There is no restriction at all, however, on the types of the parameters; Example 12.3 demonstrates a function with an array parameter.

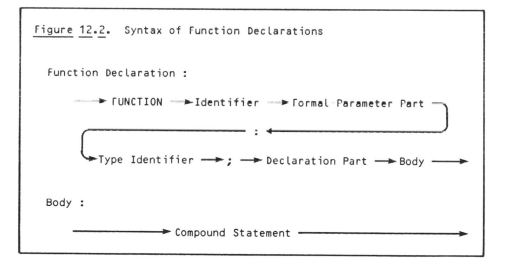

Figure 12.2. Syntax of Function Declarations

Function Declaration :

```
        ──► FUNCTION ──►Identifier ──► Formal Parameter Part ─┐
   ┌─────────────────────── : ◄──────────────────────────────┘
   └─►Type Identifier ──► ; ──► Declaration Part ──► Body ──►
```

Body :

```
        ─────────────► Compound Statement ─────────────────►
```

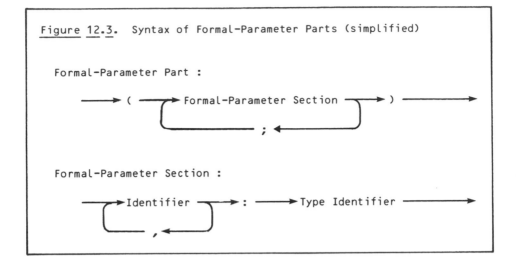

Figure 12.3. Syntax of Formal-Parameter Parts (simplified)

Formal-Parameter Part :

(→ Formal-Parameter Section →)

;

Formal-Parameter Section :

Identifier → : → Type Identifier

,

12.3 DECLARATIONS INSIDE FUNCTIONS

The examples in the previous section illustrate functions whose results can be computed essentially by obeying a single statement involving the formal parameters. More commonly, several statements are needed to work out the result and these statements may require variables of their own, variables which are of no concern to the rest of the program. Such variables could be declared in the program's declaration part, as global variables. However, doing this would make the working of the function dependent on something outside of itself; it would no longer be self-contained. To avoid this, Pascal allows a function to have its own internal declaration part, as we can see in Figure 12.2. As well as variables, we can declare constants, types, and even further functions, inside the function declaration, and these will be available for use only within the function. Thus the function resembles a complete program in miniature – it is an example of a subprogram.

Example 12.3

Assuming the type definitions

```
MONTHS = (JAN,FEB,MAR,APR,MAY,JUN,JUL,AUG,SEP,OCT,NOV,DEC) ;
MONTHLYSTATS = ARRAY [MONTHS] OF REAL
```

the following function returns the value of the largest element of a given array of type MONTHLYSTATS.

132

```
FUNCTION MAXIMUM ( STATS : MONTHLYSTATS ) : REAL ;
   VAR
      MAX   : REAL ;
      MONTH : MONTHS ;
   BEGIN
   MAX := STATS[JAN] ;
   FOR MONTH := FEB TO DEC DO
      IF STATS[MONTH]>MAX THEN MAX := STATS[MONTH] ;
   MAXIMUM := MAX
   END (* MAXIMUM *)
```

Note that the auxiliary variable MAX is necessary. Within a function body the name of the function normally may appear only on the left hand side of assignment statements. The function name is not a variable, and cannot be used as such in an expression.

The function could be incorporated into a complete program as follows.

```
PROGRAM YEARLYMAXIMA ( INPUT, OUTPUT ) ;

TYPE
   MONTHS = (JAN,FEB,MAR,APR,MAY,JUN,JUL,AUG,SEP,OCT,NOV,DEC) ;
   MONTHLYSTATS = ARRAY [MONTHS] OF REAL ;
VAR
   RAINFALL, TEMPERATURE : MONTHLYSTATS ;
   MONTH                 : MONTHS ;

FUNCTION MAXIMUM ( STATS : MONTHLYSTATS ) : REAL ;
   VAR
      MAX   : REAL ;
      MONTH : MONTHS ;
   BEGIN
   MAX := STATS[JAN] ;
   FOR MONTH := FEB TO DEC DO
      IF STATS[MONTH]>MAX THEN MAX := STATS[MONTH] ;
   MAXIMUM := MAX
   END (* MAXIMUM *) ;

BEGIN (* YEARLYMAXIMA *)
FOR MONTH := JAN TO DEC DO
   READLN (RAINFALL[MONTH], TEMPERATURE[MONTH]) ;
WRITELN ('MAXIMUM MONTHLY RAINFALL', MAXIMUM(RAINFALL)) ;
WRITELN ('MAXIMUM MEAN TEMPERATURE', MAXIMUM(TEMPERATURE))
END (* YEARLYMAXIMA *) .
```

(Observe the indentation of the internal declarations and statements of the function declaration relative to the word FUNCTION. This indentation helps to set them apart from the declarations and statements of the program proper.)

Note that the global variable MONTH, declared and used in the main program, is quite distinct from the local variable MONTH declared and used inside the function.

Let us see exactly what happens when the function is invoked, e.g. by the first of the WRITELN statements. Before this statement is obeyed, the storage picture will look like this:

RAINFALL | 8.9 | 8.0 | 8.4 | 7.7 | 6.5 | 3.3 | 3.4 | 3.0 | 4.8 | 6.8 | 7.5 | 8.1 |

TEMPERATURE | | | | | | | | | | | | |

MONTH | ? |

When we enter the function to evaluate the function designator MAXIMUM(RAINFALL), we require additional storage for the function result, for the formal parameter STATS, and for the local variables MAX and MONTH. The formal parameter is initialized with the value of the corresponding actual parameter, RAINFALL, but the others are initially undefined:

MAXIMUM | ? |

STATS | 8.9 | 8.0 | 8.4 | 7.7 | 6.5 | 3.3 | 3.4 | 3.0 | 4.8 | 6.8 | 7.5 | 8.1 |

MAX | ? | MONTH | ? |

– –

RAINFALL | 8.9 | 8.0 | 8.4 | 7.7 | 6.5 | 3.3 | 3.4 | 3.0 | 4.8 | 6.8 | 7.5 | 8.1 |

TEMPERATURE | | | | | | | | | | | | |

MONTH | ? |

After the body of MAXIMUM has been obeyed, the storage picture will look like this:

MAXIMUM | 8.9 |

STATS | 8.9 | 8.0 | 8.4 | 7.7 | 6.5 | 3.3 | 3.4 | 3.0 | 4.8 | 6.8 | 7.5 | 8.1 |

MAX | 8.9 | MONTH | ? |

– –

RAINFALL | 8.9 | 8.0 | 8.4 | 7.7 | 6.5 | 3.3 | 3.4 | 3.0 | 4.8 | 6.8 | 7.5 | 8.1 |

TEMPERATURE | | | | | | | | | | | | |

MONTH | ? |

The value in the box labelled MAXIMUM now becomes the value of the function designator, so in this case the value 8.9 is written. All the storage above the broken line is discarded, since it was needed only for the evaluation of the function designator, and thus we return to the original picture:

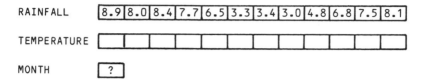

RAINFALL | 8.9 | 8.0 | 8.4 | 7.7 | 6.5 | 3.3 | 3.4 | 3.0 | 4.8 | 6.8 | 7.5 | 8.1 |

TEMPERATURE

MONTH   ?

Let us conclude by summarizing the manner in which a function designator is evaluated.

(1) The actual parameters of the function designator are paired off, from left to right, with the formal parameters of the named function. (It follows that the actual parameters and the formal parameters must be equal in number.)
(2) For the function result a storage location is created whose initial content is undefined.
(3) For each formal parameter of the function a storage location is created and initialized with the value of the corresponding actual parameter.
(4) For each local variable of the function a storage location is created whose initial content is undefined.
(5) The function body is obeyed.
(6) Finally, all storage locations created for the function result, for the formal parameters and for the local variables are discarded, but the value of the function result is retained as the value of the function designator.

EXERCISES 12

12.1. Write a program fragment, invoking the function NMROFDAYSIN (Example 12.2), which assigns to an INTEGER variable N the number of days in this month next year, given that today's month and year have been stored in variables MONTH and YEAR.

12.2. Write a function which returns the fourth power of a given REAL value.

12.3. Write a function which determines whether a given integer is prime, i.e. has no factors other than itself and 1. Write a program fragment which reads an integer and writes it together with the appropriate message 'PRIME' or 'NON-PRIME'.

12.4. Make your answers to Exercise 10.6 into functions, with MATRIX as the formal parameter of each function.

12.5. Write a function which, given a person's complete name (forename(s) followed by surname, separated by blanks) stored in an array of type ARRAY [1..LENGTH] OF CHAR, returns the initial letter of the surname.

PROGRAMMING EXERCISES 12

12.6. The integer logarithm to the base B of a positive integer N is the largest integer L such that the L-th power of B does not exceed N. Write a function which computes the integer logarithm to a given base of a given positive integer. Write a program, incorporating your function, which writes a table of integer logarithms, to the bases 2, 3 and 10, of all the integers from 1 to (say) 50.

12.7*. Write a function which, given a Roman numeral stored left-justified in a character array, returns its integer value. (Take into account combinations like IV, whose value is 4, not 6.) Make sure your function deals sensibly with incorrectly formed Roman numerals. Write a program which reads Roman numerals and writes them together with their values.

13 Procedures

13.1 THE NEED FOR PROCEDURES

In Chapter 12 we have viewed a function as a self-contained piece of program, or subprogram, which takes one or more given values and returns a single result. This result is used immediately on return from the function, for example as an operand in an expression. {This view of a function corresponds quite closely to the mathematical concept of a function.}

By "self-contained" we mean here that the declaration of a subprogram may contain many details which are of no concern outside the subprogram, such as the detailed statements used to compute the subprogram's result(s), and the constants, variables, etc., declared inside the subprogram and used in these statements. Once the subprogram has been written and we are confident of its correctness, we are interested only in the results it can provide.

Frequently we need to write subprograms which avoid the restrictions of Pascal functions, for example a subprogram with several results, or no results at all, or a subprogram whose result cannot be used as an operand in an expression (such as an array). In Pascal such subprograms can be written as procedures. Unlike a function designator, a procedure invocation does not itself have a value. Instead, a procedure is invoked by a new form of statement, called a procedure statement.

All our examples of functions have shown parameters being used in a particular way, to supply values to be used by the functions. Parameters can be used in this way with procedures too. There is also a second, very different, way of using parameters: to get results out of a procedure and stored in variables, where they can be retained for later use. Such use of parameters allows a procedure to have as many results as desired. Thus there are two major parameter mechanisms in Pascal, which are discussed in detail in Section 13.3.

We have met some procedures already, namely the predeclared procedures READ, WRITE, etc. In fact, READ and WRITE statements are special forms of procedure statements. They are, however, rather irregular in that they accept actual parameters of varying numbers and types. It is best to regard these procedures as like the irregular verbs of a natural language: each is a special case unto itself! An ordinary procedure has a fixed number of parameters, with fixed types.

13.2 PROCEDURES IN PASCAL

As we have stated already, a procedure is unlike a function in that it does not itself return a value, therefore a procedure has no result type. Apart from this, and the replacement of FUNCTION by the reserved word PROCEDURE, the syntax of a procedure declaration is similar to that of a function declaration; see Figure 13.1.

Procedure declarations, like function declarations, are inserted between the variable declarations and the body of the program. For a complete summary of the positioning of constant definitions, type definitions, variable declarations and procedure and function declarations, see the syntax of Declaration Part in Appendix 1.5.

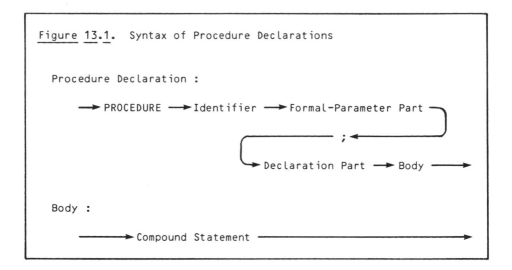

Figure 13.1. Syntax of Procedure Declarations

Procedure Declaration :

Body :

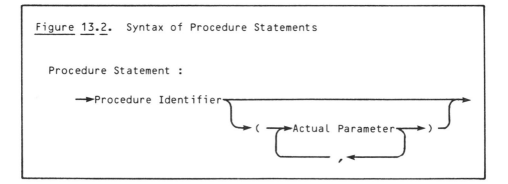

Figure 13.2. Syntax of Procedure Statements

Procedure Statement :

We invoke a procedure by means of a procedure statement. Like a function designator this specifies the identifier of the procedure to be

138

invoked, together with some actual parameters; see Figure 13.2.

Leaving aside, for the moment, the treatment of actual parameters (described in Section 13.3), the effect of obeying a procedure statement is simply to obey the body of the specified procedure.

Example 13.1

The following little procedure writes out a date in the form "day/month/year" (with only the last two digits of the year written), given the day-of-the-month, the month and the year. We assume appropriate definitions of the type identifiers DAYSOFMONTH, MONTHS and YEARS.

```
PROCEDURE WRITEDATE ( D : DAYSOFMONTH ;
                      M : MONTHS ;
                      Y : YEARS        ) ;
    BEGIN
    WRITE (D:2, '/', M:2, '/', (Y MOD 100):2)
    END (* WRITEDATE *)
```

This procedure will pass no results back when invoked; its only effect is to write some output.

The following procedure statement invokes procedure WRITEDATE to write the date given by the variables DAY, MONTH, YEAR:

```
WRITEDATE(DAY,MONTH,YEAR)
```

The following statement writes the date exactly nine months thence:

```
IF MONTH > 3 THEN
    WRITEDATE(DAY,MONTH-3,YEAR+1)
ELSE
    WRITEDATE(DAY,MONTH+9,YEAR)
```

Here is a complete program, incorporating procedure WRITEDATE, which simply reads in the three components of a date and writes that date:

```
PROGRAM DATE ( INPUT, OUTPUT ) ;

    TYPE
       DAYSOFMONTH = 1..31 ;
       MONTHS      = 1..12 ;
       YEARS       = 0..9999 ;
    VAR
       DAY   : DAYSOFMONTH ;
       MONTH : MONTHS ;
       YEAR  : YEARS ;
```

```
PROCEDURE WRITEDATE ( D : DAYSOFMONTH ;
                      M : MONTHS ;
                      Y : YEARS          ) ;
    BEGIN
    WRITE (D:2, '/', M:2, '/', (Y MOD 100):2)
    END (* WRITEDATE *) ;

BEGIN (* DATE *)
READ (DAY, MONTH, YEAR) ;
WRITEDATE(DAY,MONTH,YEAR) ;
WRITELN
END (* DATE *) .
```

Here is an alternative version of procedure WRITEDATE, which
writes the name of the month and also writes the year in full.

```
PROCEDURE WRITEDATE ( D : DAYSOFMONTH ;
                      M : MONTHS ;
                      Y : YEARS          ) ;
    BEGIN
    WRITE (D:2) ;
    CASE M OF
        1: WRITE (' JANUARY ') ;
        2: WRITE (' FEBRUARY ') ;
        3: WRITE (' MARCH ') ;
        4: WRITE (' APRIL ') ;
        5: WRITE (' MAY ') ;
        6: WRITE (' JUNE ') ;
        7: WRITE (' JULY ') ;
        8: WRITE (' AUGUST ') ;
        9: WRITE (' SEPTEMBER ') ;
       10: WRITE (' OCTOBER ') ;
       11: WRITE (' NOVEMBER ') ;
       12: WRITE (' DECEMBER ')
    END ;
    WRITE (YEAR:4)
    END (* WRITEDATE *)
```

Observe the flexibility of procedures: a new version of a procedure
such as WRITEDATE can easily be slotted into a program in place of the
old version, and the procedure statement(s) invoking it need not be
changed at all, providing only that the procedure's parameters remain
the same.

13.3 VALUE-PARAMETERS AND VARIABLE-PARAMETERS

So far we have met formal parameters used only in a particular way: to supply values to be used by a function or procedure. Such formal parameters are called value-parameters, and their mechanism is very simple: on entry to the function or procedure, each value-parameter is initialized to the value of the corresponding actual parameter.

In Example 13.1, the formal parameters of procedure WRITEDATE - D, M and Y - were all value-parameters. Thus the effect of the procedure statement

    WRITEDATE(DAY,MONTH-3,YEAR+1)

is to obey the body of WRITEDATE with D initialized to the value of DAY, M initialized to the value of MONTH-3, and Y initialized to the value of YEAR+1. Once the initializations of the value-parameters have been performed, there is no further interaction between the actual parameters and the formal parameters. If a procedure assigns a value to its own value-parameter, this assignment has no effect whatsoever on the corresponding actual parameter.

A procedure, therefore, cannot use value-parameters to pass back any results. For this purpose a new kind of formal parameter is needed, one which allows a procedure, by assigning a value to the formal parameter, to change the value of the corresponding actual parameter. Since the actual parameter must be capable of receiving a new value, it follows that the actual parameter must be a variable. So formal parameters of this kind are called variable-parameters. A variable-parameter merely represents the variable which is placed in the corresponding actual-parameter position.

A variable-parameter is distinguished by placing the word VAR in front of it in the formal parameter part of the procedure declaration.

Example 13.2

The following procedure will determine the minimum of three given INTEGER values, and pass back this minimum through the variable-parameter MIN.

```
PROCEDURE FINDMINIMUM ( A, B, C : INTEGER ;
                        VAR MIN : INTEGER  ) ;
    BEGIN
    IF A < B THEN
        MIN := A
    ELSE
        MIN := B ;
    IF C < MIN THEN
        MIN := C
    END (* FINDMINIMUM *)
```

Assuming the variable declaration

```
WEEKS, CONTRIBUTIONS, BENEFIT : INTEGER
```

an example of a procedure statement invoking FINDMINIMUM would be

```
FINDMINIMUM(600,5*CONTRIBUTIONS,25*WEEKS,BENEFIT)
```

which would have the effect of storing in BENEFIT the minimum of 600,
5*CONTRIBUTIONS and 25*WEEKS. Let us see exactly how this works.
Immediately before obeying the procedure statement, suppose we have
the following situation:

Now we enter FINDMINIMUM. A, B and C are value-parameters, so we
create storage locations for them and initialize them with the values
of the corresponding actual parameters, namely 600, 5*CONTRIBUTIONS
and 25*WEEKS respectively. On the other hand, MIN is a variable-
parameter, so rather than just receiving the current value of
BENEFIT, MIN will represent the variable BENEFIT itself. We
illustrate this by drawing an arrow from MIN to the location of
BENEFIT:

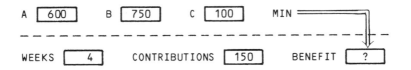

Now we start to obey the procedure body. The expression A < B
evaluates to TRUE, so we obey the statement MIN := A. Since MIN is
a variable-parameter, we store the value of the expression A in the
variable represented by MIN, i.e. in BENEFIT:

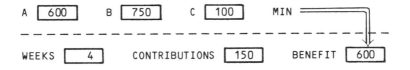

Now to evaluate the expression C < MIN, we compare the current value
of C with the current value of the variable represented by MIN, i.e.
BENEFIT; thus the expression evaluates to TRUE. We obey the
statement MIN := C, whose effect is to store the value of C in
BENEFIT:

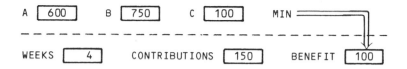

A `600`   B `750`   C `100`   MIN

WEEKS `4`   CONTRIBUTIONS `150`   BENEFIT `100`

Finally we leave the procedure, and discard the storage locations above the broken line. Thus obeying the procedure statement has had the following nett effect:

WEEKS `4`   CONTRIBUTIONS `150`   BENEFIT `100`

Since procedure FINDMINIMUM passes back only one result, of type INTEGER, we could, if we prefer, replace it by an INTEGER function with only A, B and C as formal parameters:

```
FUNCTION MINIMUM ( A, B, C : INTEGER ) : INTEGER ;
   VAR
      MIN : INTEGER ;
   BEGIN
   IF A < B THEN
      MIN := A
   ELSE
      MIN := B ;
   IF C < MIN THEN
      MIN := C ;
   MINIMUM := MIN
   END (* MINIMUM *)
```

In this version, MIN is an ordinary local variable. The same effect as our procedure statement could now be achieved by the assignment statement

```
BENEFIT := MINIMUM(600,5*CONTRIBUTIONS,25*WEEKS)
```

When a choice is available, a function is often more convenient to use than a procedure. In the following example, however, we require a subprogram with <u>two</u> results, one of which moreover is an array; for this purpose a procedure is the more appropriate choice.

Example 13.3

Suppose that we are supplied with data in the form of natural-language text, which consists of "words" separated by blanks. Let us assume that any sequence of non-blank characters constitutes a "word", and that no word is longer than MAXLENGTH characters.

When writing a program which processes natural-language text, it is a good idea to include a procedure whose task is to read a single word and to pass back the word itself and its length.

The procedure must take into account the possibility that the next word in the input data may be preceded by several blanks, so two steps will be necessary, the first to scan (and ignore) blanks, the second to scan (and store) non-blanks which comprise the word itself.

At this stage it is unnecessary to commit ourselves on how to store the word. Let us just agree that the word will be stored in a variable-parameter of type WORDS, which we shall define later.

```
PROCEDURE READWORD ( VAR NEXTWORD  : WORDS ;
                     VAR ITSLENGTH : INTEGER ) ;
   BEGIN
   read past any blanks preceding the next word ;
   read the word itself into NEXTWORD,
                 storing its length in ITSLENGTH
   END (* READWORD *)
```

Each of the two steps will be refined into a loop. The first loop continues until a non-blank character is read, and the second until a subsequent blank is read, signifying the end of the word. In each loop we must also allow for the possibility of reaching the end of the input data, so we must arrange to leave either loop whenever EOF(INPUT) becomes TRUE.

We must now commit ourselves to a definition of the type WORDS. Let us choose the definition

```
WORDS = ARRAY [1..MAXLENGTH] OF CHAR
```

which will allow us to store words up to MAXLENGTH characters in length; and let us decide to store each word left-justified in NEXTWORD. After further refinements, we may arrive at the following solution:

```
PROCEDURE READWORD ( VAR NEXTWORD  : WORDS ;
                     VAR ITSLENGTH : INTEGER ) ;
   CONST
      BLANK = ' ' ;
   VAR
      CH   : CHAR ;
      FILL : 1..MAXLENGTH ;
   BEGIN
   (* read past any blanks preceding the next word *)
      CH := BLANK ;
      WHILE NOT EOF(INPUT) AND (CH = BLANK) DO
         READ (CH) ;
```

```
(* read the word itself *)
   ITSLENGTH := 0 ;
   WHILE NOT EOF(INPUT) AND (CH <> BLANK) DO
      BEGIN
      IF ITSLENGTH < MAXLENGTH THEN
         (* store CH in NEXTWORD *)
            BEGIN
            ITSLENGTH := ITSLENGTH+1 ;
            NEXTWORD[ITSLENGTH] := CH
            END ;
      READ(CH)
      END ;
   (* fill out with blanks *)
      FOR FILL := ITSLENGTH+1 TO MAXLENGTH DO
         NEXTWORD[FILL] := BLANK
END (* READWORD *)
```

Here is a complete program, incorporating READWORD and another procedure, which simply reads words and writes them one per line. The program exploits the fact that, when no more words remain to be read, READWORD will pass back the value 0 through its variable-parameter ITSLENGTH.

```
PROGRAM COPYWORDS ( INPUT, OUTPUT ) ;

   CONST
      MAXLENGTH = 8 ;
   TYPE
      WORDS = ARRAY [1..MAXLENGTH] OF CHAR ;
   VAR
      WORD       : WORDS ;
      LENGTH     : INTEGER ;

   PROCEDURE READWORD ( VAR NEXTWORD  : WORDS ;
                        VAR ITSLENGTH : INTEGER  ) ;
      ....................
      .................... (* as above *)
      ....................

   PROCEDURE WRITEWORD ( WORD      : WORDS ;
                         ITSLENGTH : INTEGER ) ;
      VAR
         I : 1..MAXLENGTH ;
      BEGIN
      FOR I := 1 TO ITSLENGTH DO
         WRITE (WORD[I])
      END (* WRITEWORD *) ;
```

```
BEGIN (* COPYWORDS *)
READWORD(WORD,LENGTH) ;
WHILE LENGTH <> 0 DO    (* we have a word *)
   BEGIN
   WRITEWORD(WORD,LENGTH) ;  WRITELN ;
   READWORD(WORD,LENGTH)
   END
END (* COPYWORDS *) .
```

Suppose the input data is

PARIS IN THE
SPRING-TIME

When we obey the statement READWORD(WORD,LENGTH), the variable-
parameters NEXTWORD and ITSLENGTH represent the variables WORD and
LENGTH respectively; in particular, NEXTWORD represents the whole of
the array WORD:

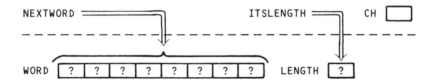

Assignment of the characters of a word to NEXTWORD[1], NEXTWORD[2],
etc., will actually result in these characters being stored in
WORD[1], WORD[2], etc. Thus after the first invocation of READWORD
we have:

WORD ['P']['A']['R']['I']['S'][' '][' '][' '] LENGTH [5]

and after the fifth invocation:

WORD [' '][' '][' '][' '][' '][' '][' '][' '] LENGTH [0]

     As an exercise, work through program COPYWORDS with the input data
given above, and show exactly what output is produced.

The following example illustrates a slightly different usage of a
variable-parameter, to update the value of an actual parameter, i.e. to
use its old value before changing it.

Example 13.4

The following little procedure can be invoked with any INTEGER

146

variable as actual parameter; its effect is to add 1 to that
variable's value.

```
PROCEDURE INCREMENT ( VAR N : INTEGER ) ;
   BEGIN
   N := N+1
   END (* INCREMENT *)
```

Suppose we wished to count the frequencies of individual upper-
case letters, and the total frequency of all other characters, in a
piece of text. Let us declare the variables

```
LETTERFREQ : ARRAY ['A'..'Z'] OF INTEGER ;
OTHERFREQ  : INTEGER ;
CH         : CHAR
```

and initialize OTHERFREQ, and each element of LETTERFREQ, to 0. Then
after storing a character in CH we can update the appropriate
frequency by:

```
IF ('A' <= CH) AND (CH <= 'Z') THEN
   INCREMENT(LETTERFREQ[CH])
ELSE
   INCREMENT(OTHERFREQ)
```

When the statement INCREMENT(LETTERFREQ[CH]) is obeyed, the
variable-parameter N represents the variable LETTERFREQ[CH], i.e. a
single element of the array. For example, when CH has the value 'C',
N represents LETTERFREQ['C']:

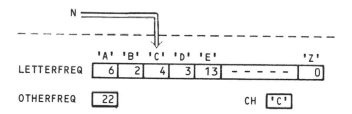

The effect of the procedure statement will then be to change the
value of LETTERFREQ['C'] from 4 to 5; the remaining elements of
LETTERFREQ will not be disturbed.

The syntax of formal parameters, including value- and variable-
parameters, is summarized in Figure 13.3. A formal-parameter section
starting with VAR defines a list of variable-parameters; a formal-
parameter section starting with an identifier defines a list of value-
parameters.

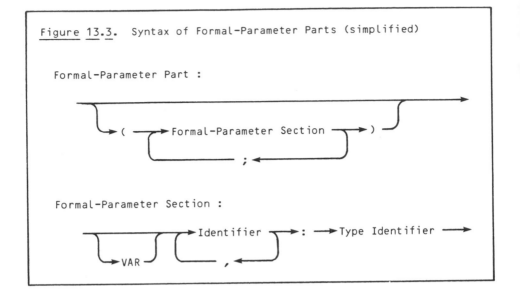

Figure 13.3. Syntax of Formal-Parameter Parts (simplified)

Formal-Parameter Part :

Formal-Parameter Section :

Let us summarize the effect of obeying a procedure statement.

(1) The actual parameters of the procedure statement are paired off, from left to right, with the formal parameters of the named procedure. (It follows that the actual parameters and the formal parameters must be equal in number.)

(2) For each value-parameter of the procedure a storage location is created and initialized with the value of the corresponding actual parameter. (It follows that the actual parameter may be any expression of a type which permits its value to be assigned to the value-parameter. Usually the actual parameter's type will be the same as the value-parameter's, but the former could be INTEGER if the latter is REAL, etc.)

(3) Each variable-parameter of the procedure is made to represent the corresponding actual parameter (which must be a variable of exactly the same type as the variable-parameter).

(4) For each local variable of the procedure a storage location is created whose initial content is undefined.

(5) The procedure body is obeyed. At this stage value-parameters behave exactly like ordinary local variables, but each reference to a variable-parameter is effectively a reference to the actual parameter it represents. (In particular, assigning a value to the variable-parameter effectively changes the value of the actual parameter.)

(6) Finally, all storage locations created for formal parameters and local variables of the procedure are discarded.

Thus the effect of obeying a procedure statement is similar to the evaluation of a function designator, except for the treatment of the function result. Compare the summary above with the summary at the end of Chapter 12. The latter, however, took only value-parameters into account.

Although it is not illegal in Pascal for a function to have variable-parameters, you will find no such examples in this book. It is more natural to use functions with only value-parameters, since these correspond more closely to the mathematical concept of functions. If a function, when invoked, changes the value of any non-local variable, either through a variable-parameter or by any other means, or performs any input or output, this phenomenon is known as a side-effect. Side-effects are generally considered to be bad programming practice, since they make programs more difficult to understand.

(A final point: our explanation of the variable-parameter mechanism has been slightly over-simplified. Some compilers make any assignment to the variable-parameter change the value of the corresponding actual parameter immediately, as described above. Other compilers allow the change to the value of the actual parameter to be delayed until exit from the procedure, though the formal parameter's own value will change immediately. The difference is only detectable in pathological programs, and Pascal is so defined that such programs are invalid.)

13.4 THE VIRTUES OF PROCEDURES AND FUNCTIONS

All the example programs in this chapter and in Chapter 12 could have been written without using any procedures or functions. You might well ask, then, why take the trouble to learn how to use them? There are a number of very good reasons why this effort is worthwhile, reasons which should become more and more convincing as you go on to write larger and larger programs.

(a) Procedures and functions can be used to build a program from small self-contained pieces, which we have called subprograms. Each subprogram can be written and tested in isolation by its author, which facilitates the task of writing and testing a large program. Equally important, each subprogram can be read and understood in isolation by another person, and this facilitates his understanding of the whole program.

(b) Procedures and functions allow us to give names (identifiers) to pieces of program. Judicious choice of identifiers for procedures and functions, as well as for constants, types and variables, can make a program read almost like prose.

(c) Once declared, a procedure or function may be invoked from several places, with different actual parameters if required. This makes it unnecessary to write similar pieces of program in several different places, which would be a very tedious and error-prone task. Note that the use of parameters provides valuable flexibility in this respect.

(d) Another source of flexibility is the ease of replacing one version of a procedure or function by another. We have already seen an example of this (Example 13.1). This flexibility is a consequence of the self-contained nature of procedures and functions.

(e) As we have seen, variables declared inside a subprogram occupy storage only while that subprogram is being obeyed. At other times this storage can be used for other purposes. (On the other hand, variables declared at the head of the program proper occupy storage for the entire duration of the program.) Thus we can economize on storage space by declaring each variable only in the subprogram where it is actually needed.

We can illustrate some of these points by comparing two versions of the same program, one version being monolithic, the other being conveniently broken down into procedures. Each program reads two square matrices, A and B, and writes their matrix product, AB.

Example 13.5

```
PROGRAM MATRIXPRODUCT1 ( INPUT, OUTPUT ) ;

CONST
   N = 10 ;
TYPE
   MATRIX = ARRAY [1..N,1..N] OF INTEGER ;
VAR
   A, B, AB : MATRIX ;
   I, J, K  : 1..N ;
   CROSS    : INTEGER ;

BEGIN (* MATRIXPRODUCT1 *)
FOR I := 1 TO N DO
   FOR J := 1 TO N DO
      READ (A[I,J]) ;
FOR I := 1 TO N DO
   FOR J := 1 TO N DO
      READ (B[I,J]) ;
FOR I := 1 TO N DO
   FOR J := 1 TO N DO
      BEGIN
      CROSS := 0 ;
      FOR K := 1 TO N DO
         CROSS := CROSS + A[I,K]*B[K,J] ;
      AB[I,J] := CROSS
      END ;
FOR I := 1 TO N DO
   BEGIN
   WRITE ('[') ;
   FOR J := 1 TO N DO
      WRITE (AB[I,J]) ;
   WRITELN ('  ]')
   END
END (* MATRIXPRODUCT1 *) .
```

Example 13.6

```
PROGRAM MATRIXPRODUCT2 ( INPUT, OUTPUT ) ;

CONST
   N = 10 ;
TYPE
   MATRIX = ARRAY [1..N,1..N] OF INTEGER :
VAR
   A, B, AB : MATRIX ;

PROCEDURE READMATRIX ( VAR M : MATRIX ) ;
   VAR
      I, J : 1..N ;
   BEGIN
   FOR I := 1 TO N DO
      FOR J := 1 TO N DO
         READ (M[I,J]) ;
   END (* READMATRIX *) ;

PROCEDURE WRITEMATRIX ( M : MATRIX ) ;
   VAR
      I, J : 1..N ;
   BEGIN
   FOR I := 1 TO N DO
      BEGIN
      WRITE ('[') ;
      FOR J := 1 TO N DO
         WRITE (M[I,J]) ;
      WRITELN ('   ]')
      END
   END (* WRITEMATRIX *) ;

PROCEDURE MULTIPLYMATRICES (     M1, M2  : MATRIX ;
                             VAR PRODUCT : MATRIX ) ;
   VAR
      I, J, K : 1..N ;
      CROSS : INTEGER ;
   BEGIN
   FOR I := 1 TO N DO
      FOR J := 1 TO N DO
         BEGIN
         CROSS := 0 ;
         FOR K := 1 TO N, DO
            CROSS := CROSS + M1[I,K]*M2[K,J] ;
         PRODUCT[I,J] := CROSS
         END
   END (* MULTIPLYMATRICES *) ;
```

```
BEGIN (* MATRIXPRODUCT2 *)
READMATRIX(A) ;
READMATRIX(B) ;
MULTIPLYMATRICES(A,B,AB) ;
WRITEMATRIX(AB)
END (* MATRIXPRODUCT2 *) .
```

MATRIXPRODUCT1 cannot be read at all without at once plunging into a morass of nested loops. Compare how easily the program body of MATRIXPRODUCT2 can be read and understood, because of its brevity and well-chosen procedure identifiers.

Compare also the variable declarations at the head of each program. In MATRIXPRODUCT1 these declarations are rather cluttered, with the important MATRIX variables placed on an equal footing with the others, which are merely auxiliary variables. In MATRIXPRODUCT2 the auxiliary variables have been relegated to the procedures where they are needed, leaving only the more important MATRIX variables at the head of the program, where they are more visible.

MATRIXPRODUCT1 contains two similar pieces of program, one for reading the matrix A, one for reading the matrix B. MATRIXPRODUCT2 avoids this duplication by substituting two procedure statements invoking the same procedure, READMATRIX, with actual parameters A and B respectively.

Although these two pieces of program are very short, it would be annoying if they had to be changed consistently (for example, if the matrix elements were to be read in column by column, instead of row by row). In MATRIXPRODUCT2 the change could be made in a single place, in the body of READMATRIX. In MATRIXPRODUCT1 changes would be necessary in two places; consequently the chance of error would be greater.

The flexibility inherent in the use of procedures would become even more apparent if the programs were to be changed to write the matrices A and B as well as their product. In MATRIXPRODUCT1 it would be necessary to grind out yet more nested loops, making the program even more unclear. In MATRIXPRODUCT2 esentially the only change would be to insert the statements

```
WRITEMATRIX(A) ;
WRITEMATRIX(B)
```

in the program body, which would not reduce its clarity at all.

A good methodical approach to writing and testing a program such as MATRIXPRODUCT2 would be to write and test the procedures one at a time. We could first write WRITEMATRIX and test it using a test program which assigns arbitrary values to the elements of A and then obeys WRITEMATRIX(A). Then we could write READMATRIX and test it using the following test program:

152

```
BEGIN (* test READMATRIX *)
READMATRIX(A) ;
WRITEMATRIX(A) ;
END .
```

Finally we could write MULTIPLYMATRICES and test it using the complete program. This approach to testing is called "bottom-up" testing.

An alternative approach is "top-down" testing, which makes use of temporary dummy versions of the procedures. The program body is written first, in its final form. Then we write WRITEMATRIX, and test it using a dummy version of READMATRIX which assigns arbitrary values to the elements of its formal parameter M, and a dummy version of MULTIPLYMATRICES whose body could be simply PRODUCT := M1. Then we replace the dummy version of READMATRIX by its final version, and test it. Finally we replace the dummy version of MULTIPLYMATRICES by its final version, and test the complete program. Observe that the same version of the program body is used at all stages of testing.

We have stressed how procedures and functions can be exploited to structure even quite small programs written by a single programmer. In the development of large programs such structuring is absolutely essential. Professional programmers often work in teams, collaborating in the construction of very large programs (1000 to 100000 statements). A very convenient method of splitting up such a task is to have each programmer independently write and test a related group of subprograms, or module. This exploits the self-contained nature of subprograms. Later, the modules are combined to form a complete program.

Another common practice of experienced programmers is to write and test subprograms of general utility, and then to deposit them in "libraries" where they become accessible to other programmers. This avoids duplication of effort, and makes sophisticated algorithms available even to inexperienced programmers. The predeclared procedures and functions of Pascal form such a library, which is available to every Pascal programmer.

13.5 THE SCOPE RULES OF PASCAL

As we have stated already, declarations of identifiers inside a procedure or function have no meaning outside that subprogram; we say that such identifiers are local to that subprogram. On the other hand, identifiers declared outside a subprogram can generally be used inside that subprogram; the constant identifier N was used in this way in Example 13.6.

It is time that we clarified these issues by spelling out what are known as the scope rules of Pascal. We shall use the program of Example 13.7 to illustrate the scope rules.

Example 13.7

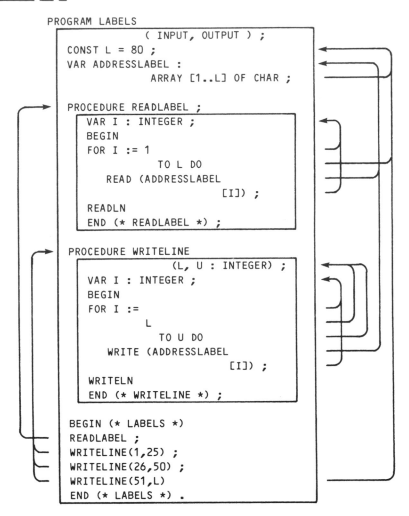

```
PROGRAM LABELS
                    ( INPUT, OUTPUT ) ;
          CONST L = 80 ;
          VAR ADDRESSLABEL :
                       ARRAY [1..L] OF CHAR ;

          PROCEDURE READLABEL ;
              VAR I : INTEGER ;
              BEGIN
              FOR I := 1
                         TO L DO
                 READ (ADDRESSLABEL
                                    [I]) ;
              READLN
              END (* READLABEL *) ;

          PROCEDURE WRITELINE
                            (L, U : INTEGER) ;
              VAR I : INTEGER ;
              BEGIN
              FOR I :=
                      L
                         TO U DO
                 WRITE (ADDRESSLABEL
                                    [I]) ;
              WRITELN
              END (* WRITELINE *) ;

          BEGIN (* LABELS *)
          READLABEL ;
          WRITELINE(1,25) ;
          WRITELINE(26,50) ;
          WRITELINE(51,L)
          END (* LABELS *) .
```

In Example 13.7 we have boxed in each procedure declaration, excluding only the procedure identifier itself; and likewise we have boxed in the whole program, excluding only the program identifier. Each of these boxes is called a block.

Observe that the blocks are nested, i.e. a block may lie entirely within another block, but blocks do not overlap in any other way. This nesting is a consequence of the syntax of Pascal.

In general, there will be one block for each procedure declaration, one block for each function declaration, and one block for the program as a whole. Let us name each block after the corresponding procedure, function or program identifier. Thus, in Example 13.7 we have an outer block, LABELS, and two inner blocks, READLABEL and WRITELINE.

154

Scope Rule <u>1</u>.   No identifier may be declared more than once in the same
block.

Nevertheless, Pascal allows the same identifier to be declared in
different blocks. In Example 13.7, L is declared in two of the blocks:
in block LABELS as a constant identifier, in block WRITELINE as a
value-parameter. Clearly, these are two distinct entities. Also, I is
declared in two of the blocks, in both cases as a variable identifier,
and coincidentally it is given the same type in both declarations.
Despite this coincidence, these two declarations introduce <u>two distinct</u>
<u>variables</u>.

How can we tell, in general, when we use an identifier which has
several declarations, to which of these declarations we are referring?

Scope Rule <u>2</u>.   If an identifier ID is used in a statement S, find the
smallest block which encloses both S and a declaration of
ID; then the occurrence of ID in S corresponds to that
declaration.

Consider the statement WRITELINE(51,L) in block LABELS. The
smallest block enclosing both this statement and a declaration of L is
block LABELS itself, where L is defined to be a constant with value 80.
The same applies to the occurrence of L in the statement "FOR I := 1 TO
L DO ...." in block READLABEL. But now consider the occurrence of L in
the statement "FOR I := L TO U DO ...." in block WRITELINE. The
smallest block enclosing both this statement and a declaration of L is
block WRITELINE, where L is declared as a value-parameter. On different
occasions this L will have the values 1, 26 and 51.

In Example 13.7, arrows have been drawn from all identifier
occurrences to the corresponding declarations.

What happens if, when applying Scope Rule 2, no block can be found
containing both the statement and a declaration of the identifier? This
is simply a programming error - the identifier has not been declared (at
least not in the correct place).

Scope Rule <u>3</u>.   An identifier may be used only within a block where it is
declared.

In Example 13.7, U cannot be used in block LABELS nor in block
READLABEL; it can be used only in block WRITELINE, where it is declared.

These three scope rules apply equally to all identifiers: constant
identifiers, type identifiers, variable identifiers, formal parameters,
and even procedure and function identifiers.

Identifiers declared in a particular block are described as <u>local</u> to
that block. Identifiers declared in an enclosing block are described as
<u>non-local</u> to the inner block. Identifiers declared in the outermost
block (the program proper) are described as <u>global</u>, since (potentially)
they can be used anywhere.

We can now clarify the status of the predeclared constants, types,
procedures and functions. Imagine these to be declared in an invisible
block enclosing every program:

```
CONST
   MAXINT = ...
TYPE
   INTEGER = ....
   BOOLEAN = (FALSE,TRUE) ;
   ...............


PROCEDURE READ ......
   ........
   ........


FUNCTION EOF ......
   ........
   ........


..................
..................


PROGRAM ........
   .........
   BEGIN
   .........
   .........
   END .
```

In terms of the scope rules, therefore, the predeclared constants,
types, functions and procedures are not really special. We can, if we
wish, re-declare any of their identifiers for our own purposes.
Normally, however, this would not be wise, since it would make their
original declarations in the invisible outer block inaccessible; but see
Example 13.8.

We have already seen some examples illustrating how the scope rules
can be exploited in practical programming. In Example 13.6 auxiliary
variables named I and J were declared in each of the three procedures.
In Example 13.3 the identifier WORD was used both for a global variable
and for a formal parameter. As these examples illustrate, the scope
rules allow identifiers for formal parameters, local variables, etc., to
be chosen freely within each block, and if they happen to be the same as
identifiers declared in other blocks, the coincidence does not affect
the meaning of the program. Nevertheless, this facility should be used
with restraint, since using one identifier indiscriminately for a
variety of purposes in different places may make the program difficult
to understand.

Here is another example of the usefulness of the scope rules.

Example 13.8

Suppose that someone has written a program which writes a series of

156

tables, one table per page (for example, tables of mathematical functions, or tables of students' examination marks grouped by subject). In skeleton form, the program might look like this:

```
PROGRAM TABLES ( INPUT, OUTPUT ) ;

   ......
   ......

BEGIN
PAGE ;
write the first table ;
PAGE ;
write the second table ;
   ........
   ........
END .
```

PAGE is a predeclared procedure, whose effect is to force subsequent output on to a fresh page.

Now suppose that most of the tables being written turn out to occupy only a few lines, and moreover computer paper is becoming very expensive; so, in order to economize on paper, we decide to separate the tables by lines across the page, rather than by writing the tables on separate pages.

We could modify the program by replacing each invocation of PAGE by appropriate WRITELN statements. A much neater solution, however, is to insert our own declaration of the procedure PAGE:

```
PROGRAM TABLES ( INPUT, OUTPUT ) ;

   ......
   ......

PROCEDURE PAGE ;
   BEGIN                    (* paper-saving version *)
   WRITELN ; WRITELN ;
   WRITELN ('----------------------------------------------') ;
   WRITELN ;  WRITELN
   END (* PAGE *) ;

BEGIN (* TABLES *)
PAGE ;
write the first table ;
PAGE ;
write the second table ;
   ........
   ........
END (* TABLES *) .
```

The scope rules ensure that each procedure statement PAGE invokes our own procedure and not the predeclared version in the invisible outer block.

This solution is very flexible; if desired, we could go back to writing one table per page simply by removing the procedure declaration. No change to the rest of the program is necessary.

This example also illustrates the use of a parameterless procedure. Compare the declaration of PAGE with the syntax diagrams of Figures 13.1 and 13.3, and compare the procedure statements invoking it with the syntax diagram of Figure 13.2.

EXERCISES 13

13.1. Write a procedure which writes N blank lines, where N is its parameter. Write a statement which invokes your procedure to write four blank lines.

13.2. The Pascal READ statement cannot be used to read a BOOLEAN value. Write a procedure which reads a BOOLEAN value, represented in the input data by one of the characters 'F' or 'T', and passes it back through a variable-parameter. The procedure should skip any blanks preceding the 'F' or 'T'.

13.3. Write a procedure which interchanges the values of its two parameters (which may be of any type T).

13.4. Assume the type definition

    CENTRES = (FRANKFURT,LONDON,NEWYORK,PARIS,TOKYO,ZURICH)

(a) Write a procedure which locates the maximum and minimum elements of a parameter of type ARRAY [CENTRES] OF REAL; the subscripts of the maximum and minimum elements are to be passed back through the parameters MAXCENTRE and MINCENTRE respectively. (Assume that no two elements are exactly equal.)
(b) Assume further the type definition

    CURRENCIES = (DEUTSCHMARK,FFRANC,SFRANC,STERLING,USDOLLAR,YEN)

and assume that each element of an array CURRENCYVALUE, whose type is ARRAY [CURRENCIES, CENTRES] OF REAL, contains the value of one currency at one trading centre. Write a program fragment, invoking your procedure, which determines at which centres a dealer could most profitably buy and sell Sterling respectively, and computes his percentage profit on the deal.

13.5. Assume the type definitions

    INDEXRANGE = 1..N ;
    LISTS   = ARRAY [INDEXRANGE] OF ITEMS

158

Write a procedure SEARCH which searches LIST (a parameter of type LISTS) for an element which matches TARGET (a parameter of type ITEMS); the subscript of the matched element is to be passed back through LOCATION (a parameter of type INDEXRANGE), if the search is successful, and FOUND (a BOOLEAN parameter) is to be set accordingly.

PROGRAMMING EXERCISES 13

13.6. Write a program which reads the number of a year and the day-of-the-week on which 1 January falls, and which writes a complete calendar for that year. Include in your program a procedure which, given the name of a month, the number of days in that month, and the day-of-the-week on which the first day of that month falls, writes a calendar for that month, and passes back the day-of-the-week on which the month ends.

13.7. Write a function which returns the group code of a given character CH according to the Soundex system (see Example 11.2). Enclose your function in a procedure which, given a name stored left-justified in a parameter of type WORDS (see Example 13.3), stores the Soundex code of that name in a parameter of type ARRAY [1..4] OF CHAR. If the Soundex code is longer than four characters, it is to be truncated at the right; if it is shorter, it is to be extended to four characters with '0's.

Write a program, including your procedure and procedure READWORD (see Example 13.6), which reads names and writes them together with their Soundex codes.

13.8. Write a procedure which, given a pair of characters which form the abbreviation of a chemical element, passes back, through a parameter of type (HYDROGEN,HELIUM,.....), an indication of which element that character pair represents. ('H' followed by a blank for hydrogen, 'H' followed by 'e' for helium, etc.) Take only a few of the more common elements into account.

Write a procedure which reads a molecular formula, enclosed in parentheses, such as (Na2SO4), and passes back the molecular weight of the compound it represents. Assume that the molecular formula itself contains no parentheses.

Write a program which uses your procedure to read a number of molecular formulas, one per line of input, and writes their molecular weights.

14 Advanced use of functions and procedures

{This chapter should be omitted altogether on a first reading.}

14.1 RECURSIVE FUNCTIONS AND PROCEDURES

Any subprogram (function or procedure) may invoke other subprograms, as we have already seen (Example 12.2). Programmers exploit this possibility to build hierarchical programs, in which the main program invokes subprograms A1, A2, A3, ... to perform subsidiary tasks; these subprograms in turn invoke subprograms B1, B2, B3, ... to perform simpler tasks; and so on down to any desired depth.

This is by no means the only way of exploiting the use of subprograms. In particular, a subprogram may invoke itself! Such a subprogram is said to be recursive. This idea seems paradoxical at first sight: how can a subprogram achieve anything by invoking itself? Yet recursive subprograms allow very elegant solutions to a certain class of programming problems. The best way to understand this idea is to study some examples.

Example 14.1

Consider the expression "M raised to the power of N", where M and N are integers, N being positive. Let us write this expression, in functional notation, as POWER(M,N). This function has the value

POWER(M,N) = M * M ...... * M   (N-1 multiplications)

Mathematicians avoid this awkward notation by resorting to a different form of definition:

$$POWER(M,N) \quad = \quad \begin{cases} M & \text{if } N=1 \\ M * POWER(M,N-1) & \text{if } N>1 \end{cases}$$

i.e. the function is defined in terms of itself! In fact, the function is defined recursively.

The recursive definition can be transcribed directly into a Pascal function declaration:

```
FUNCTION POWER ( M : INTEGER ;
                 N : POSITIVEINTEGER ) : INTEGER ;
   BEGIN
   IF N = 1 THEN
      POWER := M
   ELSE
      POWER := M * POWER(M,N-1)
   END (* POWER *)
```

How does this recursive function ever succeed in yielding a result? The answer is that, every time the function invokes itself, its second actual parameter (N-1) is one less than before (N). So, although the function repeatedly invokes itself, it will eventually invoke itself with 1 as its second actual parameter, whereupon the function yields a result directly.

Let us trace the action of the function when it is invoked to evaluate POWER(4,3); this should yield 4*4*4, i.e. 64.

To evaluate POWER(4,3), we initialize the value-parameters M and N to 4 and 3 respectively, then obey the body of POWER. We can see that the function result will be evaluated as 4*POWER(4,2).

> To evaluate POWER(4,2), we initialize the value-parameters M and N to 4 and 2 respectively, then obey the body of POWER. We can see that the function result will be evaluated as 4*POWER(4,1).

>> To evaluate POWER(4,1), we initialize the value-parameters M and N to 4 and 1 respectively, then obey the body of POWER. We can see that the function result will be evaluated directly to 4.

> Thus POWER(4,2) evaluates to 4*4, i.e. 16.

Thus POWER(4,3) evaluates to 4*16, i.e. 64.

Of course, the function POWER can easily be programmed without resort to recursion; compare Example 6.1.

Many computations, like Example 14.1, can be programmed either recursively or using a loop. Programmers usually prefer to avoid recursion when they have a choice, because a recursive subprogram tends to use up both more space (a complete set of storage locations must be allocated every time it invokes itself) and more time (through overheads incurred on entering and leaving the subprogram) than an equivalent non-recursive subprogram.

Nevertheless, there are certain computations which are "naturally" recursive, in the sense that they are awkward to program without recursion. The following example illustrates such a problem.

Example 14.2

Finding a path through a maze is a popular problem. Let us assume that the maze is a rectangular enclosure divided into squares, each square being either covered by hedge or not. We may move from square to square in any direction (except diagonally), but we may not cross a hedge. Let us assume that the entrance is at the north-west corner of the maze and that the exit is at its south-east corner.

We could represent the maze in a computer by a two-dimensional character array, e.g.:

```
. . H H H . . . . .
H . . . H . H H H .
. . H . H . H . . .        where 'H' represents hedge
H H . . . . H H H H         and '.' represents walkway
. . . H H H . . . .
. H . . . . H H .
```

Write a program to find a path (if one exists) from the entrance to the exit.

Let us generalize the problem slightly: find a path from <u>any</u> given square to the exit. We can refine this problem as follows:

```
(* find a path from square S to the exit *)
   IF square S is the exit square THEN
      success!
   ELSE
      BEGIN
      IF square S is not on the eastern boundary THEN
         try heading East ;
      IF no success yet AND
            square S is not on the southern boundary THEN
         try heading South ;
      IF no success yet AND
            square S is not on the western boundary THEN
         try heading West ;
      IF no success yet AND
            square S is not on the northern boundary THEN
         try heading North
      END
```

Let us further refine "try heading East" (the others will be analogous):

```
(* try heading East *)
   IF the eastern neighbouring square is walkway THEN
         find a path from the eastern neighbouring square to the exit
```

But "find a path from the eastern neighbouring square to the exit" is analogous to the original problem "find a path from square S to the exit"! So let us introduce a procedure, SEEKEXITFROM, with the coordinates of a square as its parameters, whose task is to find a path from that square to the exit. This procedure will be recursive.

The following is a complete solution to the problem for a 6-by-10 maze, omitting only the details of reading and writing a picture of the maze.

```
PROGRAM MAZE ( INPUT, OUTPUT ) ;

CONST
   NORTHLIMIT = 1 ;
   SOUTHLIMIT = 6 ;
   WESTLIMIT  = 1 ;
   EASTLIMIT  = 10 ;
   ENTRYLATITUDE = NORTHLIMIT ;     ENTRYLONGITUDE = WESTLIMIT ;
   EXITLATITUDE  = SOUTHLIMIT ;     EXITLONGITUDE  = EASTLIMIT ;
   WALKWAY   = '.' ;
   HEDGE     = 'H' ;
   FOOTSTEP  = 'o' ;
   PATHMARK  = '*' ;
TYPE
   LONGITUDES = WESTLIMIT..EASTLIMIT ;
   LATITUDES  = NORTHLIMIT..SOUTHLIMIT ;
VAR
   MAZE          : ARRAY [LATITUDES, LONGITUDES] OF CHAR ;
   SUCCESSFUL    : BOOLEAN ;
```

```
        PROCEDURE SEEKEXITFROM ( LAT  : LATITUDES ;
                                LONG : LONGITUDES ) ;
   (* find a path from square (LAT,LONG) to the exit *)
      BEGIN
      IF (LONG = EXITLONGITUDE) AND (LAT = EXITLATITUDE) THEN
         SUCCESSFUL := TRUE
      ELSE
         BEGIN
         MAZE[LAT,LONG] := FOOTSTEP ;
         IF LONG <> EASTLIMIT THEN
            (* try heading East *)
               IF MAZE[LAT,LONG+1] = WALKWAY THEN
                  SEEKEXITFROM(LAT,LONG+1) ;
         IF NOT SUCCESSFUL AND (LAT <> SOUTHLIMIT) THEN
            (* try heading South *)
               IF MAZE[LAT+1,LONG] = WALKWAY THEN
                  SEEKEXITFROM(LAT+1,LONG) ;
         IF NOT SUCCESSFUL AND (LONG <> WESTLIMIT) THEN
            (* try heading West *)
               IF MAZE[LAT,LONG-1] = WALKWAY THEN
                  SEEKEXITFROM(LAT,LONG-1) ;
         IF NOT SUCCESSFUL AND (LAT <> NORTHLIMIT) THEN
            (* try heading North *)
               IF MAZE[LAT-1,LONG] = WALKWAY THEN
                  SEEKEXITFROM(LAT-1,LONG)
         END ;
      IF SUCCESSFUL THEN
         MAZE[LAT,LONG] := PATHMARK
      END (* SEEKEXITFROM *) ;

   BEGIN (* MAZE *)
   read MAZE ;
   SUCCESSFUL := FALSE ;
   SEEKEXITFROM(ENTRYLATITUDE,ENTRYLONGITUDE) ;
   IF SUCCESSFUL THEN
      write MAZE
   ELSE
      WRITELN ('NO WAY THROUGH MAZE')
   END (* MAZE *) .
```

The procedure contains some necessary additional details. The
statement MAZE[LAT,LONG] := FOOTSTEP marks each square of the maze
as it is visited; this is essential to ensure that we do not go round
the maze in circles! The statement MAZE[LAT,LONG] := PATHMARK
marks each square which lies on the path from the entrance to the
exit. Thus the final picture of the maze will show this path, and
also any blind alleys which were followed during the search, e.g.:

```
* * H H H o o o o o
H * * * H o H H H o
. . H * H o H o o o     where '*' marks a step on the path
H H * * o o H H H H     and 'o' marks a step up a blind alley
. . * H H H * * * *
. H * * * * * H H *
```

From these examples we may extrapolate to the following general principles concerning recursive subprograms:

(a) A recursive subprogram must, in at least one degenerate case, perform its task without invoking itself recursively. In Example 14.1, the degenerate case is N=1. In Example 14.2, one degenerate case is when the current square is the exit square; in addition, the procedure will not invoke itself recursively when every neighbouring square either is hedge-covered or has been marked.

(b) A recursive subprogram must invoke itself only in such a way as to approach one of the degenerate cases mentioned in (a). In Example 14.1, the function invokes itself with a second parameter (N) which is positive but smaller than before, i.e. it has moved closer to the case N=1. In Example 14.2, every entry to the procedure marks a square in such a way that the square will not be visited again.

14.2 FUNCTIONAL-PARAMETERS AND PROCEDURAL-PARAMETERS

We have already seen that a subprogram may invoke another subprogram. Now, just as a value-parameter allows a subprogram to work with different given values on different occasions, and just as a variable-parameter allows a subprogram to work with different variables on different occasions, sometimes we wish to allow a subprogram to invoke different functions or different procedures on different occasions. In other words, we wish sometimes to parameterize a function or procedure. Pascal makes this possible by providing two additional parameter mechanisms, functional-parameters and procedural-parameters.

We illustrate this idea with just one example.

Example 14.3

Let us write a procedure which approximately evaluates the integral of F(x) between given limits A and B, where F is assumed to be a continuous finite REAL function with a single REAL parameter.

We can visualize this integral as the area bounded by the curve y = F(x) and the straight lines y = 0, x = A and x = B:

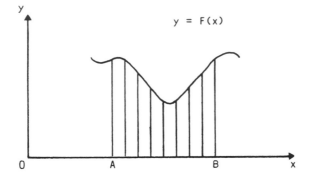

y = F(x)

A simple method of approximating the integral is to choose a suitable positive integer N and divide the interval [A,B] into N equal intervals, each of width W = (B-A)/N, as illustrated above. This divides the area of interest into strips which resemble right-angled trapezia, and it is easy to derive the following approximate formula for the area under the curve:

(F(A)/2 + F(A+W) + F(A+2*W) + ... + F(B)/2) * W

This is called the <u>trapezoidal rule</u>.

Since our procedure must deal with <u>any</u> given function F, F will be a functional-parameter.

```
PROCEDURE INTEGRATE ( FUNCTION   F : REAL ;
                             A, B : REAL ;
                      VAR INTEGRAL : REAL ) ;
(* evaluates approximately the integral of F(x)
   between limits A and B, using the trapezoidal
   rule with 8 intervals *)
   CONST
      N = 8 ;
   VAR
      W, SUM : REAL ;
      I      : INTEGER ;
   BEGIN
   W := (B-A)/N ;
   SUM := (F(A)+F(B))/2 ;
   FOR I := 1 TO N-1 DO
      SUM := SUM + F(A+I*W) ;
   INTEGRAL := SUM * W
   END (* INTEGRATE *)
```

The formal-parameter section "FUNCTION F : REAL" specifies that F is a functional-parameter and that the result type of F is REAL; it says nothing about the parameters of F itself. Inside the body of INTEGRATE, F is invoked just like an ordinary function, by function designators such as F(A) and F(A+I*W).

166

When we invoke INTEGRATE by a procedure statement, the actual parameter corresponding to F must also be a function with a REAL result. For example, we could integrate SIN(x) between limits 0 and PI/2 by the procedure statement

```
INTEGRATE(SIN,0,PI/2,INT)
```

The effect of this procedure statement is to make the functional-parameter F stand for the actual function SIN, i.e. each function designator such as F(A) actually results in the evaluation of SIN(A). Likewise, if we invoke INTEGRATE by the procedure statement

```
INTEGRATE(GROT,LOW,HIGH,INT)
```

where GROT is a declared function, then the functional-parameter F stands for GROT, and the function designator F(A) actually results in the evaluation of GROT(A).

From these examples we may deduce the rules governing the use of functional-parameters. If F is a functional-parameter and G is used as an actual parameter corresponding to F, then
(a) G must be a function (of course!);
(b) G must have the same result type as F;
(c) all the formal parameters of G must be value-parameters; and
(d) every function designator invoking F must have actual parameters which are compatible with the formal parameters of G.
    The syntax of formal-parameter sections, including functional- and procedural-parameters, is summarized in Appendix 1.5.

EXERCISES 14

14.1. The factorial function N! may be defined recursively:

$$N! = \begin{cases} 1 & \text{if } N <= 1 \\ N * (N-1)! & \text{if } N > 1 \end{cases}$$

Transcribe this definition into a recursive function. Write an alternative non-recursive version of this function.

14.2. (a) Write a function which returns the minimum value of a given INTEGER function F (which takes a single INTEGER parameter), between given limits LOWLIMIT and HIGHLIMIT. (b) Write a declaration of the INTEGER function

```
QUADRATIC(p) = p*p - 2*p - 3
```

and write a statement which writes the minimum value of this function between limits -4 and +4.

14.3*. If you have written a procedure to read a molecular formula (Programming Exercises 13), modify the procedure so that it accepts parentheses within the formula, such as (Al2(SO4)3). (Hint: on detecting a left parenthesis, the procedure should invoke itself recursively.)

14.4*. "The Towers of Hanoi" is a game played with three poles and a set of discs, all differently sized, which fit on to the poles. Initially all the discs are on pole 1, as shown below; the object of the game is to move all the discs on to pole 2. Only one disc may be moved at a time, and no disc may ever be placed on a smaller disc.

Consider the more general problem of moving N discs from pole SOURCE to pole DESTINATION, using pole SPARE as a spare. This problem can be solved recursively by the following strategy:
(1) move (N-1) discs from pole SOURCE to pole SPARE, using pole DESTINATION as a spare;
(2) move a single disc from pole SOURCE to pole DESTINATION;
(3) move (N-1) discs from pole SPARE to pole DESTINATION, using pole SOURCE as a spare.
Transcribe this strategy into a recursive procedure which writes a suitable message each time a single disc is moved. Write a program which uses your procedure to solve the Towers of Hanoi problem with four discs.

V More data structures
15 Records

15.1 THE NEED FOR RECORDS

The concept of a record is familiar in everyday life. Examples include the information about a student held by a university's records office, or information about a book contained in a library catalogue. Such records might be kept as entries in a loose-leaf folder, on index cards, or stored in a computer system.

The concept of a record is very useful in programming, too. When we talk about records in everyday life, however, there is a connotation of long-term storage. This connotation is not necessarily present when we talk about records in programming. Here we shall view a record simply as a fixed collection of information relating to a single object, where sometimes we wish to refer to the information as a whole, and at other times we wish to refer, by name, to the individual pieces of information. The latter are known as fields.

Example 15.1

A date consists of three components, the day-of-the-month, the month, and the year. Sometimes we are interested in individual components, e.g. answering queries like "What month is it?" At other times we are interested in the date as a whole, as a single piece of information, e.g. "What is to-day's date?" A date may be considered as a record with three fields.

Example 15.2

A population registry office would be interested in the following information about people in its area:
(a) surname,
(b) forename,
(c) date of birth,
(d) sex, and
(e) marital status.
This information about one person can be considered to comprise a record with five fields.

The concept of a record is most fruitful when we consider similar records relating to several similar objects. For example, we might talk about the registry office's records for several different people, such as "my record" or "Bill's record". Each of these records will contain the same fields, so we can talk about "my surname", or "Bill's date of birth", referring to individual fields. In each case we combine a possessive ("my" or "Bill's"), indicating which record we are talking about, with a noun ("surname" or "date of birth"), indicating which field of that record we are talking about. Similarly we can talk about different dates, such as "to-day" or "the date of the next eclipse", and about individual fields of these dates, such as "the year of the next eclipse".

It is most important to understand the distinction between records and arrays. Firstly, the fields of a record may have different types, whereas the elements of an array must all have the same type. Secondly (a consequence of this), the fields of a record must be selected by name, whereas the elements of an array are selected by subscripts, which may be variable. It would make sense to talk about the I-th element of an array, for example, but not about the I-th field of a registry office record, since we could not be sure what type of information we were talking about.

15.2 RECORDS IN PASCAL

A record type in Pascal is specified by writing down the identifiers and types of its fields (using syntax similar to that of variable declarations), and enclosing the lot between the reserved words RECORD and END. There is no restriction on the types of the fields.

To refer to an individual field of a record we use a field selector, in which the record variable is suffixed by a period and the field identifier.

Example 15.1

The type definition

```
DATES = RECORD
          DAY   : 1..31 ;
          MONTH : 1..12 ;
          YEAR  : 0..9999
        END
```

could be used to declare variables whose values are dates:

```
TODAY, MANANA, NEXTECLIPSE : DATES
```

Each of these record variables can be visualized as a box divided into three compartments, named DAY, MONTH, and YEAR:

```
            DAY  MONTH  YEAR                      DAY  MONTH  YEAR
TODAY   <|   3  |  5  |  1978  |>   NEXTECLIPSE <|  1  |   4  | 1980  |>
```

We shape the ends of these boxes to distinguish them clearly from
arrays.

An example of a field selector is TODAY.MONTH, which selects the
field MONTH of the record variable TODAY. In the diagram, the
current values of the fields of TODAY are TODAY.DAY=3, TODAY.MONTH=5,
and TODAY.YEAR=1978.

Example 15.2

The structure of our registry office's records could be specified by
the type definition

```
PERSONALDETAILS =
    RECORD
        SURNAME,
            FORENAME    : ARRAY [1..12] OF CHAR ;
        BIRTHDATE      : DATES ;
        SEX            : (MALE,FEMALE) ;
        MARITALSTATUS : (SINGLE,MARRIED,DIVORCED.WIDOWED)
    END
```

The variable declaration

```
MYDETAILS, YOURDETAILS : PERSONALDETAILS
```

declares two variables of this type.

The following program fragment will write some data from the
record YOURDETAILS:

```
WRITE (YOURDETAILS.FORENAME, ' ',
       YOURDETAILS.SURNAME, ' IS ') ;
CASE YOURDETAILS.SEX OF
    MALE:    WRITE ('MALE  ') ;
    FEMALE:  WRITE ('FEMALE')
END
```

The following statement updates one field of MYDETAILS:

```
MYDETAILS.MARITALSTATUS := MARRIED
```


The syntax of record types is summarized in Figure 15.1. A record
type may be used, like any other type, in type definitions and variable
declarations.

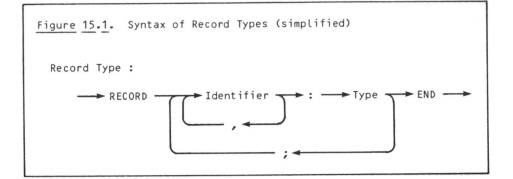

Figure 15.1. Syntax of Record Types (simplified)

Record Type :

    ⟶ RECORD ⟶ Identifier ⟶ : ⟶ Type ⟶ END ⟶

The syntax of field selectors is summarized in Figure 15.2. A field selector may be used anywhere an ordinary variable may be used, as illustrated in Example 15.2.

Figure 15.2. Syntax of Field Selectors

Field Selector :

    ⟶ Record Variable ⟶ . ⟶ Field Identifier ⟶

In a field selector such as YOURDETAILS.SURNAME, we say that the field identifier SURNAME is qualified by the record variable YOURDETAILS. Normally a field identifier must always be qualified in statements; for example,

    WRITE (SURNAME)

would be ambiguous, since we do not know whether SURNAME here refers to MYDETAILS.SURNAME or YOURDETAILS.SURNAME or something else altogether.

Within each record type, every field must of course have a distinct identifier. However, field identifiers may be the same as identifiers given to constants, variables, procedures, etc. The requirement to qualify the field identifiers ensures that no ambiguity arises.

15.3 OPERATIONS ON COMPLETE RECORDS

We have seen that individual record fields may be used just like
ordinary variables. A major advantage of collecting data together in
records, however, is that we may choose sometimes to treat the records
as a whole, without regard to their individual fields. Thus we are
interested in what operations Pascal allows on complete records.

The simplest operation on complete records is <u>assignment</u>, which just
amounts to copying one record into another. Pascal allows assignment of
one record variable to another, provided they are of the same type.

Example 15.3

Assuming the type definition of DATES from Example 15.1, and the
variable declarations

    TODAY, LETTERDATE : DATES

the single assignment statement

    LETTERDATE := TODAY

copies the whole of the record TODAY into the record LETTERDATE. It
is equivalent to the three assignments of individual fields:

    LETTERDATE.DAY   := TODAY.DAY ;
    LETTERDATE.MONTH := TODAY.MONTH ;
    LETTERDATE.YEAR := TODAY.YEAR

but it is obviously clearer and more concise than the latter.

Assuming the type definition of PERSONALDETAILS from Example 15.2,
and the variable declaration

    NEWBORN : PERSONALDETAILS

observe that the field NEWBORN.BIRTHDATE is itself a record, of type
DATES. Thus we can write the assignment statement

    NEWBORN.BIRTHDATE := TODAY

Even more usefully, Pascal allows whole records to be made parameters
to functions and procedures - either as value-parameters or as
variable-parameters.

Example 15.4

Let us write a procedure which will inspect the registry office records of a man and a woman to determine whether they may legally marry, and if so to update their records accordingly. The procedure will take the two records as parameters. Since it may update these records, they must be made variable-parameters.

{Disclaimer: the following is intended for illustration only. Marriage laws vary considerably from state to state. The following is based on the current law of Scotland.}

```
      PROCEDURE MARRY ( VAR HUSBAND, WIFE : PERSONALDETAILS ;
                        VAR LEGAL        : BOOLEAN          ) ;
         BEGIN
            LEGAL := (HUSBAND.SEX = MALE)
                 AND (WIFE.SEX = FEMALE)
                 AND (HUSBAND.MARITALSTATUS <> MARRIED)
                 AND (WIFE.MARITALSTATUS <> MARRIED) ;
            IF LEGAL THEN
               (* update the records *)
               BEGIN
               HUSBAND.MARITALSTATUS := MARRIED ;
               WIFE.MARITALSTATUS := MARRIED ;
               WIFE.SURNAME := HUSBAND.SURNAME
               END
         END (* MARRY *)
```

The actual parameters corresponding to HUSBAND and WIFE must be record variables of the same type as the formal parameters. For example, given the variable declarations

```
   NAPOLEON, JOSEPHINE : PERSONALDETAILS ;
   LEGAL               : BOOLEAN
```

we may write the procedure statement

```
   MARRY(NAPOLEON,JOSEPHINE,LEGAL)
```

We can make procedure MARRY more elaborate by checking in addition that both partners have reached the age of majority. For this purpose it will be convenient to introduce a function which, given a person's birth date, computes that person's age. The birth date will be a value-parameter to this function. (Let us assume that today's date is available in a global variable TODAY.)

174

```
PROCEDURE MARRY ( VAR HUSBAND, WIFE : PERSONALDETAILS ;
                    VAR LEGAL        : BOOLEAN         ) ;
    CONST
       AGEOFMAJORITY = 16 ;

    FUNCTION AGE ( DATEOFBIRTH : DATES ) : INTEGER ;
       BEGIN
       IF (TODAY.MONTH > DATEOFBIRTH.MONTH)
          OR ((TODAY.MONTH = DATEOFBIRTH.MONTH)
             AND (TODAY.DAY >= DATEOFBIRTH.DAY)) THEN
          AGE := TODAY.YEAR - DATEOFBIRTH.YEAR
       ELSE
          AGE := TODAY.YEAR - DATEOFBIRTH.YEAR - 1
       END (* AGE *) ;

BEGIN (* MARRY *)
    LEGAL := (HUSBAND.SEX = MALE)
         AND (WIFE.SEX = FEMALE)
         AND (HUSBAND.MARITALSTATUS <> MARRIED)
         AND (WIFE.MARITALSTATUS <> MARRIED)
         AND (AGE(HUSBAND.BIRTHDATE) >= AGEOFMAJORITY)
         AND (AGE(WIFE.BIRTHDATE) >= AGEOFMAJORITY) ;
    IF LEGAL THEN
       (* update the records *)
          BEGIN
          HUSBAND.MARITALSTATUS := MARRIED ;
          WIFE.MARITALSTATUS := MARRIED ;
          WIFE.SURNAME := HUSBAND.SURNAME
          END
END (* MARRY *)
```

15.4 THE WITH STATEMENT

When writing a program fragment to process a single record, we tend to
find ourselves using the same record variable time and time again to
qualify field identifiers. Since this can become rather tedious, Pascal
provides a convenient shorthand, in the form of the WITH statement.

Example 15.5

The program fragment in Example 15.2 could be abbreviated as follows:

```
WITH YOURDETAILS DO
   BEGIN
   WRITE (FORENAME, ' ', SURNAME, '    ') ;
   CASE SEX OF
      MALE:    WRITE ('MALE ') ;
      FEMALE:  WRITE ('FEMALE')
   END (* CASE *)
   END (* WITH *)
```

We simply write the name of the record variable (YOURDETAILS) between WITH and DO, then inside the WITH statement there is no need to qualify the identifiers of that record variable's fields.

The syntax of WITH statements is summarized in Figure 15.3. WITH and DO are both reserved words.

Figure 15.3. Syntax of WITH Statements (simplified)

WITH Statement :

⟶ WITH ⟶ Record Variable ⟶ DO ⟶ Statement ⟶

Within a WITH statement, any unqualified identifier which is the identifier of a field of the record variable actually refers to that field. So, inside the WITH statement of Example 15.5, the unqualified identifier SURNAME, which is the identifier of a field of the record variable YOURDETAILS, actually refers to the field YOURDETAILS.SURNAME.

A WITH statement is the only place where a field identifier may be used unqualified.

When we are processing more than one record of the same type, we can abbreviate the field selectors of only one of these records.

Example 15.6

The function AGE of Example 15.4 may be recast as follows:

176

```
FUNCTION AGE ( DATEOFBIRTH : DATES ) : INTEGER ;
  BEGIN
  WITH DATEOFBIRTH DO
    IF (TODAY.MONTH > MONTH)
      OR (TODAY.MONTH = MONTH)
        AND (TODAY.DAY >= DAY)  THEN
      AGE := TODAY.YEAR - YEAR
    ELSE
      AGE := TODAY.YEAR - YEAR - 1
  END (* AGE *)
```

Here, DAY, MONTH and YEAR, where unqualified, refer to the fields
of DATEOFBIRTH. There is no ambiguity since the corresponding fields
of TODAY are still qualified.

WITH statements play a part in the scope rules of Pascal (Section
13.5). The component statement of a WITH statement acts as a block in
which the field identifiers of the record variable may be imagined to be
declared as ordinary variables. The behaviour of WITH statements can
now be understood by applying the normal scope rules of Pascal.

15.5 DATA STRUCTURES

A data structure is just an organized collection of data. Arrays and
records are different kinds of data structures, with particular
properties, and later we shall meet other kinds of data structures, such
as files. An array is a data structure whose components are homogeneous
and are selected by (variable) subscripts. A record is a data structure
whose components are non-homogeneous and are selected by name. The fact
that the components of arrays and records may themselves be structured
allows us to build up data structures as complex as we need.

Data structures form a subject of study in their own right, a subject
whose proper treatment is well beyond the scope of this book. We shall
confine ourselves here to examples illustrating some data structures
which turn up frequently in programming.

A record with fields which are themselves records is sometimes called
a hierarchical record.

Example 15.7

The record type PERSONALDETAILS of Example 15.2 contains a field,
BIRTHDATE, which is itself a record, of type DATES. Thus records of
type PERSONALDETAILS have a hierarchical structure, as illustrated
below:

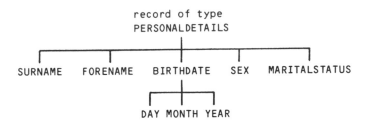

record of type
PERSONALDETAILS

SURNAME   FORENAME   BIRTHDATE   SEX   MARITALSTATUS

DAY MONTH YEAR

The field MYDETAILS.BIRTHDATE is itself a record variable, so we may select a field from it, such as MYDETAILS.BIRTHDATE.YEAR. The following statements are all equivalent:

```
WRITE (MYDETAILS.BIRTHDATE.YEAR)

WITH MYDETAILS DO
   WRITE (BIRTHDATE.YEAR)

WITH MYDETAILS.BIRTHDATE DO
   WRITE (YEAR)
```

Hierarchical records are often processed by nested WITH statements, e.g.:

```
WITH MYDETAILS DO
   BEGIN
   SEX := MALE ;
   MARITALSTATUS := MARRIED ;
   WITH BIRTHDATE DO
      BEGIN
      DAY := 5 ;  MONTH := 11 ;  YEAR := 1946
      END
   END
```

Tables are very useful data structures, of which we have already met some rather simple examples (Chapter 10.) A table may have several items of data in each entry, i.e. each table entry may itself be a record.

Example 15.8

The internal telephone directory of a small organization might be stored as a table declared as follows:

```
DIRECTORY : ARRAY [1..MAXENTRIES] OF
              RECORD
                  NAME    : ARRAY [1..16] OF CHAR ;
                  DEPT    : ARRAY [1..12] OF CHAR ;
                  NUMBER : 0..9999
              END
```

DIRECTORY might be visualized as follows, in the case that
MAXENTRIES=5:

	NAME	DEPT	NUMBER
DIRECTORY	'FINDLAY, W. '	'COMPUTING '	7458
	'WATT, D.A. '	'COMPUTING '	7458
	'WATT, H.D. '	'COM.MEDICINE'	227
	'WEBB, J.R.L. '	'MATHEMATICS '	7176
	'YOUNG, N.J. '	'MATHEMATICS '	7417

Assuming that the actual number of directory entries is stored in
the variable

    NMROFENTRIES : 0..MAXENTRIES

let us write a program fragment which writes the name and department
of the employee whose internal telephone number is N, or writes a
suitable message if no-one has this number.

This is an example of linear search. We declare

    ENTRY   : INTEGER ;
    SEARCHING : BOOLEAN

Now we can write:

```
(* find who has telephone number N *)
   SEARCHING := TRUE ;
   ENTRY := 1 ;
   WHILE SEARCHING AND (ENTRY <= NMROFENTRIES) DO
      WITH DIRECTORY[ENTRY] DO
         IF NUMBER = N THEN
            BEGIN
            SEARCHING := FALSE ;
            WRITELN (NAME, DEPT, N)
            END
         ELSE
            ENTRY := SUCC(ENTRY) ;
   IF SEARCHING THEN
      WRITELN ('NO-ONE HAS NUMBER ', N)
```

Inside the loop we examine one directory entry, DIRECTORY[ENTRY].
Since the latter is itself a record variable, we can conveniently
make use of a WITH statement to access the individual fields of this
entry without qualification. Thus, for example,

179

```
     WRITELN (NAME, DEPT, N)
```

above is equivalent to

```
     WRITELN (DIRECTORY[ENTRY].NAME,
              DIRECTORY[ENTRY].DEPT, N)
```

The telephone directory could alternatively have been stored in three separate arrays:

```
     NAME   : ARRAY [1..MAXENTRIES] OF ARRAY [1..16] OF CHAR ;
     DEPT   : ARRAY [1..MAXENTRIES] OF ARRAY [1..10] OF CHAR ;
     NUMBER : ARRAY [1..MAXENTRIES] OF 0..9999
```

But these declarations do not reflect the logical structure of the directory. They are more cumbersome than the original declaration, and so too would be the program fragment which searches the directory. (Convince yourself of this by rewriting it accordingly.)

15.6 VARIANT RECORDS

{This section should be omitted on first reading.}

All the records we have met so far have been completely rigid in their structure, i.e. all records of one type have had the same number of fields, with the same names and the same types.

Sometimes we find it convenient to use records with a more flexible structure. Pascal allows us to use variant records, in which the number and types of the fields may vary to some extent according to circumstances.

Example 15.9

A lending library might keep the following information in its catalogue about each item in stock:
(a) reference number,
(b) title,
(c) name of author/composer,
(d) name of publisher,
(e) class of item - book or recording,
(f) number of edition (books only),
(g) year of publication (books only),
(h) name of performer (recordings only).

We could represent this information by a record with eight fields, but that would be wasteful, since only six or seven fields will be used in any one case.

Using a variant record, we can make the class of the library item determine what fields are actually present in each record:

```
ITEMCLASSES  = (BOOK,RECORDING) ;

LIBRARYITEMS =
   RECORD
      REF        : 0..999999 ;
      TITLE      : ARRAY [1..30] OF CHAR ;
      AUTHOR     : ARRAY [1..16] OF CHAR ;
      PUBLISHER  : ARRAY [1..20] OF CHAR ;
      CASE CLASS : ITEMCLASSES OF
         BOOK:
             ( EDITION : 1..50 ;
               YEAR    : -2000..1999 ) ;
         RECORDING:
             ( PERFORMER : ARRAY [1..20] OF CHAR )
   END
```

Up to CASE the fields are defined normally. The clause "CASE CLASS : ITEMCLASSES OF" defines a special field CLASS, of type ITEMCLASSES, which is called a tag field. This gives each record of type LIBRARYITEMS the following special property: the number and types of the fields following the tag field will depend upon the tag field's current value. Specifically, when the tag field's current value is BOOK, the tag field is assumed to be followed by two fields, EDITION and YEAR; on the other hand, when its current value is RECORDING, it is assumed to be followed by a single field, PERFORMER.

Thus the internal structure of the record

ITEM : LIBRARYITEMS

will depend upon the current value of ITEM.CLASS:

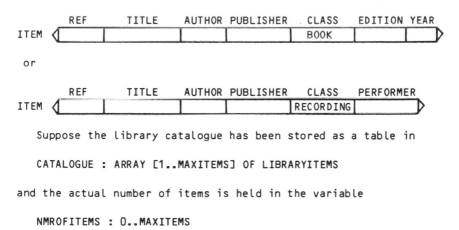

or

Suppose the library catalogue has been stored as a table in

CATALOGUE : ARRAY [1..MAXITEMS] OF LIBRARYITEMS

and the actual number of items is held in the variable

NMROFITEMS : 0..MAXITEMS

If we declare

ITEM : 1..MAXITEMS

then the following program fragment will write out the catalogue:

```
WRITELN (' REF.  ','TITLE                         ',
         'AUTHOR            ','PUBLISHER           ',
         'OTHER DETAILS') ;
WRITELN ;
FOR ITEM := 1 TO NMROFITEMS DO
   WITH CATALOGUE[ITEM] DO
      BEGIN
      WRITE (REF:6, '   ', TITLE, AUTHOR, PUBLISHER) ;
      CASE CLASS OF
         BOOK:
            WRITELN ('EDITION ', EDITION:2, YEAR:8) ;
         RECORDING:
            WRITELN ('PERFORMED BY ', PERFORMER)
      END (* CASE *)
      END
```

Note that it would be a serious error to attempt to access the field PERFORMER, for example, when the tag field's value is BOOK, for then the field PERFORMER does not exist. (See the diagram above.) That is why the program fragment above inspected the tag field of each record (using a CASE statement), in order to deduce which further fields were available for examination.

The complete syntax of record types (including variant records) is given in Appendix 1.6. A tag field may be of any ordinal type, but note that its type must be specified by a type identifier.

Example 15.10

Given that the input data consists of English-language text, let us write a procedure to read and store a single "token", where a token is a word, a period, a comma, a semicolon, or a colon. Assume that a word is a sequence of consecutive letters. All other characters are to be ignored.
On reading a token, the procedure should note what kind of token it is. In the case that the token is a word, the procedure should in addition store its spelling. In the other cases, however, no further information is needed. The natural way to represent a token, therefore, is by a variant record:

```
TOKENKINDS = (WORD,PERIOD,COMMA,SEMICOLON,COLON) ;
TOKENS =
   RECORD
      CASE KIND : TOKENKINDS OF
         WORD:
            ( SPELLING : ARRAY [1..MAXLENGTH] OF CHAR ) ;
         PERIOD, COMMA, SEMICOLON, COLON:
            ( )
   END
```

This illustrates two points:
(a) the tag field may be the first field of a record; and
(b) the tag field may be the last field of the record for some values
   of the tag field — this is specified simply by putting nothing
   between the parentheses.
   Given this definition of TOKENS, we can write the procedure as
follows:

```
PROCEDURE READTOKEN ( VAR TOKEN : TOKENS ) ;
   VAR
      LENGTH : INTEGER ;

   FUNCTION ISLETTER ( CH : CHAR ) : BOOLEAN ;
      BEGIN
      ISLETTER := ('A' <= CH) AND (CH <= 'Z')
      END (* ISLETTER *) ;

   BEGIN (* READTOKEN *)
   (* skip characters up to the beginning of a token,
      or end of input, whichever comes sooner         *)
      WHILE NOT (EOF(INPUT) OR ISLETTER(CH) OR (CH='.') OR
               (CH=',') OR (CH=';') OR (CH=':')) DO
         READ (CH) ;
   IF NOT EOF(INPUT) THEN
      WITH TOKEN DO
         IF ISLETTER(CH) THEN
            BEGIN
            KIND := WORD ;
            (* store the spelling of the word *)
               LENGTH := 0 ;
               REPEAT
                  LENGTH := LENGTH + 1 ;
                  IF LENGTH <= MAXLENGTH THEN
                     SPELLING[LENGTH] := CH ;
                  READ (CH)
               UNTIL EOF(INPUT) OR NOT ISLETTER(CH) ;
            (* pad out the spelling with blanks *)
               FOR LENGTH := LENGTH+1 TO MAXLENGTH DO
                  SPELLING[LENGTH] := ' '
            END
```

```
          ELSE
            BEGIN
            CASE CH OF
               '.':  KIND := PERIOD ;
               ',':  KIND := COMMA ;
               ';':  KIND := SEMICOLON ;
               ':':  KIND := COLON
            END (* CASE *) ;
            READ (CH)
            END
       END (* READTOKEN *)
```

Assignment of the value WORD to the tag field TOKEN.KIND brings the field TOKEN.SPELLING into existence. Only thereafter is assignment to (elements of) TOKEN.SPELLING legitimate.

This procedure assumes the existence of a non-local variable CH which has been suitably initialized, either to the first character of the input or (harmlessly) to a blank. The procedure would not work properly if CH were a local variable. For example, if the input starts

       I, CLAUDIUS

then on the first invocation of READTOKEN, after the word "I" has been read and stored, the value of CH is ','. On the next invocation of READTOKEN, the value of CH would be undefined (since local variables are always initially undefined on entry to a subprogram), so the comma would have been been lost. Therefore, CH must be a non-local variable to ensure that it preserves its value between successive invocations of READTOKEN. {This last point has no connection with variant records, but it is important nevertheless!}

EXERCISES 15

15.1. (a) Write a definition of a record variable suitable for storing payroll details of an employee, namely the employee's name, number, grade (manual, skilled, clerical or managerial) and rate of pay. (b) Write a program fragment which writes these details in a suitable format.

15.2. (a) Rewrite procedure WRITEDATE (Example 13.1) to accept a single parameter of type DATES (Example 15.1). (b) Write a program fragment which invokes your procedure to write today's date followed by the date exactly nine months hence.

15.3. (a) Write a definition of a record type suitable for describing the position (latitude and longitude) of a point on the Earth's surface. (b) Write a function which returns the true time difference between two given points on the Earth's surface. (c) Write a procedure which reads a point's position, presented as two signed real numbers. (d) Write a procedure which writes the position of a given point in degrees and minutes, using conventional notation (e.g. the latitudes +45.5 and -45.5 should be written as 45:30N and 45:30S respectively). (e) Write a program fragment which reads the positions of two points, and which writes these positions together with the true time difference between them.

{Attempt the following exercise only after reading Section 15.6.}

15.4. (a) Write a definition of a record type suitable for describing a plane figure, namely its shape plus the following: (i) for a circle, its radius, (ii) for a rectangle, the lengths of its two sides, or (iii) for a triangle, the lengths of all its sides. (b) Write a function which returns the area of a given plane figure.

PROGRAMMING EXERCISES 15

15.5. Write a procedure which reads personal details from a single line of input data and passes them back through a single parameter of type PERSONALDETAILS (Example 15.2). Assume that a person's sex is represented in the input data by a single character 'M' or 'F', and marital status by a single character 'C', 'M', 'D' or 'W'. Write a procedure which writes similar details in a suitable format. Write a program to test these procedures and procedure MARRY (Example 15.4).

15.6*. An entry in a city telephone directory consists of a name, an address and a telephone number. An address in turn consists of a street number, a street name and a three-character district code. A telephone number consists of a three-digit exchange code and a four-digit line number. Write a program which reads directory entries (supplied in any format you choose) and writes them neatly and compactly in two columns on each page. You may assume that the entries are supplied in alphabetical order. The written entries must be arranged in order down the columns. On the last page the two columns should be as equal as possible.

16 Packed data and strings

16.1 PACKED DATA

Up to now we have pictured single items of data, i.e. numbers, characters, Boolean values, etc., as occupying one "box" or storage location each. This is the natural or <u>unpacked</u> arrangement for storing such data.

Sometimes, however, when we are dealing with bulky data structures, it is expedient to consider more economical use of storage. In certain circumstances, this can be achieved by squeezing several items of data into each storage location. Since it is not the purpose of this book to explain exactly how numbers, characters and so on are represented in computer storage, we shall illustrate this idea by analogy.

Consider the example of a <u>date</u>, consisting of a day, month and year. Normally this would occupy three storage locations, e.g.:

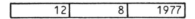

Observe, however, that the day and the month each need only two (decimal) digits, and the year needs only four digits. If our computer happens to be able to accomodate eight-digit integers, we can combine all three components of the date into one eight-digit integer which can occupy a single storage location:

> 12081977

Even if our computer can accomodate only six-digit integers (say), we still need only two storage locations, if we combine just the day and the month:

> | 1208| 1977 |

In each case, we say that the data is <u>packed</u>. When data is packed, it is still possible to access individual items, but such access is more difficult since it will require the stored numbers to be broken down into their constituent digits. Thus the saving of space has been bought at the expense of slowing down access to individual items.

16.2 THE PACKED ATTRIBUTE IN PASCAL

In Pascal, any data structure may be specified as packed simply by prefixing ARRAY or RECORD, as the case may be, by the reserved word PACKED.

Example 16.1

Recall the type DATES defined in Example 15.1. We may specify that its fields are to be packed simply by prefixing RECORD by PACKED:

```
DATES = PACKED RECORD
               DAY   : 1..31 ;
               MONTH : 1..12 ;
               YEAR  : 0..9999
           END
```


Example 16.2

In a hotel room reservation system, it might be convenient to use a BOOLEAN array FREE, such that FREE[ROOM] indicates whether room ROOM is free or not. If the number of rooms to be controlled is large, it would make sense to pack this data:

```
FREE : PACKED ARRAY [1..NMROFROOMS] OF BOOLEAN
```

On a typical computer, this packing would reduce the storage required for the array by a factor of around 32!

Notice that there is no way in Pascal to specify exactly how the data is to be packed. The Pascal compiler will <u>automatically</u> choose a suitable arrangement, which will depend on the size of the items to be packed and on the capacity of the computer's storage locations.

Using the attribute PACKED makes no difference whatsoever to the meaning of a program, in the sense that the program will produce the same results whether PACKED is present or absent. The only difference PACKED makes is to the efficiency of the program: less space will be required to store its data, but the program will run more slowly.

Generally speaking, you should not concern yourself too much at this stage with the problems of balancing decreased storage space and increased run-time. The main reason for mentioning the PACKED attribute here is to introduce the important topic of the next section.

16.3 STRINGS AND STRING HANDLING

A <u>string</u> is just a packed character array. We have used strings already, in WRITE statements such as

    WRITE ('CENSUS SUMMARY')

Here the string 'CENSUS SUMMARY' is just a constant of type

    PACKED ARRAY [1..14] OF CHAR

(14 being the length of the string). String constants can be used in other ways as well, as illustrated by Example 16.3.

Example 16.3

Given the following declarations (note the constant definition):

    CONST
        RUNNINGTITLE = 'PROLOGUE   ' ;
    TYPE
        TITLES = PACKED ARRAY [1..12] OF CHAR ;
    VAR
        ANOTHERTITLE : TITLES ;

    PROCEDURE CENTRETITLE (TITLE : TITLES) ;
        (* c.f. Example 10.10 *)

we may write statements like:

    ANOTHERTITLE := 'HAMLET   '

    CENTRETITLE('CATCH 22   ')

    CENTRETITLE(RUNNINGTITLE)

Note that in all cases the length of the string must be <u>exactly</u> what is expected; hence the padding blanks in these examples.

You will be familiar with the ordinary <u>alphabetical ordering</u> of words; for example, names in a telephone directory would be ordered as follows:

    Dahl
    Dijkstra
    Hoare
    Knuth
    Wilkes
    Wirth

The names are first ordered on their first letters; names which have the same first letters are ordered on their second letters; and so on. If we assume an ordering is defined for all characters (not just letters) then we can generalize this to the lexicographic ordering of strings.

As you know already, individual characters may be compared using the comparison operators "=", "<>", "<", "<=", ">=", and ">". In fact we may also compare complete strings using these same operators. For example, if NAME has the value 'WIRTH   ', then the expressions

```
NAME = 'WIRTH   '        NAME <> 'DIJKSTRA'
NAME > 'WILKES  '        NAME >= 'DAHL    '
```

all have the value TRUE.

Example 16.4

A list of names is supplied as input data, each name being left-justified in the first 20 characters of a line. The names are in no particular order. Let us write a program which will read all the names and write them out in lexicographic order, assuming that there are no more than (say) 1000 names.

This is an example of sorting, a very common theme in programming. A bewildering variety of sorting techniques have been devised. Here we shall illustrate one of the simplest, called insertion sort.

We can store the names in an array. Let us arrange to read the names one at a time, and to insert each name immediately in its correct place in the array (rather than just store the names in the order they are read). For example, if the array already contains the names

| "Dijkstra" | "Knuth" | "Wirth" | | – – – – – – – – – |

and the next name is "Hoare", this name will be inserted between "Dijkstra" and "Knuth". This will require the names "Knuth" and "Wirth" to be shifted up to make room for the new name:

| "Dijkstra" | "Hoare" | "Knuth" | "Wirth" | – – – – – – – – – |

In this way the names will always be in correct order.
Here is a skeleton solution:

```
BEGIN
make the list empty ;
WHILE NOT EOF(INPUT) DO
   BEGIN
   read an item ;
   insert the new item in its correct position
   END ;
write all the items in order
END .
```

The key section will be the refinement of "insert the new item in its correct position". Let us use a variable NMROFITEMS to keep track of the number of items stored in the array.

```
(* insert the new item in its correct position *)
   find the position, NEWPOSITION,
               where the new item will be inserted ;
   shift up the items in positions
               NEWPOSITION to NMROFITEMS ;
   place the new item in position NEWPOSITION ;
   NMROFITEMS := NMROFITEMS+1
```

Since this program fragment involves details, and variables such as NEWPOSITION, of purely local interest, it is a good candidate for a procedure. Likewise, the refinements of "read an item" and "write all the items in order" should also be made into procedures.

Here is a complete solution, which takes into account the possibility that the array might become completely filled:

```
PROGRAM SORTITEMS ( INPUT, OUTPUT ) ;

CONST
   MAXITEMS   = 1000 ;
   NAMELENGTH = 20 ;
TYPE
   ITEMS = PACKED ARRAY [1..NAMELENGTH] OF CHAR ;
VAR
   NMROFITEMS : 0..MAXITEMS ;
   LIST       : ARRAY [1..MAXITEMS] OF ITEMS ;
   NEWITEM    : ITEMS ;

PROCEDURE READITEM ( VAR ITEM : ITEMS ) ;
   VAR
      POS : 1..NAMELENGTH ;
   BEGIN
   FOR POS := 1 TO NAMELENGTH DO
      READ (ITEM[POS]) ;
   READLN
   END (* READITEM *) ;
```

```
PROCEDURE INSERTITEM ( NEWITEM : ITEMS ) ;
   VAR
      POSITION, NEWPOSITION : 1..MAXITEMS ;
      SEARCHING             : BOOLEAN ;
   BEGIN
   (* find the position where the new item
                            will be inserted *)
      POSITION := 1 ;
      SEARCHING := TRUE ;
      WHILE SEARCHING AND (POSITION <= NMROFITEMS) DO
         IF NEWITEM < LIST[POSITION] THEN
            SEARCHING := FALSE
         ELSE
            POSITION := SUCC(POSITION) ;
      NEWPOSITION := POSITION ;
   (* shift up the items in succeeding positions *)
      FOR POSITION := NMROFITEMS DOWNTO NEWPOSITION DO
         LIST[SUCC(POSITION)] := LIST[POSITION] ;
   (* place the new item in position *)
      LIST[NEWPOSITION] := NEWITEM ;
   NMROFITEMS := NMROFITEMS+1
   END (* INSERTITEM *) ;

PROCEDURE WRITEITEMS ;
   VAR
      POSITION : 1..MAXITEMS ;
   BEGIN
   FOR POSITION :- 1 TO NMROFITEMS DO
      WRITELN (LIST[POSITION])
   END (* WRITEITEMS *) ;

BEGIN (* SORTITEMS *)
(* make the list empty *)
   NMROFITEMS := 0 ;
WHILE NOT EOF(INPUT) AND (NMROFITEMS < MAXITEMS) DO
   BEGIN
   (* read an item *)
      READITEM(NEWITEM) ;
   (* insert the new item in its correct position *)
      IF NMROFITEMS < MAXITEMS THEN
         INSERTITEM(NEWITEM)
   END ;
(* write all the items in order *)
   WRITEITEMS
END (* SORTITEMS *) .
```

Have you noticed that this program has an interesting property?
Although it serves to illustrate string comparisons, it can easily be
adapted to sort single characters, integer numbers, real numbers,
months, or any other items which can be ordered! It is necessary

only to change the definition of the type identifier ITEMS, the body
of procedure READITEM, and possibly the body of procedure WRITEITEMS.
It can even be adapted to sort more complex items like dates (Example
15.1) or telephone directory entries (Example 15.8), although that
would force us to replace the simple comparison

    NEWITEM < LIST[POSITION]

in procedure INSERTITEM by something more complex. (See Exercises
16.)

    Generally speaking, character arrays should always be packed, to take
advantage of the ability in Pascal to compare strings directly, as in
Example 16.4. On typical computers, packing compresses character arrays
by a factor of about 4, and the copying and comparison of strings is
speeded up by a similar factor.

EXERCISES 16

16.1. Write a procedure which reads a string enclosed in quotes (") and
stores it in a parameter of type STRINGS = PACKED ARRAY [1..MAXLENGTH]
OF CHAR. The quotes themselves are not to be stored, and all characters
preceding the opening quote are to be ignored. The string is to be
filled out with blanks if it is too short, or truncated if it is too
long. How does your procedure behave at end-of-file?

16.2. Write a function, with a parameter of type STRINGS (as above),
which returns the length of the text stored in that parameter, excluding
padding blanks.

16.3. In commercial data processing, strings consisting entirely of
decimal digits often crop up. If it is desired to perform simple
arithmetic on such strings, it is often quicker to perform decimal
arithmetic directly on the strings than first to determine their INTEGER
values. Write a procedure which, given two parameters of type PACKED
ARRAY [1..NMROFDIGITS] OF CHAR which are assumed to consist entirely of
decimal digits (e.g. '007863224508'), stores their sum in a third
parameter of the same type. The algorithm you use for manual addition
can be adopted. Your procedure should have a fourth, BOOLEAN, parameter
which indicates whether the sum is too big for NMROFDIGITS digits.

16.4. Modify the program SORTITEMS (Example 16.4):
(a) to sort integers;
(b) to sort dates (see Example 15.1);
(c) to sort telephone directory entries (see Example 15.8) by name;
(d) to sort telephone directory entries by number.

16.5. Sometimes it is useful to be able to write "banner headlines", larger than normal characters. For example, "PASCAL" might be written as:

```
PPP    AA    SSS   CCC   AA   L
P  P   A  A  S     C     A  A  L
PPP    AAAA  SS    C     AAAA L
P      A  A     S  C     A  A  L
P      A  A  SSS   CCC   A  A  LLLL
```

Design a complete set of letters for banner headlines, and write a procedure which, given a short string of characters, writes a banner headline. Test your procedure by writing a program which writes a banner headline corresponding to each line of input data.

16.6. Insertion sort is most suitable for sorting items as they are read in. The following algorithm is more suitable for sorting, in situ, items already held in elements LIST[1], ..., LIST[LENGTH] of an array:

```
FOR INDEX := 1 TO LENGTH-1 DO
   BEGIN
   determine which item of LIST[INDEX], ...
           ..., LIST[LENGTH] should come first in order ;
   exchange this item with LIST[INDEX]
   END
```

This algorithm is called exchange sort. Write a procedure, with parameters LIST and LENGTH, which performs an exchange sort. Enclose your procedure in a test program which reads items into an array, sorts them in situ, and finally writes them. Use your program
(a) to sort integers;
(b) to sort strings.

16.7*. Write a procedure, to the same specification as the procedure SEARCH of Exercises 13, which searches an ordered list of items LIST[1], ..., LIST[N] for a given item TARGET. Linear search is a very inefficient solution here, since it fails to exploit the ordering of the list. (Would you use linear search to look up a dictionary?) Use the following algorithm:

```
      consider the interval 1..N ;
FOUND := FALSE ;
WHILE NOT FOUND AND
      the interval under consideration is not empty DO
   BEGIN
   select a point MID near the middle
         of the interval under consideration ;
   IF item TARGET would be ordered before LIST[MID] THEN
      consider the sub-interval up to MID-1
   ELSE IF item TARGET would be ordered after LIST[MID] THEN
      consider the sub-interval from MID+1
   ELSE  (* item TARGET matches LIST[MID] *)
      FOUND := TRUE
   END
```

This algorithm is called <u>binary search</u>, since it works by successively halving the interval under consideration. Incorporate your procedure in a test program which first sets up a directory (c.f. Example 15.8) ordered by name, and then looks up the numbers corresponding to names read from the input data.

17 Files

17.1 FILES AND FILE STRUCTURES

All the programs you have seen or written so far have had one thing in common: they have used at most one stream of input data, INPUT, and one stream of results, OUTPUT. Such simple programs are quite unrepresentative of most computer applications.

In fact, most of the data handled by computer systems is never seen (directly) by people! Instead, results generated by one program are often intended just to be read subsequently by another program, or even by the same program. For such purposes, computer time can be saved by not bothering to generate the results in a form suitable for human reading, but rather storing them on media more suitable for both reading and writing by the computer (e.g. magnetic tape or disks).

It is helpful to take a somewhat abstract view of the sets of data read and written by programs. We call such sets of data files, whether they are stored on magnetic tape or disk, keyed in at a terminal, punched on a deck of cards, printed on paper, or whatever. From this point of view, a deck of cards prepared at a key-punch is an example of a file which happens to be capable only of being read, and a set of printed results is an example of a file which happens to be capable only of being written. Other files may be capable of being both written and read.

The following examples illustrate some typical applications of files.

Example 17.1

A bank might maintain a file containing details of each account open at the bank, such as the account number, the customer's name and address and the current balance of the account.

This file will have to be processed at the end of each month to update the balances as a result of debit and credit transactions on the accounts, and to produce monthly bank statements for the customers. The monthly program would therefore read two files:
(a) details of the transactions, possibly punched on cards; and
(b) a file containing details of all accounts as they stood at the start of the month.
The program would write two files:
(c) printed bank statements addressed to the customers; and
(d) an updated copy of (b) with amended balances.

The file (d) would then be kept for reading by the same program at the end of the next month.

Other programs might make use of the same accounts file, such as a program to open new accounts, to close old accounts, and to record changes of address.

Example 17.2

A reference library might run a computer system to assist users to find books containing information they want. The user of such a system would type, on the keyboard of a computer terminal, queries like "List all books about computer programming". This is an example of information retrieval.

The information retrieval program would read two files:
(a) a file containing relevant details of all books in stock; and
(b) the queries typed by the user on his keyboard.
It would write one file:
(c) the information requested by the user, perhaps displayed on a screen, or typed on paper so that it can be taken away.

Again, it will be necessary to allow other programs to manipulate the same file of book details, such as a program to add details of newly acquired books.

These examples illustrate the fact that data may have an existence in its own right, independently of any individual program. Rather than data always being generated for the benefit of specific programs, programs are often written to manipulate data which exists already!

A number of different file structures are possible, of which the simplest is the serial file. A serial file consists simply of a sequence of components, all of the same type. The accounts file of Example 17.1 might be a serial file whose components are records. INPUT and OUTPUT are serial files whose components are single characters. Serial files have the property that their components must be read, or written, in strict sequence, starting from the first component; so, for example, it is not possible to read the 100th component until the first 99 components have already been read.

{Such an file structure would not be appropriate for the information retrieval system of Example 17.2, since it would be very inefficient to have to scan through perhaps the whole file to find details about a single book. A different file structure, one which permits direct access to a specified component, is required in this and similar applications. We shall not consider such file structures here.}

We shall picture a serial file which currently is being read as follows:

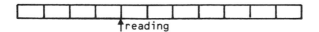
↑reading

The file position, here shown as an arrow, indicates what progress has been made in reading the file; here four components have been read so far. If all components of the file have already been read, we describe the situation as end-of-file:

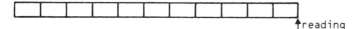

Any attempt to read a component beyond end-of-file will cause the program to fail.

We shall picture a serial file which currently is being written as follows:

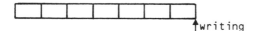

Writing a component to this file makes it longer:

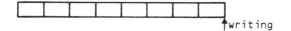

Observe that, while a serial file is being written, the file position is always at end-of-file.

As a data structure, a serial file is similar to an array in that all its components have the same type, but there the similarity ends. It is important to understand the distinctions between arrays and serial files. First, the size of an array is fixed, whereas the size of a serial file varies as it is written, starting at zero components and expanding (virtually) without limit. Second, the elements of an array may be accessed at random, whereas only one component of a serial file is accessible at any time (the component immediately to the right of the file position).

17.2 FILES IN PASCAL

Pascal concerns itself only with serial files, so henceforth we shall use the terms "file" and "serial file" synonymously.

As it appears to a Pascal program, a file is much like an ordinary variable: it has an identifier and it is declared in a variable declaration; its type will specify that it _is_ a file, and will also specify the type of its components.

Example 17.3

Recall the bank accounts files of Example 17.1. Given a type declaration like

```
ACCOUNTS =
    RECORD
        NAME      : PACKED ARRAY [1..NAMELENGTH] OF CHAR ;
        ADDRESS   : PACKED ARRAY [1..ADDRESSLENGTH] OF CHAR ;
        BALANCE   : REAL
    END
```

we could declare a bank accounts file as follows:

```
ACCOUNTSFILE : FILE OF ACCOUNTS
```

This variable declaration specifies that ACCOUNTSFILE will identify a (serial) file whose components are of type ACCOUNTS.

The syntax of file types is summarized in Figure 17.1. FILE and OF are both reserved words. There is no restriction on the choice of component type.

Figure 17.1. Syntax of File Types

File Type :

    ───▶ FILE ──▶ OF ──▶ Component Type ──▶

Component Type :

    ──────────▶ Type ──────────▶

A file is generated by writing components to it, one at a time. This is achieved by using the following predeclared procedures:

REWRITE(F)   makes the file F ready for writing; F now contains zero components.

WRITE(F,x)   appends to the file F a component whose value is that of the expression x. The type of x must be compatible with the component type of F.

The effect of WRITE(F,x) is illustrated below:

198

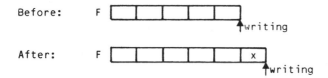

Before: F

↑writing

After: F

↑writing

It is not possible to write to any file until it has been initialized for writing by REWRITE. The only exception to this rule is the file OUTPUT; the statement REWRITE(OUTPUT) is performed automatically, and must <u>not</u> be included in any program.

Once a file has been generated, it may be read by the same program or another program. This is achieved by using the following predeclared procedures:

RESET(F)   prepares the file F for reading, by moving the file position to the first component.

READ(F,V)   copies the next component of the file F into the variable V, then advances the file position past this component. The type of V must be compatible with the component type of F.

After obeying RESET(F), F looks like this:

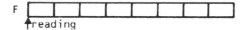

F

↑reading

The effect of READ(F,V) is illustrated below:

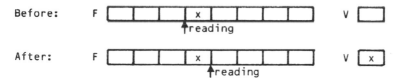

Before: F   x   V

↑reading

After: F   x   V   x

↑reading

It is not possible to read from any file until it has been re-initialized for reading by RESET. The only exception to this rule is the file INPUT; the statement RESET(INPUT) is performed automatically, and must <u>not</u> be included in any program.

READ(F,V) will fail if F is already at end-of-file. In order to anticipate this we must be able to test for end-of-file, and for this purpose the BOOLEAN predeclared function EOF(F) is provided. In the last diagram, EOF(F) is FALSE, but it will become TRUE after a further four components have been read.

Apart from these and other predeclared procedures and functions, we can write our own subprograms with files as parameters. Pascal does not, however, allow whole file variables to be used in any other way; in particular, assignment of files is forbidden.

Example <u>17.4</u>

A company might keep a payroll file containing the following details of each of its employees: name, employee number, grade (manual, skilled, clerical, or managerial), pay rate, tax code, and number of weeks (or months) of service. This file would be used for printing out payslips, for supplying data to the tax authority, for calculating pension entitlement, etc.

The following program calculates the week's pay of all weekly-paid employees (i.e. all except managers). Tax is be deducted automatically according to the formula (pay - tax code) * 33%. The program writes out a table showing the name, number, gross pay, tax deduction and nett pay of each employee. It also generates an updated file taking account of the extra week's service.

```
PROGRAM WEEKLYPAY ( OLDPAYROLL, NEWPAYROLL , OUTPUT ) ;

CONST
   TAXRATE = 0.33 ;
TYPE
   GRADES    = (MANUAL,SKILLED,CLERICAL,MANAGERIAL) ;
   EMPLOYEERECORDS =
           RECORD
               NAME    : PACKED ARRAY [1..16] OF CHAR ;
               NUMBER  : 0..9999 ;
               GRADE   : GRADES ;
               PAYRATE : REAL ;
               TAXCODE : INTEGER ;
               SERVICE : INTEGER
           END ;
VAR
   OLDPAYROLL, NEWPAYROLL : FILE OF EMPLOYEERECORDS ;
   ONEEMPLOYEE            : EMPLOYEERECORDS ;
   NETTPAY, TAXDEDUCTION  : REAL ;
```

```
BEGIN
RESET (OLDPAYROLL) ;
REWRITE (NEWPAYROLL) ;
WRITELN ('NAME            ', ' NUMBER',
        '  GROSS PAY', '          TAX', '    NETT PAY') ;
WRITELN ;
WHILE NOT EOF(OLDPAYROLL) DO
   BEGIN
   READ (OLDPAYROLL, ONEEMPLOYEE) ;
   WITH ONEEMPLOYEE DO
      IF GRADE <> MANAGERIAL THEN
         BEGIN
         TAXDEDUCTION := (PAYRATE - TAXCODE) * TAXRATE ;
         NETTPAY := PAYRATE - TAXDEDUCTION ;
         WRITELN (NAME, NUMBER:8, PAYRATE:12:2,
                  TAXDEDUCTION:12:2, NETTPAY:12:2) ;
         SERVICE := SERVICE + 1
         END ;
   WRITE (NEWPAYROLL, ONEEMPLOYEE)
   END
END .
```

This example illustrates the purpose of the program parameters; they
are the identifiers of files used by the program. However, only files
which are assumed to exist before the program is run (such as OLDPAYROLL
in the example), or which are to be kept after the program is run (such
as NEWPAYROLL in the example), should be listed as program parameters.
Some programs use files for _temporary_ storage of large quantities of
data, taking advantage of the (virtually) unlimited size of files: such
files should not be listed as program parameters.

Program parameters may stand for different files in different runs of
the program. Consider program WEEKLYPAY, for example; the actual file
represented by NEWPAYROLL in one week's run would be the same file as
that represented by OLDPAYROLL in the following week's run.

All files, whether program parameters or not, must appear in variable
declarations in the usual way. Again, INPUT and OUTPUT are exceptions
to this rule: they must _not_ be declared even if they are used.

The syntax of program parameters is summarized in Appendix 1.1.

17.3 TEXT FILES

Text files, i.e. files whose components are characters, are of special
interest since they are the normal means of communication between people
and computers. Pascal provides a predefined type

    TEXT = FILE OF CHAR

to facilitate declarations of text files.

Everything said in Section 17.2 applies to text files as well as to other files, except (let us repeat) that INPUT and OUTPUT must not be initialized by RESET or REWRITE and must not appear in variable declarations. These files are in fact predeclared:

INPUT, OUTPUT : TEXT

Because of their role in communication with people, text files have a special property not shared by other files. Text files are considered to be composed of lines, i.e. character sequences terminated by line boundaries (shown here as "↓"):

| 'T' | 'R' | 'Y' | ',' | ↓ | 'T' | 'R' | 'Y' | ' ' | 'A' | 'G' | 'A' | 'I' | 'N' | ↓ |

If this text file were printed, it would look like this:

TRY,
TRY AGAIN

A line boundary is not considered to be a normal character, i.e. it is not possible to store a line boundary in a CHAR variable. The only way to generate a line boundary is by means of the predeclared procedure WRITELN(T), which appends a line boundary to the text file T.

If we attempt to read a line boundary, then we actually get a blank. The effect of READ(T,C) at a line boundary is illustrated below:

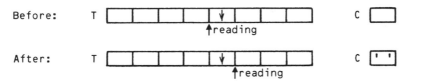

We may wish to distinguish between a line boundary and a genuine blank. For this purpose the BOOLEAN predeclared function EOLN(T) is provided. EOLN(T) is TRUE if and only if the file position of the text file T is immediately before a line boundary. Thus EOLN(T) is TRUE in the first of the diagrams above, and is FALSE in the second (unless there happen to be two consecutive line boundaries).

Finally, the effect of READLN(T) is to move the file position past the next line boundary:

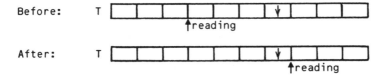

The following example illustrates character-by-character processing of a text file.

Example 17.5

Write a program to count the blanks and the non-blanks in a given text file.

```
PROGRAM COUNT ( TEXTFILE , OUTPUT ) ;

CONST
   BLANK = ' ' ;
VAR
   TEXTFILE                   : TEXT ;
   CH                         : CHAR ;
   NMROFBLANKS, NMROFNONBLANKS : INTEGER ;

BEGIN
NMROFBLANKS := 0 ;
NMROFNONBLANKS := 0 ;
RESET (TEXTFILE) ;
WHILE NOT EOF(TEXTFILE) DO
   BEGIN
   WHILE NOT EOLN(TEXTFILE) DO
      BEGIN
      READ (TEXTFILE, CH) ;
      IF CH = BLANK THEN
         NMROFBLANKS := NMROFBLANKS + 1
      ELSE
         NMROFNONBLANKS := NMROFNONBLANKS + 1
      END ;
   READLN (TEXTFILE)       (* ignore the line boundary *)
   END ;
WRITELN ('NUMBER OF BLANKS:    ', NMROFBLANKS) ;
WRITELN ('NUMBER OF NONBLANKS: ', NMROFNONBLANKS)
END .
```

The predeclared procedures provided for handling text files are very flexible in the number and types of parameters they allow. We have seen this already, as long ago as Chapter 4, but this flexibility applies to all text files, not just to INPUT and OUTPUT.
(a) READ and READLN may be invoked without an explicit file parameter, in which case the file is taken to be INPUT. Similarly, WRITE, WRITELN and PAGE may be invoked without an explicit file parameter, in which case the file is taken to be OUTPUT.
(b) READ, READLN, WRITE and WRITELN may be invoked with parameters of various types. This is because, for many purposes, reading and writing one character at a time is too low-level. For example, we want to be able to read and write (decimal) numbers, each consisting of several characters in a text file. Here is a summary of all the

allowable parameter types:

READ, READLN	WRITE, WRITELN
CHAR	CHAR
INTEGER	INTEGER
REAL	REAL
	BOOLEAN
	any character array

On reading in INTEGER or REAL mode, blanks and line boundaries preceding the number are ignored.

(c) READ, READLN, WRITE and WRITELN may be invoked with several parameters of these types, in addition to the (optional) file parameter.

A complete summary of input and output via text files may be found in Appendix 4.

We are now in a position to explain precisely why, as noted in Sections 6.2 and 8.1, the EOF test can safely be used to detect the end of a list of numbers in a text file T only when the most recent input operation was READLN, rather than READ. (The same applies when reading strings or anything else, other than single characters, from a text file.) If READ were used instead of READLN in Example 6.4, then after the last number had been read the file position would still not have passed the last line boundary, so EOF(T) would still be FALSE:

T `'2' '3' ↓ ' ' '7' ↓ ' ' '1' '3' ↓ '2' '5' '6' ↓`

              ↑reading

When READLN is used, the last READLN advances the file position just past the last line boundary, where EOF(T) becomes TRUE.

Often the data in a text file consists of words or numbers separated by blanks and/or line boundaries. When reading such a text file, it is very convenient that the line boundaries are transmitted as blanks, since we can completely ignore the distinction between blanks and line boundaries. Thus the procedure of Example 13.3 will work even though it takes no account of line boundaries.

17.4 FILE BUFFERS

{This section should be omitted on a first reading.}

We have seen, in Section 17.2, that the statement READ(F,V) has two effects: it copies the next component of F into the variable V, then it advances the file position of F. For certain kinds of file processing, it is convenient to be able to separate the second step from the first. For such purposes, the concept of the file buffer is useful.

Consider a file F which is being read; the file buffer of F, which is denoted F↑, is a copy of the component of F immediately to the right of the file position:

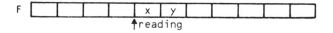

F↑ ⬚ x

The file buffer can be used just like any variable, so its content may be inspected directly without bothering to copy it into another variable.

The file position may be advanced (<u>automatically</u> updating the file buffer) by means of the standard procedure GET(F), whose effect on F (above) is as follows:

F ⬚⬚⬚⬚⬚ x y ⬚⬚⬚⬚⬚
          ↑reading

F↑ ⬚ y

It may now be seen that the statement READ(F,V) is equivalent to:

BEGIN V := F↑ ; GET(F) END

Example 17.6

Recall the payroll file described in Example 17.4. It is required to update the payroll file to include details of new employees. To this end a second file has been generated, consisting of records similar to those of the payroll file, containing details of the new employees. All employees are assumed to have distinct employee numbers, and in both files the records are assumed to be arranged in ascending order by employee number. Write a program to generate an updated payroll file, in which the records are also ordered by employee number.

For example, if the employee numbers in the two input files are as follows:

    Old payroll: 3, 7, 8, 9, 11, 12, 15, 19
    New employees: 1, 2, 5, 6, 10, 14

then the new payroll file should contain the following, in order:

    New payroll: 1, 2, 3, 5, 6, 7, 8, 9, 10, 11, 12, 14, 15, 19

This is an example of <u>merging,</u> a very common theme in commercial data processing.

```
PROGRAM MERGE ( UPDATES, OLDPAYROLL, NEWPAYROLL ) ;

TYPE
   GRADES    = (MANUAL,SKILLED,CLERICAL,MANAGERIAL) ;
   EMPLOYEES =
         RECORD
            NAME    : PACKED ARRAY [1..16] OF CHAR ;
            NUMBER  : 0..9999 ;
            GRADE   : GRADES ;
            PAYRATE : REAL ;
            TAXCODE : INTEGER ;
            SERVICE : INTEGER
         END ;
VAR
   UPDATES, OLDPAYROLL, NEWPAYROLL : FILE OF EMPLOYEES ;

BEGIN
RESET (UPDATES) ;
RESET (OLDPAYROLL) ;
REWRITE (NEWPAYROLL) ;
(* merge until one file is exhausted *)
   WHILE NOT (EOF(UPDATES) OR EOF(OLDPAYROLL)) DO
      IF UPDATES↑.NUMBER > OLDPAYROLL↑.NUMBER THEN
         BEGIN
         WRITE (NEWPAYROLL, OLDPAYROLL↑) ;
         GET (OLDPAYROLL)
         END
      ELSE
         BEGIN
         WRITE (NEWPAYROLL, UPDATES↑) ;
         GET (UPDATES)
         END ;
(* copy any records left in either file *)
   WHILE NOT EOF(OLDPAYROLL) DO
      BEGIN
      WRITE (NEWPAYROLL, OLDPAYROLL↑) ;
      GET (OLDPAYROLL)
      END ;
   WHILE NOT EOF(UPDATES) DO
      BEGIN
      WRITE (NEWPAYROLL, UPDATES↑) ;
      GET (UPDATES)
      END
END .
```

This program serves to illustrate the use of file buffers and GET. It must be admitted, however, that the program would <u>not</u> be acceptable in the real world of commercial data processing, since it naively accepts all the assumptions about the two input files. Files are generated by programs which may be incorrect, they are recorded on media which may occasionally be unreliable, and they are read and written by devices which may also be unreliable. A realistic file-processing program must, therefore, check that the assumptions about its input files are indeed met, writing appropriate error messages if they are not. (See Exercises 17.)

A file which is being written also has associated with it a file buffer, in which the value of each new component is stored until the file position is advanced:

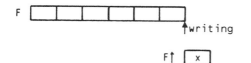

The file buffer may be used like any variable, so we may store some value in it, then update it later if we wish.

The file position is advanced by means of the standard procedure PUT(F). This appends the contents of the file buffer to the file itself, and leaves the file buffer undefined:

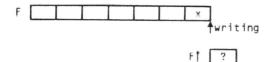

It may now be seen that the statement WRITE(F,x) is equivalent to:

BEGIN F↑ := x ; PUT(F) END

EXERCISES 17

17.1. Write a program fragment which counts the components in a file F of type FILE OF ITEMS.

17.2. Write a procedure which searches a given file F, of type FILE OF INTEGER, for a component which matches a given value TARGET, setting a BOOLEAN parameter accordingly.

17.3. Write a program fragment which writes your name and address, complete with line boundaries, to a text file T.

17.4. Write a program which reads a text file and writes it on OUTPUT with line numbering on the left.

17.5. Modify program MERGE (Example 17.6) so that it writes an error message every time it finds an employee record out of sequence in either input file.

17.6*. The Drinkers' Club maintains a file containing the names, addresses, etc. of all its members, ordered by name. The Temperance Society maintains a similar file containing details of its members. Write a program which writes on OUTPUT details of everyone who is a member of both groups.

PROGRAMMING EXERCISES 17

{To run the following programs, you will have to find out how to create and access files at your computer installation.}

17.7. A bank accounts file (as in Example 17.3) is to be created from scratch. The first NAMELENGTH characters of each line of INPUT contain a customer's name (left-justified), the next ADDRESSLENGTH characters contain the customer's address, and the remainder of the line contains the customer's account number. Every customer starts with a balance of zero. Write a program which reads this data and generates the bank accounts file.

17.8*. Write a program to update a bank accounts file and produce printed bank statements, as described in Example 17.1. Details of each transaction are supplied as a single line of INPUT containing the customer's account number followed by the amount of the transaction (positive for a credit transaction, negative for a debit transaction). Each bank statement must contain the customer's name, address and account number, original balance, list of transactions, and updated balance. A bank statement is to be printed for every customer, even where there are no transactions. Both the accounts file and the set of transactions are supposed to be ordered on the customer's account number; your program must print an error message every time an account number is found to be out of sequence, and take some appropriate recovery action.

18 Sets

{This chapter should be omitted entirely on a first reading.}

SETS AND THEIR USE IN PROGRAMMING

The concept of a <u>set</u> is one of the most basic in mathematics. A set is best defined, for our purposes, as a collection of distinct objects all of the same type. The objects contained in a set are called the <u>members</u> of that set. {June, July, August} and {3, 5, 7, 11, 13, 17, 19} are examples of sets: the first has three members, which are months; the second has seven members, which are integers. A set with no members at all is called the <u>empty set</u>.

The following operations can be performed upon sets.

(a) <u>Test for membership</u>: a given value either is a member of a given set or is not. Thus June is a member of the set {June, July, August}; May is not.

(b) <u>Test for inclusion</u>: a set A is included in a set B (alternatively, A is a <u>subset</u> of B) if and only if every member of A is also a member of B. Thus {June, July, August}, {July} and the empty set are all subsets of {June, July, August}.

(c) <u>Set intersection</u>: the intersection of two sets A and B is the set of all values which are members of both A and B. Thus the intersection of {June, July, August} and {December, March, June, September} is the single-member set {June}.

(d) <u>Set union</u>: the union of two sets A and B is the set of all values which are members of A or of B or of both. Thus the union of {June, July, August} and {December, March, June, September} is the set {March, June, July, August, September, December}.

(e) <u>Set difference</u>: the difference of two sets A and B is the set of all values which are members of A but not of B. Thus the difference of {June, July, August} and {December, March, June, September} is the set {July, August}.

The use of sets permits elegant formulation of many programming problems. The following example illustrates a common situation.

Example 18.1

Suppose we have a variable MONTH, and suppose further that we wish to write down a loop which will continue as long as MONTH has one of the

values April, June, September or November. The "obvious" solution
is:

```
    WHILE    (MONTH = April)
         OR (MONTH = June)
         OR (MONTH = September)
         OR (MONTH = November) DO
      ..........
      ..........
```

A much neater formulation is this:

```
    WHILE   MONTH is a member of
              {April, June, September, November}  DO
      ..........
      ..........
```

Moreover, this formulation can easily be generalized, for example:

```
    WHILE   MONTH is a member of MONTHSOFINTEREST  DO
      ..........
      ..........
```

where MONTHSOFINTEREST is a set variable, i.e. a variable whose value
(in this case) will be a set of months.

18.2 SETS IN PASCAL

Unlike most other programming languages, Pascal allows the programmer to
take advantage of the elegance of set notation. We can declare set
variables, and we can compose set expressions using the operations of
test for membership, set inclusion, set intersection, set union and set
difference.

Example 18.2

   Given the type definition

```
      MONTHS = (JANUARY,FEBRUARY,MARCH,APRIL,MAY,JUNE,JULY,
                AUGUST,SEPTEMBER,OCTOBER,NOVEMBER,DECEMBER)
```

   we can declare some set variables as follows:

```
      MONTHSOFINTEREST, SUMMERMONTHS : SET OF MONTHS
```

   This declares that the variables MONTHSOFINTEREST and SUMMERMONTHS
   will take values which are sets, and that each member of these sets
   will be of type MONTHS; the latter is called the base type of the
   sets. Alternatively, we may give the set type a name using a type

definition:

    SETOFMONTHS = SET OF MONTHS

and then declare the variables as follows:

    MONTHSOFINTEREST, SUMMERMONTHS : SETOFMONTHS

The syntax of set types is summarized in Figure 18.1. SET and OF are both reserved words.

Figure 18.1. Syntax of Set Types

Set Type:

    ──→ SET ──→ OF ──→ Base Type ──→

Base Type:

    ─────────→ Ordinal Type ─────────→

Unfortunately, Pascal imposes the restriction that every set's base type must be ordinal; thus, for example, we cannot use sets of real numbers, nor sets of strings (which would definitely be useful), nor sets of sets, in a Pascal program. Moreover, each Pascal compiler is free to impose a limit on the number of different values of the base type, in order to allow set operations to be performed efficiently. This limit (which is typically around 64) may exclude some useful set types like SET OF CHAR.

In Pascal we denote a set value using notation similar to the mathematical notation, only replacing the curly brackets by square brackets. For example,

    SUMMERMONTHS := [JUNE,JULY,AUGUST]

assigns a set value (with three members) to the set variable SUMMERMONTHS. This particular set denotation can be abbreviated:

    SUMMERMONTHS := [JUNE..AUGUST]

assigns to SUMMERMONTHS a set value whose members are JUNE to AUGUST inclusive.

We are not restricted to using constants in a set denotation. For example, if I and N are INTEGER variables, we can test whether the value of I lies in the range N to N+6 inclusive by means of the test

    IF I IN [N..N+6] THEN ......

which is a neat alternative to the more usual

    IF (I >= N) AND (I <= N+6) THEN ......

The empty set is denoted by []. The syntax of set denotations is summarized in Figure 18.2. A set denotation may be used as a factor in a set expression.

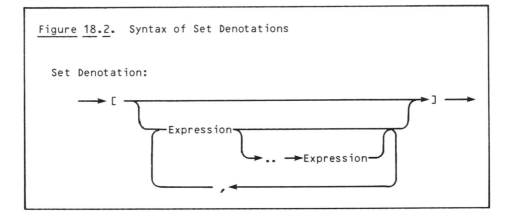

Figure 18.2. Syntax of Set Denotations

Set Denotation:

The last example has introduced the test for membership, denoted in Pascal by the comparison operator IN. Here is another example of its use, showing how the last loop in Example 18.1 would be expressed in Pascal:

    WHILE MONTH IN MONTHSOFINTEREST DO
       ....
       ....

In general, the type of the left operand of IN must be some ordinal type T, and the type of its right operand must then be SET OF T. Just like any other comparison operator, IN yields a result which is TRUE or FALSE. IN has the same priority as the other comparison operators.

The comparison operators "=", "<>", "<=" and ">=" (but not "<" nor ">") may be used with set operands. Let A and B be sets. A = B evaluates to TRUE if and only if A and B have exactly the same members; A <> B is defined in the opposite sense. A <= B means "A is a subset of B"; A >= B means "B is a subset of A".

Set expressions may be composed using the following set operators:

```
*      which with set operands denotes set intersection;
+        "    "   "     "        "     "   union;
-        "    "   "     "        "     "   difference.
```

A set value may be assigned to a set variable, and sets may be passed
as parameters to subprograms. In set assignments, set comparisons, set
expressions and set parameters, all the set variables and operands
concerned must have the same type. A function may not have a set as its
result, nor may sets be read from or written to text files.

Example 18.3

Assume the variable declarations

    HOLIDAYMONTHS, WETMONTHS, DRYMONTHS : SETOFMONTHS

The following statements illustrate some uses of set expressions:

```
HOLIDAYMONTHS := [JULY..SEPTEMBER] ;
DRYMONTHS := [JANUARY..DECEMBER] - WETMONTHS ;
    (*  Any month which is not wet is assumed to be dry *)
IF HOLIDAYMONTHS <= DRYMONTHS THEN
                    (* i.e. every summer month is dry *)
    take beachwear on holiday
ELSE IF HOLIDAYMONTHS * DRYMONTHS <> [] THEN
                    (* i.e. some summer months are dry *)
    take an umbrella as well as beachwear
ELSE                (* every summer month is wet *)
    stay at home
```


Example 18.4

Suppose that the departments of a hypothetical large organization are
numbered from 1 to 20, and that the organization maintains a file
containing details of each of its employees, including his name and
the number of the department in which he works. Occasionally it may
be desired to create a file containing details only of employees
working in a given subset of the departments. Let us write a program
to do so, given as input data the numbers of the desired departments,
one department number per line.

```
              PROGRAM EXTRACT ( INPUT, MASTERFILE, EXTRACTEDFILE ) ;

              CONST
                 MAXDEPTCODE = 20 ;
              TYPE
                 DEPTCODES       = 1..MAXDEPTCODE ;
                 SETOFDEPTCODES  = SET OF DEPTCODES ;
                 EMPLOYEERECORDS = RECORD
                                       DEPT : DEPTCODES
                                   (* ......................
                                       name and other details
                                   ...................... *)
                                   END ;
              VAR
                 MASTERFILE, EXTRACTEDFILE : FILE OF EMPLOYEERECORDS ;
                 ONEEMPLOYEE               : EMPLOYEERECORDS ;
                 DESIREDDEPTS              : SETOFDEPTCODES ;

              PROCEDURE READDEPTS ( VAR DEPTSET : SETOFDEPTCODES ) ;
                 VAR
                    DEPT : INTEGER ;
                 BEGIN
                 DEPTSET := [] ;
                 WHILE NOT EOF(INPUT) DO
                    BEGIN
                    READLN (DEPT) ;
                    IF DEPT IN [1..MAXDEPTCODE] THEN
                       (* add DEPT to DEPTSET *)
                           DEPTSET := DEPTSET + [DEPT]
                    END
                 END (* READDEPTS *) ;

              BEGIN (* EXTRACT *)
              READDEPTS(DESIREDDEPTS) ;
              RESET(MASTERFILE) ;
              REWRITE(EXTRACTEDFILE) ;
              WHILE NOT EOF(MASTERFILE) DO
                 BEGIN
                 READ (MASTERFILE, ONEEMPLOYEE) ;
                 IF ONEEMPLOYEE.DEPT IN DESIREDDEPTS THEN
                    WRITE (EXTRACTEDFILE, ONEEMPLOYEE)
                 END
              END (* EXTRACT *) .
```

This example illustrates one method of building up a set: in
procedure READDEPTS, the set variable DEPTSET is initialized to the
empty set, then members (read from the input file in this case) are
successively added to DEPTSET using the set union operator "+".

EXERCISES 18

18.1. A group of people have been numbered 1 to N. Write down declarations of variables OLDPEOPLE, MALES, SMOKERS and DRINKERS which can take values which are sets of people in this group. Assuming that appropriate values have been assigned to these variables, write set expressions whose values will be:
(a) the whole group;
(b) the set of non-smokers;
(c) the set of old smoking drinking males;
(d) the set of those who smoke or drink (or both);
(e) the set consisting of all the old people plus those males who smoke or drink.
Write a statement which writes the message 'BAD INSURANCE RISK' if a given person PERSON is in set (e).

18.2. Write a function which determines whether a given colour occurs in your national flag or not, by testing for membership of a suitably chosen set of colours.

18.3. Write a function which determines whether a given character is a letter, a digit, a blank, punctuation, or other.

19 Pointers and linked lists

{This chapter should be omitted entirely on a first reading.}

19.1 POINTERS

Recall the program of Example 16.4, in which a set of names was sorted by inserting each name, as it was read, into its correct position in a list of names. This program served well enough to illustrate string handling and the basic idea of insertion sort.

From the point of view of efficiency, however, the solution using an array is rather unsatisfactory. This is because (among other reasons) inserting an item in its correct position forces us to shift the items in this and succeeding positions of the array up one position. As the list of items lengthens, the program will run more and more slowly. This is likely to be unacceptable if the number of items to be sorted becomes very large (say 1000 or more).

The shifting is necessary because the position of each entry in the array is implied by its subscript: the item following LIST[I] is LIST[I+1]. So when we wish to insert a new item between these two items, we must place the new item in LIST[I+1], having shifted the item previously in LIST[I+1] into LIST[I+2], the item previously in LIST[I+2] into LIST[I+3], etc.

A completely different way to represent the list is to make each entry in the list explicitly refer to the entry which follows it in the list, as shown here by arrows:

For obvious reasons, these references are called pointers. The advantage of using pointers becomes apparent when we update the list by inserting a new item, e.g. inserting "Hoare" between "Dahl" and "Knuth". All that needs to be done is (1) to create a new entry containing "Hoare" and containing a pointer to the "Knuth" entry (which will be its follower), and (2) to redirect the pointer in the "Dahl" entry to refer to the new entry. The entries for "Knuth", "Wirth", etc. need not be disturbed at all:

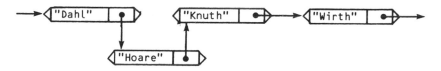

A list of records linked by pointers in this way is known as a <u>linked</u> <u>list</u>.

It must be emphasized that pointers are data which can be assigned and compared. Thus lists and more complex data structures built up using pointers can often be manipulated simply by redirecting the pointers, which is faster than moving around bulky data like strings.

19.2 DYNAMIC DATA STRUCTURES

When we declare a variable, say V, at the head of a block, we obtain a storage location named V:

V

We can access this storage location simply by naming it, e.g. if V is a record:

    WITH V DO ....

On the other hand, the storage locations in the linked list of Section 19.1 are anonymous. Such locations are accessed not by name but through the pointers which refer to them. Thus, if P is a pointer which refers to a record, the form of the WITH statement must be:

    WITH the record referenced by P DO ....

Anonymous locations have the great advantage that they can be explicitly created <u>at</u> <u>any</u> <u>time</u> <u>while</u> <u>the</u> <u>program</u> <u>is</u> <u>running</u>. (By contrast, a named location is automatically created on entry to the block where it is declared, and destroyed on exit from that block – see Section 13.5.) Data structures composed of anonymous locations linked by pointers are called <u>dynamic</u> <u>data</u> <u>structures</u>, since they can expand and contract freely as required. A linked list is a simple example of a dynamic data structure.

Thus we see a further advantage to the use of a linked list rather than an array in programs like the insertion sort, where the number of items to be stored is unpredictable: the linked list can be made just as long as required (no more, no less); whereas the size of an array is fixed in advance, so an arbitrary limit on the number of items must be imposed.

19.3 POINTERS IN PASCAL

Suppose we wish to set up a linked list containing items of type ITEMS. The type definition

        ITEMPOINTERS = ↑ ITEMRECORDS

defines ITEMPOINTERS to be a <u>pointer</u> <u>type</u>: each value of type ITEMPOINTERS will be a pointer to an (anonymous) storage location of type ITEMRECORDS. Since for our purposes each such storage location must contain a pointer as well as an item of type ITEMS, ITEMRECORDS must be defined to be a record type:

        ITEMRECORDS = RECORD
                      ITEM : ITEMS ;
                      NEXT : ITEMPOINTERS
                    END

We can make the field ITEM contain one of the items, and the field NEXT contain a pointer to the following entry in the linked list.

   Each entry in the list will thus be referenced by the previous entry, but how will the first entry be referenced? For this purpose we need a variable (or parameter or field) such as

        LISTHEAD : ITEMPOINTERS

in which we can store a pointer to the first entry. Finally, how can we indicate that the last entry in the list has no follower? For purposes like this, Pascal provides the special pointer value NIL, which refers to no location at all. (NIL is a reserved word.) Thus we can mark the last entry in the linked list by storing NIL in the field NEXT of this entry:

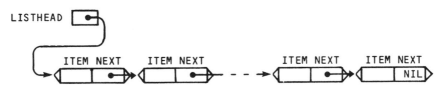

We can represent an empty linked list (i.e. one with no entries at all) simply by storing NIL in LISTHEAD itself:

LISTHEAD [NIL]

   Pointer values in Pascal can be assigned, and compared using the comparison operators "=" and "<>". (Two pointer values are equal if they are both NIL or if they refer to the same location.) Pointers may also be passed as parameters, and a function may have a pointer result.

   Assuming the variable declaration

        P, Q : ↑ T

and assuming that suitable pointer values (i.e. not NIL) have been assigned to P and Q, the locations referenced by P and Q can be accessed by P↑ and Q↑ respectively. For example, if T is a record type, we can write

    WITH P↑ DO ....

P↑ and Q↑ are examples of <u>referenced variables</u>.
    It is most important to distinguish between P, which denotes a location containing a pointer value, and P↑, which denotes the location referenced by the value of P (provided P <> NIL). The following situation illustrates the distinction:

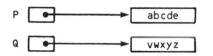

The assignment statement P := Q assigns a <u>pointer value</u>, as a result of which P now refers to the same location as Q:

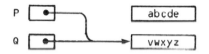

On the other hand, the assignment statement P↑ := Q↑ copies the content of the location referenced by Q into the location referenced by P:

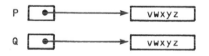

(Both P↑ := Q and P := Q↑ are meaningless and are forbidden by Pascal.)
    The syntax of pointer types is summarized in Figure 19.1, and that of referenced variables in Figure 19.2. Note that a type <u>identifier</u> is compulsory in a pointer type, and that this type identifier is an exception to the general rule that every identifier must be declared before it is used (see Example 19.3).

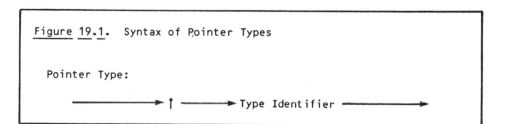

Figure 19.1. Syntax of Pointer Types

    Pointer Type:

Figure 19.2. Syntax of Referenced Variables

Referenced Variable:

—————————▶ Pointer Variable ——————▶ ↑ —————————▶

The variable declaration

P : ↑ T

creates a storage location for P only. P's value is initially
undefined; it does not yet refer to any storage location:

P [?]

Storage locations can be created dynamically using the predeclared
procedure NEW; for example, NEW(P) creates a new location which is
referenced by P:

The content of this new location is initially undefined, but a value of
type T may subsequently be stored in this location by assignment to P↑.

19.4 LINKED LIST PROCESSING

In this section we illustrate the use of pointers by examples of
manipulation of linked lists.

Example 19.1

Assume the definitions of the types ITEMPOINTERS and ITEMRECORDS from
Section 19.3. Let us write a function which, given as a parameter a
pointer LISTHEAD to the first entry of a linked list of items,
returns the number of items in the linked list.

This problem is a simple illustration of serial processing of a
linked list. We need a local pointer variable, say ENTRY, which will
be made to refer to each entry of the linked list in turn. The
serial processing can be performed by a loop which is terminated when
ENTRY = NIL. A WHILE loop will allow for an empty list.

220

```
FUNCTION LISTLENGTH ( LISTHEAD : ITEMPOINTERS ) : INTEGER ;
VAR
   ITEMCOUNT : INTEGER ;
   ENTRY     : ITEMPOINTERS ;
BEGIN
ITEMCOUNT := 0 ;
ENTRY := LISTHEAD ;
WHILE ENTRY <> NIL DO
   WITH ENTRY↑ DO
      BEGIN
      ITEMCOUNT := ITEMCOUNT+1 ;
      ENTRY := NEXT
      END ;
LISTLENGTH := ITEMCOUNT
END (* LISTLENGTH *)
```

Example 19.2

Assume the definitions of the types ITEMPOINTERS and ITEMRECORDS from Section 19.3. Let us write a procedure which, given as parameters an item TARGETITEM and a pointer LISTHEAD to the first entry of a linked list of items, returns in a variable parameter a pointer to the entry containing TARGETITEM (or NIL is there is no such entry in the linked list). We do not assume that the items in the list are in any particular order.

This problem illustrates linear search in a linked list. (Compare Example 10.7.)

```
PROCEDURE SEARCHLIST (     TARGETITEM : ITEMS ;
                           LISTHEAD   : ITEMPOINTERS ;
                       VAR TARGETLOC  : ITEMPOINTERS ) ;
   VAR
      ENTRY     : ITEMPOINTERS ;
      SEARCHING : BOOLEAN ;
   BEGIN
   ENTRY := LISTHEAD ;
   SEARCHING := TRUE ;
   WHILE SEARCHING AND (ENTRY <> NIL) DO
      WITH ENTRY↑ DO
         IF ITEM = TARGETITEM THEN
            SEARCHING := FALSE
         ELSE
            ENTRY := NEXT ;
   IF SEARCHING THEN
      TARGETLOC := NIL
   ELSE
      TARGETLOC := ENTRY
   END (* SEARCHLIST *)
```

Example 19.3

Let us modify the program of Example 16.4 to use a linked list instead of an array.

```
PROGRAM SORTITEMS ( INPUT, OUTPUT ) ;

CONST
   NAMELENGTH = 20 ;
TYPE
   ITEMS       = PACKED ARRAY [1..NAMELENGTH] OF CHAR ;
   ITEMPOINTERS = ↑ ITEMRECORDS ;
   ITEMRECORDS  = RECORD
                     ITEM : ITEMS ;
                     NEXT : ITEMPOINTERS
                  END ;
VAR
   LISTHEAD : ITEMPOINTERS ;
   NEWITEM  : ITEMS ;

PROCEDURE INSERTITEM ( NEWITEM : ITEMS ) ;
   VAR
      ENTRY, PRIORENTRY, NEWENTRY : ITEMPOINTERS ;
      SEARCHING                   : BOOLEAN ;
   BEGIN
   (* find the position where the new item will be inserted *)
      ENTRY := LISTHEAD ;
      SEARCHING := TRUE ;
      WHILE SEARCHING AND (ENTRY <> NIL) DO
         WITH ENTRY↑ DO
            IF NEWITEM < ITEM THEN
               SEARCHING := FALSE
            ELSE
               BEGIN
               PRIORENTRY := ENTRY ;
               ENTRY := NEXT
               END ;
   (* create the new entry and insert it in position *)
      NEW(NEWENTRY) ;
      NEWENTRY↑.ITEM := NEWITEM ;
      NEWENTRY↑.NEXT := ENTRY ;
      IF ENTRY = LISTHEAD THEN
         LISTHEAD := NEWENTRY
      ELSE
         PRIORENTRY↑.NEXT := NEWENTRY
   END (* INSERTITEM *) ;
```

```
PROCEDURE READITEM ( VAR ITEM : ITEMS ) ;
   ....................
   .................... (* as in Example 16.4 *)
   ....................

PROCEDURE WRITEITEMS ;
   VAR
      ENTRY : ITEMPOINTERS ;
   BEGIN
   ENTRY := LISTHEAD ;
   WHILE ENTRY <> NIL DO
      WITH ENTRY↑ DO
         BEGIN
         WRITELN (ITEM) ;
         ENTRY := NEXT
         END
   END (* WRITEITEMS *) ;

BEGIN (* SORTITEMS *)
(* make the list empty *)
   LISTHEAD := NIL ;
WHILE NOT EOF(INPUT) DO
   BEGIN
   (* read an item *)
      READITEM(NEWITEM) ;
   (* insert the new item in its correct position *)
      INSERTITEM(NEWITEM)
   END ;
(* write all the items in order *)
   WRITEITEMS
END (* SORTITEMS *) .
```

Apart from procedure WRITEITEMS, the substantial changes to the
program are localized in procedure INSERTITEM. The search leaves
ENTRY pointing to the entry which will follow the new entry. Since
the pointer field NEXT in the previous entry must be redirected when
the new entry is inserted (except in the case where the new entry is
inserted at the beginning of the linked list), the procedure uses an
additional pointer variable, PRIORENTRY, to refer to the previous
entry in the linked list. The statement NEW(NEWENTRY) creates a
new storage location (of type ITEMRECORDS) and stores a pointer to
this location in NEWENTRY. Convince yourself of the correctness of
INSERTITEM by working through it by hand, choosing suitable test
cases, i.e. insertion at the beginning, in the middle and at the end
of the linked list.

19.1. (a) Write type definitions describing a linked list whose entries contain integers. (b) Write a function which, given a pointer to the first entry of such a linked list, returns the sum of the integers stored in the list.

19.2. Write a program which reads a line of characters and writes them in reverse order. Use a linked list, and insert each character as it is read at the head of the list.

19.3. Program SORTITEMS (Example 19.3) can be improved further if we can avoid searching the whole list to decide where to insert the new item. One way to do this, when the items are names, is to have twenty-six linked lists, one for each initial letter. It becomes necessary to have an array of list heads, one for each linked list. Modify the program along these lines.

PROGRAMMING EXERCISES 19

19.4*. Write a program which maintains a stock inventory held in the form of a linked list. The list must consist of one entry for each different component in stock, where each entry contains the component number, the number of units in stock, and the reorder level for that component. The inventory is initially empty. Each line of input specifies an operation on the inventory, the operation being identified by the first character in the line:

Code	Operation requested	Additional data on the same line
'N'	New component	Component number, initial number of units in stock, reorder level.
'D'	Delete component	Component number.
'A'	Add to stock	Component number, number of units added.
'R'	Remove from stock	Component number, number of units removed.
'P'	Print inventory	None.

Invalid and impossible operations should give rise to suitable error messages, and operation 'R' should give rise to a warning message if the number of units in stock falls below the reorder level.

19.5*. Modify your inventory program so that operation 'P' lists the contents of the inventory in order of component number. (The best way to do this is to keep the list ordered at all times, by suitable implementation of operation 'N'.)

VI Programming methodology
20 Programming methodology: case studies

20.1 PROGRAMMING BY STEPWISE REFINEMENT: A REVIEW

In Chapter 7 we stressed the advantages of programming methodically. By systematically developing a program from its specification we aim to arrive at a program which is easy to understand and relatively free from errors.

The example programs in the intervening chapters have been developed by the methods introduced in Chapter 7. However, these examples were intended primarily to illustrate the features of the programming language Pascal, rather than to illustrate the process of program development itself. By now you will be acquainted with the principal features of Pascal, but your experience of program development is probably limited to rather small programs. Now that we have all the necessary programming tools at our disposal, it is time to see how programming problems of a more realistic size can be tackled methodically.

Let us recap on the technique of programming by stepwise refinement. We start by devising and writing down a skeleton solution, a "program" which contains commands expressed in English, in addition to Pascal statements and control structures. We call this "program" Level 1. Having completed Level 1, we refine some of these commands, by breaking them down into program fragments which may themselves be expressed partly in Pascal and partly in English. (We must of course ensure that the old commands are broken down into commands which are in some sense "simpler", so that we have taken a step nearer to a complete solution.) By substituting these refinements into Level 1, we obtain a more detailed "program", which we call Level 2. We continue in this way, successively fleshing out our skeleton solution by refinement, until finally, at Level n, we arrive at a solution expressed entirely in Pascal.

The point of writing commands in English is that for the time being we concern ourselves only with what these commands will do, and only at a later stage decide how they will perform their tasks. Thus the fundamental advantage of programming by stepwise refinement is that it enables a programming problem to be solved in small, manageable steps. The task of testing the solution is also broken down into manageable sub-tasks. We can hand-test the refinements individually, and if we are satisfied that they are individually correct, we can be reasonably sure that the complete solution is also correct (provided of course that the refinements have been combined correctly).

If you have tended to ignore this advice while doing the programming exercises, preferring a haphazard approach to a systematic one, you will probably have learned your lesson the hard way! It is likely that your programs contained a lot of errors, which were detected only by exhaustive testing on a computer (or, still worse, remain undetected!), and that correcting these errors was a tedious affair. Even if, being an embryonic programming genius, you have been able to solve small programming problems by inspiration, you will find that inspiration alone is just not adequate for solving larger programming problems; a systematic approach becomes absolutely essential.

In this chapter we present two case studies, each describing the solution of a problem complex enough to illustrate the practical difficulties of program development. The lessons to be learned from these case studies are summarized and generalized in the last section of the chapter.

To derive the maximum benefit from each case study, we recommend that you first read and thoroughly understand the problem specification; then attempt to solve the problem yourself; and only finally, read the solution. These solutions are not unrealistic "model" solutions; they are fully worked through, and they illustrate the errors and indecisions that are more or less inevitable in program development.

20.2 CASE STUDY II: TEXT FORMATTING

Problem Specification

Write a program which will read natural-language text and write it out in paragraphs, with each line justified on both the left and the right margins. The text is supplied in free format, with successive words being separated by one or more blanks and/or line boundaries. Each punctuation mark, such as a period or a comma, may be assumed to follow immediately the preceding word, i.e. without intervening blanks. A new paragraph is indicated by the special "word" /PAR/, but the text does not necessarily start with a new paragraph.

The number of characters to be written on each line of output is to be read from a line preceding the input text.

On output, as many words as possible are to be written on each line, with successive words on the same line separated by one or more blanks. Each punctuation mark must immediately follow the preceding word (and must be on the same line). Each line is to be right-adjusted, if necessary, by writing extra blanks between words, the extra blanks being distributed as evenly as possible. No word may be split between two lines. The first line of each paragraph must be indented six spaces on the left, and must be preceded by a blank line. The last line of each paragraph, and the last line of the whole text, are not to be right-adjusted.

Assume that no word is longer than twenty characters. The program should ensure that the specified line width is sufficient to accomodate the longest possible word plus a punctuation mark.

For example, if the input text is

```
THE PRINCIPLES OF NEWSPEAK
/PAR/
NEWSPEAK WAS THE OFFICIAL LANGUAGE OF OCEANIA
AND HAD BEEN DESIGNED TO MEET THE IDEOLOGICAL NEEDS
OF INGSOC.
/PAR/
IN THE YEAR 1984
THERE WAS NOT AS YET ANYONE
WHO USED NEWSPEAK AS HIS SOLE MEANS OF COMMUNICATION,
EITHER IN SPEECH OR IN WRITING.
IT WAS EXPECTED THAT NEWSPEAK WOULD HAVE FINALLY
SUPERCEDED OLDSPEAK
(OR STANDARD ENGLISH, AS WE SHOULD CALL IT)
BY ABOUT THE YEAR 2050.
```

then the written text on lines of 30 spaces should look like this:

```
THE PRINCIPLES OF NEWSPEAK

        NEWSPEAK     WAS      THE
OFFICIAL LANGUAGE  OF  OCEANIA
AND HAD BEEN DESIGNED TO  MEET
THE   IDEOLOGICAL   NEEDS    OF
INGSOC.

        IN THE YEAR  1984  THERE
WAS NOT AS YET ANYONE WHO USED
NEWSPEAK AS HIS SOLE MEANS  OF
COMMUNICATION,    EITHER     IN
SPEECH OR IN WRITING.  IT   WAS
EXPECTED THAT  NEWSPEAK  WOULD
HAVE   FINALLY    SUPERCEDED
OLDSPEAK (OR STANDARD ENGLISH,
AS WE SHOULD CALL IT) BY ABOUT
THE YEAR 2050.
```

Solution

This is one of those problems in which close inspection of the specification reveals possibilities for simplification. A little thought should convince you that there is nothing special about the treatment of punctuation. If we combine each punctuation mark with the preceding word as a single character string, then our program will meet the output specification without taking any special account of punctuation. Therefore, we shall treat any sequence of non-blank characters in the input text as a single "word".

 The nature of the problem suggests that the heart of Level 1 will be some sort of loop. As always, the first question we must answer is "What should be done during each repetition of the loop?" A number of answers are possible:

(a) deal with a single character;
(b) deal with a single word;
(c) generate a complete line of output;
(d) deal with a complete paragraph.

Surely option (a) can be rejected immediately, since the action to be taken on each character read will vary wildly according to circumstances, such as whether the character is blank or non-blank.

Option (b) is quite attractive: the input text can be viewed as a sequence of words (counting /PAR/ as a word), so it is natural to use a loop which processes one word per repetition.

Option (c) is less attractive: although the output text may be viewed as a sequence of lines, this partitioning is not at all apparent in the input text.

Option (d) like option (b) is quite attractive, for both the input and the output texts may equally naturally be viewed as sequences of paragraphs. As each paragraph in turn contains a number of words, a nested loop will be necessary to deal with individual words.

A good guiding principle in such circumstances is to opt for the solution which most accurately reflects the structures of both the input and the output data. Here it is not immediately clear whether option (b) or option (d) is better.

An experienced programmer might be able to choose between the alternatives by thinking ahead, mentally making one or two further refinements in each case, and judging which alternative will lead to the better solution. {This is much the same mental process as that adopted by a chessplayer, who must choose between alternative moves by thinking ahead a few moves and judging which alternative will lead to the better position.} Until we learn such foresight, we are forced to try both alternatives in turn and compare the results. {This, at least, is a strategy denied to chessplayers!}

Level 1b

```
BEGIN
read the line width and make sure it is sensible ;
attempt to read a word ;
WHILE we have a word DO
   BEGIN
   IF the word is "/PAR/" THEN
      start a new paragraph
   ELSE
      output the word followed by a blank, right-adjusting
         the old line and starting a new line if necessary ;
   attempt to read a word
   END
END .
```

The wording "attempt to read a word" is a self-reminder. Even when EOF(INPUT) is FALSE, we cannot be sure that the remainder of the input text contains any words; it might be all blanks. This also explains why "attempt to read a word" must be obeyed before entering the loop, and subsequently at the end of each repetition.

Level 1d

```
BEGIN
read the line width and make sure it is sensible ;
attempt to read a word ;
WHILE we have a word DO
   BEGIN
   IF the word is "/PAR/" THEN
      BEGIN
      start a new paragraph ;
      attempt to read a word
      END ;
   process a paragraph
   END
END .
```

Since "process a paragraph" in Level 1d is "bigger" than anything in Level 1b, we shall refine it first.

Refinement 1d.1: process a paragraph

This involves processing a number of words (possibly none) up to the end of the input text or the start of the next paragraph, whichever comes sooner.

```
WHILE we have a word AND the word is not "/PAR/" DO
   BEGIN
   output the word followed by a blank, right-adjusting
      the old line and starting a new line if necessary ;
   attempt to read a word
   END
```

Level 2d

This is obtained by substituting Refinement 1d.1 into Level 1d:

```
BEGIN
read the line width and make sure it is sensible ;
attempt to read a word ;
WHILE we have a word DO
    BEGIN
    IF the word is "/PAR/" THEN
        BEGIN
        start a new paragraph ;
        attempt to read a word
        END ;
    (* process a paragraph *)
        WHILE we have a word AND the word is not "/PAR/" DO
            BEGIN
            output the word followed by a blank, right-adjusting
                the old line and starting a new line if necessary ;
            attempt to read a word
            END
    END
END .
```

The elements in Level 2d which remain to be refined are similar
to those in Level 1b, but it is clear that the latter is a more
concise solution, and it is Level 1b (henceforth labelled simply
Level 1) which we shall adopt.

Testing Level 1

Let us hand-test Level 1 with the example data. The following table
shows each word read followed by the current line of output after
dealing with that word (Ø denotes a blank).

Word	Current line of output
THE	THEØ
PRINCIPLES	THEØPRINCIPLESØ
OF	THEØPRINCIPLESØOFØ
NEWSPEAK	THEØPRINCIPLESØOFØNEWSPEAKØ
/PAR/	ØØØØØØ

{This is the start of a new paragraph.}

NEWSPEAK	ØØØØØØNEWSPEAKØ
WAS	ØØØØØØNEWSPEAKØWASØ
THE	ØØØØØØNEWSPEAKØWASØTHEØ
OFFICIAL	OFFICIALØ

{The previous line, already 23 characters long,
cannot accomodate the word "OFFICIAL", so it will
have been right-adjusted in some way, and a new line
started.}

230

```
LANGUAGE       OFFICIALØLANGUAGEØ
  ...
  ...
  ...
YEAR           THEØYEARØ
2050.          THEØYEARØ2050.
```

There being no more words, the program terminates.

Refinements from Level 1

Refinement 1.1: output the word followed by a blank, right-
adjusting the old line and starting a new line if
necessary

```
BEGIN
IF the word will not fit into the current line THEN
   BEGIN
   right-adjust the current line ;
   start a new line
   END ;
append the word to the current line ;
IF a blank will fit into the current line THEN
   append a blank to the current line
END
```

Notice that there is no need to take immediate action if there is
no room for the blank: the next word (if there is one) will
certainly start a new line.

Testing Refinement 1.1

Assume that the line width is 30 and that the current line contains
24 characters. The following table shows the contents of the
current line after dealing with each of several words of varying
length.

Word	Current line of output	Length
THE	????????????????????????THEØ	28
MEANS	??????????????????????????MEANSØ	30

{The next word, if any, will force this line to be
right-adjusted.}

ANYONE	??????????????????????????ANYONE	30

{There was no room for the blank. Again, the next
word, if any, will force this line out.}

{The word is too long to fit into the current line. The current line is right-adjusted, and a new line is started before appending the word.}

Level 2

This is obtained by substituting Refinement 1.1 into Level 1:

```
BEGIN
read the line width and make sure it is sensible ;
attempt to read a word ;
WHILE we have a word DO
   BEGIN
   IF the word is "/PAR/" THEN
      start a new paragraph
   ELSE
      (* output the word followed by a blank, right-adjusting
          the old line and starting a new line if necessary *)
         BEGIN
         IF the word will not fit into the current line
         THEN
            BEGIN
            right-adjust the current line ;
            start a new line
            END ;
         append the word to the current line ;
         IF a blank will fit into the current line THEN
            append a blank to the current line
         END ;
   attempt to read a word
   END
END .
```


Refinements from Level 2

We must now decide how to organize the output. The most important point to observe is that we must not write individual words immediately they are appended to the line, because that would make it impossible to go back and insert extra blanks between words when it is necessary to right-adjust the line. Therefore we must keep the current line of output in store until we are ready to right-adjust it. The most natural representation for the current line is a string, LINE. This forces us to choose an upper limit on the line width, but then the paper on which we are writing will have a limited width anyway! We must be able to tell whether a word will fit into the current line, so we need a variable, POSITION, to keep track of the number of characters placed in the line. We also need a variable, LINEWIDTH, to hold the line width.

We now decide on the representation of each word. We are interested in the word's spelling, of course, but also its length, so that we may easily predict whether it will fit into the current line. The spelling can be stored left-justified in a string, as usual, and should be padded out with blanks to facilitate word comparison (see Refinement 2.7). The spelling and length can neatly be combined into a record, WORD.

We introduce the global declarations

```
WORD : RECORD
          SPELLING : PACKED ARRAY [1..MAXWORDLENGTH] OF CHAR ;
          LENGTH   : 0..MAXWORDLENGTH
       END ;
LINE       : PACKED ARRAY [1..MAXLINEWIDTH] OF CHAR ;
POSITION   : 0..MAXLINEWIDTH ;
LINEWIDTH : INTEGER
```

where MAXWORDLENGTH and MAXLINEWIDTH are appropriately defined constants.

Refinement 2.1: append the word to the current line

```
PROCEDURE APPENDWORD ;
   VAR
      POS : 1..MAXLINEWIDTH ;
   BEGIN
   FOR POS := 1 TO WORD.LENGTH DO
      BEGIN
      POSITION := POSITION + 1 ;
      LINE[POSITION] := WORD.SPELLING[POS]
      END
   END (* APPENDWORD *)
```

Refinement 2.2: append a blank to the current line

```
PROCEDURE APPENDBLANK ;
   BEGIN
   POSITION := POSITION + 1 ;
   LINE[POSITION] := BLANK
   END (* APPENDBLANK *)
```

Refinement 2.3: start a new line

```
PROCEDURE STARTLINE ;
   BEGIN
   POSITION := 0
   END (* STARTLINE *)
```

Refinement 2.4: start a new paragraph

```
PROCEDURE STARTPARAGRAPH ;
   CONST
      INDENT = 6 ;
   BEGIN
   write the current line without adjustment ;
   WRITELN ;
   FOR POSITION := 1 TO INDENT DO  LINE[POSITION] := BLANK ;
   POSITION := INDENT
   END (* STARTPARAGRAPH *)
```

Since Refinements 2.1 to 2.4 all introduce messy details which are best kept away from the main program body, we have wrapped each of them up as a procedure.

We could have chosen to make WORD a parameter to procedure APPENDWORD. Since this particular program deals with only one word at a time, however, we have allowed APPENDWORD to access the global variable WORD directly.

Refinement 2.5: the word will not fit into the current line

Refinement 2.6: a blank will fit into the current line

We can take advantage of the similarity of Refinements 2.5 and 2.6 by introducing a function:

```
FUNCTION ROOMFOR ( NMROFCHARS : INTEGER ) : BOOLEAN ;
   BEGIN
   ROOMFOR := POSITION + NMROFCHARS <= LINEWIDTH
   END (* ROOMFOR *)
```

Now, for example, "the word will not fit into the current line" refines to NOT ROOMFOR(WORD.LENGTH).

Refinement 2.7: the word is "/PAR/"

```
WORD.SPELLING = '/PAR/'
```

Level 3

This is obtained by substituting these refinements into Level 2.

234

```
CONST
   BLANK         = ' ' ;
   MAXWORDLENGTH = 21 ;      (* allows for punctuation *)
   MAXLINEWIDTH  = 80 ;      (* assumed paper width *)
VAR
   WORD : RECORD
             SPELLING : PACKED ARRAY [1..MAXWORDLENGTH] OF CHAR;
             LENGTH   : 0..MAXWORDLENGTH
          END ;
   LINE       : PACKED ARRAY [1..MAXLINEWIDTH] OF CHAR ;
   POSITION   : 0..MAXLINEWIDTH ;
   LINEWIDTH  : INTEGER ;


PROCEDURE APPENDWORD ;
   ....................
   .................... (* as above *)
   ....................


PROCEDURE APPENDBLANK ;
   ....................
   .................... (* as above *)
   ....................


PROCEDURE STARTLINE ;
   ....................
   .................... (* as above *)
   ....................


PROCEDURE STARTPARAGRAPH ;
   ....................
   .................... (* as above *)
   ....................


FUNCTION ROOMFOR ( NMROFCHARS : INTEGER ) : BOOLEAN ;
   ....................
   .................... (* as above *)
   ....................
```

```
BEGIN (* TEXTFORMATTER *)
read LINEWIDTH and make sure it is sensible ;
attempt to read a word into WORD ;
WHILE we have a word DO
    BEGIN
    IF WORD.SPELLING = '/PAR/          ' THEN
        STARTPARAGRAPH
    ELSE
        (* output the word followed by a blank, right-adjusting
            the old line and starting a new line if necessary *)
        BEGIN
        IF NOT ROOMFOR(WORD.LENGTH) THEN
            BEGIN
            right-justify the current line ;
            STARTLINE
            END ;
        APPENDWORD ;
        IF ROOMFOR(1) THEN
            APPENDBLANK
        END ;
    attempt to read a word into WORD
    END
END .
```

Testing Level 3

Refinements 2.1 to 2.6 being so short, there is little point in testing them individually. Instead we should test the whole of Level 3.

We should now discover an error almost immediately! When we attempt to output the first word of the text, we will find that POSITION is initially undefined. Our mistake was omitting to include "start a new line" in the initialization sequence, as far back as Level 1; the mistake has become apparent only now because we did not realize previously that "start a new line" would involve (re-)initializing a variable. Go back and insert "start a new line" before the main loop in Levels 1 and 2, and STARTLINE in Level 3.

If we hand-test Level 3 exhaustively, then we will discover another error (or perhaps we may be alerted to it by the discovery of the previous error!). The very last line of the output text is not written! Go back and insert "write the current line without adjustment" after the main loop in Levels 1, 2 and 3.

Refinements from Level 3

The remaining refinements are concerned with input and output.

Refinement 3.1:   read LINEWIDTH and make sure it is sensible

```
READLN (LINEWIDTH) ;
IF LINEWIDTH < MAXWORDLENGTH THEN
   LINEWIDTH := MAXWORDLENGTH
ELSE IF LINEWIDTH > MAXLINEWIDTH THEN
   LINEWIDTH := MAXLINEWIDTH
```

Refinement 3.2:   attempt to read a word into WORD

This is identical to Example 13.3, apart from the representation of the word, so a little adaptation of procedure READWORD is all that is necessary. The adapted procedure could have a single variable parameter, WORD, but since this program deals with only one word at a time, we shall just let WORD be global to the procedure.

Refinement 3.3:   we have a word

As a consequence of the way procedure READWORD has been programmed, we can refine this simply as

```
WORD.LENGTH <> 0
```

Refinement 3.4:   write the current line without adjustment

```
PROCEDURE BREAKLINE ;
   VAR
      POS : 1..MAXLINEWIDTH ;
   BEGIN
   FOR POS := 1 TO POSITION DO
      WRITE (LINE[POSITION]) ;
   WRITELN
   END (* BREAKLINE *)
```

Refinement 3.5:   right-adjust the current line

We have a line of characters which is to be expanded to a width of LINEWIDTH characters exactly. This is achieved by distributing extra blanks as evenly as possible among the inter-word gaps on the line. The specification is deliberately vague about this distribution, so we are free to choose a strategy which is easy to implement.

Let us consider each gap in turn: if NMROFGAPS is the number of gaps not yet widened, and EXTRABLANKS is the number of blanks remaining to be distributed, then we can widen the gap under consideration by (EXTRABLANKS DIV NMROFGAPS) blanks and then decrease EXTRABLANKS accordingly. It is easy to prove that this distribution expands the line to exactly LINEWIDTH characters.

If, moreover, we scan the line (and its gaps) from left to right, then we can write the words and the widened gaps as we deal with them, so there is no need to shift characters within LINE itself.

There may be a blank at the end of the current line (if APPENDBLANK was obeyed more recently than APPENDWORD) - if so, this blank is to be discarded. There may also be some blanks at the beginning of the current line (if the line is the first of a paragraph) - if so, these blanks are not to be considered as a gap to be widened. We shall find it convenient to introduce two variables, LEFTMOST and RIGHTMOST, and make them indicate the first and last non-blank characters of the line.

```
PROCEDURE ADJUSTLINE ;
   VAR
      EXTRABLANKS,
         NMROFGAPS, WIDENING    : 0..MAXLINEWIDTH ;
      LEFTMOST, RIGHTMOST, POS : 1..MAXLINEWIDTH ;
   BEGIN
   make LEFTMOST the position of the leftmost non-blank ;
   make RIGHTMOST the position of the rightmost non-blank ;
   make NMROFGAPS the number of inter-word gaps ;
   EXTRABLANKS := LINEWIDTH - RIGHTMOST ;
   FOR POS := 1 TO RIGHTMOST DO
      IF there is an inter-word gap at position POS THEN
         BEGIN
         WIDENING := EXTRABLANKS DIV NMROFGAPS ;
         write (WIDENING+1) blanks ;
         EXTRABLANKS := EXTRABLANKS - WIDENING ;
         NMROFGAPS := NMROFGAPS - 1
         END
      ELSE
         WRITE (LINE[POS]) ;
   WRITELN
   END (* ADJUSTLINE *)
```

Testing Refinement 3.5

The test cases to be considered are:
(a) a line which is the first line of a paragraph;
(b) a line which is not the first of a paragraph;
(c) a line which is already completely filled;
(d) a line which requires extra blanks between words;
(e) a line with only one word.

Test case (a) is considered here. The rest are left to you as an exercise. Test case (e) is of particular interest; does ADJUSTLINE deal with this case satisfactorily?

Suppose that LINEWIDTH=30, that POSITION=29, and that the first 29 characters of LINE are

ƁƁƁƁƁƁINƁTHEƁYEARƁ1984ƁTHEREƁ

Then LEFTMOST should be set to 7 and RIGHTMOST to 28. Thus EXTRABLANKS is set to 2. Counting the inter-word gaps should set NMROFGAPS to 4 (since the leading blanks do not count as a gap). As we go round the loop, we write "␢␢␢␢␢␢IN" before coming to the first gap. We calculate WIDENING=0, so we write 1 blank, EXTRABLANKS remains at 2, and NMROFGAPS is decremented to 3. After further writing "THE" we come to the second gap. We calculate WIDENING=0, so we write 1 blank, EXTRABLANKS remains at 2, and NMROFGAPS is decremented to 2. After further writing "YEAR" we come to the third gap. This time we calculate WIDENING=1, so we write 2 blanks, EXTRABLANKS is reduced to 1, and NMROFGAPS is decremented to 1. After further writing "1984" we come to the fourth gap. We calculate WIDENING=1, so we write 2 blanks, and EXTRABLANKS and NMROFGAPS are reduced to 0. After further writing "THERE" the loop terminates. So the written line is

␢␢␢␢␢␢IN␢THE␢YEAR␢␢1984␢␢THERE

Since ADJUSTLINE is self-contained, let us complete its refinement separately.

Refinement 3.5.1: make LEFTMOST the position of the leftmost non-blank

```
LEFTMOST := 1 ;
WHILE LINE[LEFTMOST] = BLANK DO
    LEFTMOST := SUCC(LEFTMOST)
```

Refinement 3.5.2: make RIGHTMOST the position of the rightmost non-blank

```
RIGHTMOST := POSITION ;
WHILE LINE[RIGHTMOST] = BLANK DO
    RIGHTMOST := PRED(RIGHTMOST)
```

Refinement 3.5.3: make NMROFGAPS the number of inter-word gaps

Since exactly one blank has been placed between consecutive words in LINE, this can be done simply by counting the blank characters between the first and last words:

```
NMROFGAPS := 0 ;
FOR POS := LEFTMOST TO RIGHTMOST DO
    IF LINE[POS] = BLANK THEN
        NMROFGAPS := NMROFGAPS + 1
```

Refinement 3.5.4: there is an inter-word gap at position POS

    (POS > LEFTMOST) AND (LINE[POS] = BLANK)

The latter part of this condition is based on the same observation as Refinement 3.5.3. The first part ensures that we are looking at an inter-word gap rather than a blank introduced at the start of a paragraph.

Testing Refinements 3.5.1 to 3.5.4

Test these refinements as an exercise.

Level 4

This is the final program, obtained by substituting these refinements into Level 3.

```
PROGRAM TEXTFORMATTER ( INPUT , OUTPUT ) ;

CONST
   BLANK         = ' ' ;
   MAXWORDLENGTH = 21 ;   (* allows for punctuation *)
   MAXLINEWIDTH  = 80 ;   (* assumed paper width *)
VAR
   WORD : RECORD
                SPELLING : PACKED ARRAY [1..MAXWORDLENGTH] OF CHAR;
                LENGTH   : 0..MAXWORDLENGTH
             END ;
   LINE      : PACKED ARRAY [1..MAXLINEWIDTH] OF CHAR ;
   POSITION  : 0..MAXLINEWIDTH ;
   LINEWIDTH : INTEGER ;

PROCEDURE READWORD ;
   VAR
      CH : CHAR ;
   BEGIN
   (* read past any blanks preceding the next word *)
      CH := BLANK ;
      WHILE NOT EOF(INPUT) AND (CH = BLANK) DO
         READ (CH) ;
```

```
        (* read the word itself *)
        WITH WORD DO
           BEGIN
           LENGTH := 0 ;
           SPELLING := '                    ' ;
           WHILE NOT EOF(INPUT) AND (CH <> BLANK) DO
              BEGIN
              IF LENGTH < MAXWORDLENGTH THEN
                 BEGIN
                 LENGTH := LENGTH + 1 ;
                 SPELLING[LENGTH] := CH
                 END ;
              READ(CH)
              END
           END
    END (* READWORD *) ;

PROCEDURE APPENDWORD ;
   VAR
      POS : 1..MAXWORDLENGTH ;
   BEGIN
   FOR POS := 1 TO WORD.LENGTH DO
      BEGIN
      POSITION := POSITION + 1 ;
      LINE[POSITION] := WORD.SPELLING[POS]
      END
   END (* APPENDWORD *) ;

PROCEDURE APPENDBLANK ;
   BEGIN
   POSITION :- POSITION + 1 ;
   LINE[POSITION] := BLANK
   END (* APPENDBLANK *) ;

PROCEDURE STARTLINE ;
   BEGIN
   POSITION := 0
   END (* STARTLINE *) ;

FUNCTION ROOMFOR ( NMROFCHARS : INTEGER ) : BOOLEAN ;
   BEGIN
   ROOMFOR := POSITION + NMROFCHARS <= LINEWIDTH
   END (* ROOMFOR *) ;
```

```
PROCEDURE BREAKLINE ;
   VAR
      POS : 1..MAXLINEWIDTH ;
   BEGIN
   FOR POS := 1 TO POSITION DO
      WRITE (LINE[POS]) ;
   WRITELN
   END (* BREAKLINE *) ;

PROCEDURE ADJUSTLINE ;
   VAR
      EXTRABLANKS,
         NMROFGAPS, WIDENING   : 0..MAXLINEWIDTH ;
      LEFTMOST, RIGHTMOST, POS : 1..MAXLINEWIDTH ;
   BEGIN
   (* make LEFTMOST the position of the leftmost non-blank *)
      LEFTMOST := 1 ;
      WHILE LINE[LEFTMOST] = BLANK DO
         LEFTMOST := SUCC(LEFTMOST) ;
   (* make RIGHTMOST the position of the rightmost non-blank *)
      RIGHTMOST := POSITION ;
      WHILE LINE[RIGHTMOST] = BLANK DO
         RIGHTMOST := PRED(RIGHTMOST) ;
   (* make NMROFGAPS the number of inter-word gaps *)
      NMROFGAPS := 0 ;
      FOR POS := LEFTMOST TO RIGHTMOST DO
         IF LINE[POS] = BLANK THEN
            NMROFGAPS := NMROFGAPS + 1 ;
   EXTRABLANKS := LINEWIDTH - RIGHTMOST ;
   FOR POS := 1 TO RIGHTMOST DO
      IF (POS > LEFTMOST) AND (LINE[POS] = BLANK)
         (* this character is an inter-word gap *) THEN
         BEGIN
         WIDENING := EXTRABLANKS DIV NMROFGAPS ;
         WRITE (BLANK:(WIDENING+1)) ;
         EXTRABLANKS := EXTRABLANKS - WIDENING ;
         NMROFGAPS := NMROFGAPS - 1
         END
      ELSE
         WRITE (LINE[POS]) ;
   WRITELN
   END (* ADJUSTLINE *) ;
```

```
PROCEDURE STARTPARAGRAPH ;
   CONST
      INDENT = 6 ;
   BEGIN
   (* write the current line without adjustment *)
      BREAKLINE ;
   WRITELN ;
   FOR POSITION := 1 TO INDENT DO  LINE[POSITION] := BLANK ;
   POSITION := INDENT
   END (* STARTPARAGRAPH *) ;

BEGIN (* TEXTFORMATTER *)
(* read LINEWIDTH and make sure it is sensible *)
   READLN (LINEWIDTH) ;
   IF LINEWIDTH < MAXWORDLENGTH THEN
      LINEWIDTH := MAXWORDLENGTH
   ELSE IF LINEWIDTH > MAXLINEWIDTH THEN
      LINEWIDTH := MAXLINEWIDTH ;
STARTLINE ;
(* attempt to read a word into WORD *)
   READWORD ;
WHILE (* we have a word *) WORD.LENGTH <> 0 DO
   BEGIN
   IF WORD.SPELLING = '/PAR/             ' THEN
      STARTPARAGRAPH
   ELSE
      (* output the word followed by a blank, right-adjusting
          the old line and starting a new line if necessary *)
         BEGIN
         IF NOT ROOMFOR(WORD.LENGTH) THEN
            BEGIN
            (* right-justify the current line *)
               ADJUSTLINE ;
            STARTLINE
            END ;
         APPENDWORD ;
         IF ROOMFOR(1) THEN
            APPENDBLANK
         END ;
   (* attempt to read a word into WORD *)
      READWORD
   END ;
(* write the current line without adjustment *)
   BREAKLINE
END .
```

Problem Specification

The transferable vote system is a method of conducting an election in such a way that the successful candidate requires the support of an absolute majority of the voters, even when there are more than two candidates. Instead of voting for just one candidate, each voter is required to complete a ballot placing all the candidates in order of preference. In the first count of votes, only the first choice of each voter is considered. If no candidate obtains an overall majority in this count, then the candidate with the fewest votes is eliminated, and a recount is carried out in which votes cast for the eliminated candidate are ignored, i.e. the second choices of those voters who voted first for the eliminated candidate are now counted. Eliminations and recounts are continued in this way until one candidate has obtained an overall majority (or until all candidates still in contention have exactly equal votes, in which case a tie is declared).

For example, suppose the votes cast in a three-candidate election are as follows:

	1st choice	2nd choice	3rd choice
Voter A	3	1	2
Voter B	2	3	1
Voter C	2	1	3
Voter D	1	3	2
Voter E	2	1	3
Voter F	3	2	1
Voter G	1	3	2
Voter H	3	1	2
Voter I	2	3	1

in which the candidates have been numbered 1, 2 and 3. Then in the first count candidate 1 gets 2 votes, candidate 2 gets 4 votes, and candidate 3 gets 3 votes. There is no overall majority, so candidate 1 is eliminated. Both the voters (D and G) whose first choice was this candidate gave candidate 3 as their second choices, so in the recount candidate 2 gets 4 votes and candidate 3 gets 5 votes. Therefore candidate 3 is the winner.

If after any count several candidates have the same, smallest, number of votes, then any one of them may be eliminated.

Write a program to determine the winner (if any) of a transferable vote election. Assume that each ballot is presented as a single line of input, with the candidate numbers arranged in order of preference as above. Assume that these lines are preceded by a line containing the number of candidates. The program must reject invalid ballots, a valid ballot being one on which every candidate has been placed in exactly one position. (For example, with three candidates, 2 2 1 and 3 1 4 are invalid ballots.)

Solution

The problem specification implies that the ballots are liable to be examined repeatedly, once on each count. Our very first deduction, therefore, is that it will not be sufficient to examine the ballots one by one as they are read in, as in the simpler vote-counting problem of Example 10.1. Instead we must first store all the valid ballots.

The heart of the solution will be a loop in which a candidate is eliminated and the votes are recounted as often as necessary, as required by the specification. This leads us to Level 1:

Level 1

```
VAR
   NMROFCANDIDATES : INTEGER ;
BEGIN
READLN (NMROFCANDIDATES) ;
read all the ballots, storing the valid ones ;
count the votes ;
WHILE there is no overall majority AND
      not all candidates still in contention are exactly tied DO
   BEGIN
   eliminate the candidate with fewest votes ;
   recount the votes, ignoring eliminated candidates
   END ;
IF there is an overall majority THEN
   declare the winner
ELSE
   report an exact tie
END .
```

Testing Level 1

Let us hand-test the logic of Level 1 in all possible cases.
(a) All the candidates have equal votes. In this case we skip the loop; then, since there is no overall majority, we report a tie.
(b) One candidate has an overall majority. In this case also, we skip the loop; this time we declare the winner.
(c) Neither (a) nor (b) applies. Then there must be more than two candidates still in contention. In this case, we enter the loop, eliminate one of the candidates, and recount; this must reduce to case (a) or (b), or to (c) with fewer candidates.
When only two candidates are left, either (a) or (b) must apply. Since we eliminate one candidate on each repetition, therefore, the loop must eventually terminate.

Refinements from Level 1

Now we may proceed to refine Level 1. Sooner or later, we shall have to decide how to store the ballots, but we can postpone this decision until we see how to organize the vote counting and recounting. Always postpone decisions about how to store data until you know how the data will be manipulated!

Refinement 1.1: count the votes

We simply consider each ballot in turn, and credit a vote to the candidate who is the first choice on that ballot.

Before rushing ahead with this refinement, we should examine the refinement of "recount the votes, ignoring eliminated candidates" to see if we can profit from its similarity.

Refinement 1.2: recount the votes, ignoring eliminated candidates

This is similar to 1.1, except that instead of the first-choice candidate every time, we credit the most favoured candidate who has not yet been eliminated.

1.1 is just a special case of 1.2, since initially no candidates will have been eliminated, so we can use the same piece of program. This piece of program will use variables (such as those for accumulating the vote-counts) that will be irrelevant elsewhere, so we should wrap it up as a procedure; this will also save us from substituting the same piece of program in two places in Level 1.

Examining the logic of Level 1, we can see that the following information must be extracted from the vote counting to be used by the rest of the program: (a) the most and least successful candidates still in contention, (b) whether the former obtained an overall majority, and (c) whether all candidates still in contention are tied. This information can be returned through variable-parameters.

```
      PROCEDURE COUNTVOTES ( VAR LEADER, TRAILER : CANDIDATES ;
                             VAR OVERALLMAJORITY,
                                      ALLTIED : BOOLEAN ) ;
        BEGIN
        initialize all vote-counts to 0 ;
        for each valid ballot DO
           BEGIN
           determine the most favoured candidate on this
                    ballot, apart from eliminated candidates ;
           add 1 to this candidate's vote-count
           END ;
        determine which of the candidates still in contention
              received most and least votes, LEADER and TRAILER resp. ;
        OVERALLMAJORITY :=
           candidate LEADER has obtained more than half the votes ;
        ALLTIED :=
           candidates LEADER and TRAILER have obtained equal votes
        END (* COUNTVOTES *)
```

Refinement 1.1: count the votes

    consider all candidates as still in contention ;
    COUNTVOTES(LEADER,TRAILER,OVERALLMAJORITY,ALLTIED)

Refinement 1.2: recount the votes, ignoring eliminated candidates

    COUNTVOTES(LEADER,TRAILER,OVERALLMAJORITY,ALLTIED)

    In these we have assumed the global declarations

    LEADER, TRAILER   : CANDIDATES ;
    OVERALLMAJORITY, ALLTIED : BOOLEAN

The conditions "there is no overall majority" and "there is an
overall majority" can now be expressed in terms of OVERALLMAJORITY,
and "not all candidates still in contention are exactly tied"
refines to NOT ALLTIED.
    The type CANDIDATES will presumably reflect the specified
numbering of the candidates; however, there is no need to define it
more precisely at this stage.

Testing the refinements from Level 1

As an exercise, hand-test Refinements 1.1 and 1.2 using the example
data.

Level 2

This is obtained by substituting these refinements into Level 1. (The complete Level 2 program is omitted here for space reasons. Write it out yourself unless you can visualize it clearly.)

Refinements to Level 2

We cannot proceed any further without deciding how to store the ballots. The most obvious solution, perhaps, is an array each of whose elements contains a single ballot. This solution has the disadvantage that, since an array is fixed in size, it would be necessary to fix some arbitrary upper limit on the number of ballots to be accepted, in order that we can declare an array with that number of elements. But it would be difficult to choose a suitable limit: 1000 would be too small for many elections; even 100000 might not be large enough for some purposes, but it would be grossly wasteful of space when the actual number of ballots is much smaller. A little thought suggests a much better solution: a serial file. A file has the decisive advantage of being (virtually) unlimited in size. If we store the ballots in a file, we will be restricted to examining them one by one in a fixed order, but that is perfectly adequate here: examining the logic of procedure COUNTVOTES, we can see that each ballot is examined once only per count, and that the order of examination of the ballots is irrelevant. Having generated the file, we may scan it from beginning to end as often as required. So we declare

    BALLOTFILE : FILE OF BALLOTS

Each component, of type BALLOTS, will represent a single ballot. At this stage there is still no need to bother about how to represent individual ballots, so we need not define the type BALLOTS just yet.
  Since the file will be generated by the program for its own use, and will not be retained afterwards, BALLOTFILE will not be a program parameter.

Refinement 2.1: read all the ballots, storing the valid ones

We store ballots by writing them to BALLOTFILE. We shall make this refinement into a procedure, since it is naturally self-contained and distinct from the rest of the program. This procedure must return the number of valid ballots, so that the number of votes required for a clear majority can be computed.

```
PROCEDURE READALLBALLOTS
                       ( VAR NMROFVALIDBALLOTS : INTEGER ) ;
   VAR
      BALLOT : BALLOTS ;
   BEGIN
   NMROFVALIDBALLOTS := 0 ;
   REWRITE (BALLOTFILE) ;
   WHILE NOT EOF(INPUT) DO
      BEGIN
      read a single ballot into BALLOT ;
      IF this ballot is valid THEN
         BEGIN
         NMROFVALIDBALLOTS := NMROFVALIDBALLOTS + 1 ;
         WRITE (BALLOTFILE, BALLOT)
         END
      END
   END (* READALLBALLOTS *)
```

Refinement 2.2: for each valid ballot DO BEGIN ..... END

This loop must read BALLOTFILE from beginning to end. If we insert
into procedure COUNTVOTES the local declaration

```
   BALLOT : BALLOTS
```

then we can refine as follows:

```
   RESET (BALLOTFILE) ;
   WHILE NOT EOF(BALLOTFILE) DO
      BEGIN
      READ (BALLOTFILE, BALLOT) ;
      .....
      END
```

Testing the refinements from Level 2

As an exercise, hand-test Refinements 2.1 and 2.2 using suitable
test data.

Level 3

This is obtained by substituting these refinements into Level 2.
(Omitted for space reasons.)

Refinements from Level 3

Now we must decide how to represent an individual ballot, i.e. how
to define the type BALLOTS. Each ballot is a sequence of exactly
NMROFCANDIDATES candidate numbers. The ideal type definition would

be

```
BALLOTS = ARRAY [1..NMROFCANDIDATES] OF CANDIDATES
```

but unfortunately Pascal does not allow this, since NMROFCANDIDATES
is a variable! {Some programming languages, such as Algol and PL/I,
do allow arrays to have their size determined by variables. Such
arrays are called dynamic arrays.} If, however, we agree on a fixed
limit on the number of candidates, say MAXCANDIDATES = 10, then we
can define the types

```
CANDIDATES = 1..MAXCANDIDATES ;
PLACINGS   = 1..MAXCANDIDATES ;
BALLOTS    = ARRAY [PLACINGS] OF CANDIDATES
```

and only the first NMROFCANDIDATES elements of each array of type
BALLOTS will actually be used.

Refinement 3.1: read a single ballot into BALLOT

This consists of reading NMROFCANDIDATES numbers from a line of
input. Declaring a local variable

```
PLACE : PLACINGS
```

we refine as follows:

```
FOR PLACE := 1 TO NMROFCANDIDATES DO
   READ (BALLOT[PLACE]) ;
READLN
```

Refinement 3.2: this ballot is valid

A ballot is valid if (a) it contains no numbers outside the range 1
to NMROFCANDIDATES, and (b) each candidate number occurs just once.
The latter can be checked most easily by declaring

```
ALREADYCHOSEN : ARRAY [CANDIDATES] OF BOOLEAN
```

and initializing all elements to FALSE; for each candidate number
CHOICE on the ballot, we first check that ALREADYCHOSEN[CHOICE] is
still FALSE, then we set it to TRUE.
   This checking can be done most conveniently while the ballot is
being read in. In fact, we should have included check (a) in
Refinement 3.1 in the first place, since an invalid candidate number
such as 0 cannot properly be assigned to BALLOT[PLACE], which is of
type CANDIDATES = 1..MAXCANDIDATES. So let us revise Refinement
3.1.

Refinement 3.1: read a single ballot into BALLOT (revised)

Since this piece of program contains details and variables (notably
ALREADYCHOSEN) of no interest elsewhere, it should be wrapped up as
a procedure.

```
PROCEDURE READONEBALLOT ( VAR BALLOT : BALLOTS ;
                          VAR VALID  : BOOLEAN ) ;
   VAR
      CHOICE        : INTEGER ;
      PLACE         : PLACINGS ;
      ALREADYCHOSEN : ARRAY [CANDIDATES] OF BOOLEAN ;
   BEGIN
   VALID := TRUE ;
   FOR CHOICE := 1 TO NMROFCANDIDATES DO
      ALREADYCHOSEN[CHOICE] := FALSE ;
   FOR PLACE := 1 TO NMROFCANDIDATES DO
      BEGIN
      READ (CHOICE) ;
      IF (CHOICE < 1) OR (CHOICE > NMROFCANDIDATES) THEN
         VALID := FALSE
      ELSE IF ALREADYCHOSEN[CHOICE] THEN
         VALID := FALSE
      ELSE
         BEGIN
         BALLOT[PLACE] := CHOICE ;
         ALREADYCHOSEN[CHOICE] := TRUE
         END
      END ;
   READLN
   END (* READONEBALLOT *)
```

Refinement 3.2 is now trivial.

Refinement 3.3: determine the most favoured candidate on this
ballot, ignoring eliminated candidates

In refinement 2.2 we decided to store the ballot in the local
variable BALLOT. If we further declare the local variables

```
PLACE       : PLACINGS ;
MOSTFAVOURED : CANDIDATES
```

we can refine as follows:

```
PLACE := 1 ;
WHILE the candidate placed in BALLOT[PLACE]
      is one who has already been eliminated DO
   PLACE := SUCC(PLACE) ;
MOSTFAVOURED := BALLOT[PLACE]
```

This is an example of linear search. Notice that the loop condition does not include the usual "AND (PLACE <= NMROFCANDIDATES)". This is unnecessary here because at least two of BALLOT[1], ..., BALLOT[NMROFCANDIDATES] will be candidates who have not been eliminated, provided that the ballot is valid. Examination of the program logic shows that only valid ballots are considered by procedure COUNTVOTES.

Testing the refinements from Level 3

As an exercise, hand-test Refinements 3.1 and 3.3 using suitable test data.

Level 4

This is obtained by substituting these refinements into Level 3. (Omitted for space reasons.)

Refinements from Level 4

The remaining refinements are fairly straightforward. We can keep track of which candidates have been eliminated using the globally declared array

    ELIMINATED : ARRAY [CANDIDATES] OF BOOLEAN

Refinement 4.1: the candidate placed in BALLOT[PLACE] is one who has already been eliminated

    ELIMINATED[BALLOT[PLACE]]

Refinement 4.2: consider all candidates as still in contention

    FOR CONTENDER := 1 TO NMROFCANDIDATES DO
        ELIMINATED[CONTENDER] := FALSE

Refinement 4.3: eliminate the candidate with fewest votes

    ELIMINATED[TRAILER] := TRUE

Refinement 4.4: initialize all vote-counts to 0

Refinement 4.5: add 1 to this candidate's vote-count

Both these refinements can be borrowed directly from Example 10.1. We introduce the local declaration

```
COUNT : ARRAY [CANDIDATES] OF INTEGER
```

Refinement 4.6: determine which of the candidates still in
contention received most and least votes, LEADER
and TRAILER resp.

This amounts to locating the maximum and minimum of COUNT[1], ...,
COUNT[NMROFCANDIDATES], ignoring candidates who have been
eliminated.

```
        LEADERSCOUNT := 0 ;
        TRAILERSCOUNT := NMROFVALIDBALLOTS ;
        FOR CONTENDER := 1 TO NMROFCANDIDATES DO
            IF NOT ELIMINATED[CONTENDER] THEN
                BEGIN
                IF COUNT[CONTENDER] > COUNT[LEADER] THEN
                    BEGIN
                    LEADER := CONTENDER ;
                    LEADERSCOUNT := COUNT[LEADER]
                    END ;
                IF COUNT[CONTENDER] < COUNT[TRAILER] THEN
                    BEGIN
                    TRAILER := CONTENDER ;
                    TRAILERSCOUNT := COUNT[TRAILER]
                    END
                END
```

LEADERSCOUNT and TRAILERSCOUNT will be local INTEGER variables.
Their initial values have been chosen such that they are certain to
be altered, so that at the same time LEADER and TRAILER will receive
values.

The expressions "candidate LEADER has obtained more than half the
votes" and "candidates LEADER and TRAILER have obtained equal votes"
can easily be expressed in terms of LEADERSCOUNT and TRAILERSCOUNT.

Testing the Refinements from Level 4

As an exercise, hand-test Refinement 4.6 using suitable test data.

Level 5

This is obtained by substituting these refinements, and one or two
remaining minor ones, into Level 4, yielding the final program.

```
PROGRAM TRANSFERABLEVOTES ( INPUT, OUTPUT ) ;

CONST
   MAXCANDIDATES = 10 ;
TYPE
   CANDIDATES = 1..MAXCANDIDATES ;
   PLACINGS   = 1..MAXCANDIDATES ;
   BALLOTS    = ARRAY [PLACINGS] OF CANDIDATES ;
VAR
   BALLOTFILE                 : FILE OF BALLOTS ;
   NMROFCANDIDATES            : INTEGER ;
   NMROFVALIDBALLOTS          : INTEGER ;
   OVERALLMAJORITY, ALLTIED   : BOOLEAN ;
   LEADER, TRAILER, CONTENDER : CANDIDATES ;
   ELIMINATED : ARRAY [CANDIDATES] OF BOOLEAN ;

PROCEDURE COUNTVOTES ( VAR LEADER, TRAILER : CANDIDATES ;
                       VAR OVERALLMAJORITY,
                                      ALLTIED : BOOLEAN ) ;
   VAR
      COUNT  : ARRAY [CANDIDATES] OF INTEGER ;
      BALLOT : BALLOTS ;
      PLACE  : PLACINGS ;
      MOSTFAVOURED, CONTENDER    : CANDIDATES ;
      LEADERSCOUNT, TRAILERSCOUNT : INTEGER ;
   BEGIN
   (*   initialize all vote-counts to 0 *)
      FOR CONTENDER := 1 TO NMROFCANDIDATES DO
          COUNT[CONTENDER] := 0 ;
   RESET (BALLOTFILE) ;
   WHILE NOT EOF(BALLOTFILE) DO
      BEGIN
      READ (BALLOTFILE, BALLOT) ;
      (* determine the most favoured candidate on this
              ballot, apart from eliminated candidates *)
          PLACE := 1 ;
          WHILE ELIMINATED[BALLOT[PLACE]] DO
             PLACE := SUCC(PLACE) ;
          MOSTFAVOURED := BALLOT[PLACE] ;
      (* add 1 to this candidate's vote-count *)
          COUNT[MOSTFAVOURED] := COUNT[MOSTFAVOURED] + 1
      END ;
```

```
          (* determine which of the candidates still in contention
                            received most and least votes *)
          LEADERSCOUNT := 0 ;
          TRAILERSCOUNT := NMROFVALIDBALLOTS ;
          FOR CONTENDER := 1 TO NMROFCANDIDATES DO
              IF NOT ELIMINATED[CONTENDER] THEN
                  BEGIN
                  IF COUNT[CONTENDER] > COUNT[LEADER] THEN
                      BEGIN
                      LEADER := CONTENDER ;
                      LEADERSCOUNT := COUNT[LEADER]
                      END ;
                  IF COUNT[CONTENDER] < COUNT[TRAILER] THEN
                      BEGIN
                      TRAILER := CONTENDER ;
                      TRAILERSCOUNT := COUNT[TRAILER]
                      END
                  END ;
      OVERALLMAJORITY :=
              LEADERSCOUNT > NMROFVALIDBALLOTS DIV 2 ;
      ALLTIED := LEADERSCOUNT = TRAILERSCOUNT
      END (* COUNTVOTES *) ;


PROCEDURE READALLBALLOTS
                    ( VAR NMROFVALIDBALLOTS : INTEGER ) ;
      VAR
          BALLOT : BALLOTS ;
          VALID  : BOOLEAN ;

      PROCEDURE READONEBALLOT ( VAR BALLOT : BALLOTS ;
                                VAR VALID  : BOOLEAN ) ;
          VAR
              CHOICE        : INTEGER ;
              PLACE         : PLACINGS ;
              ALREADYCHOSEN : ARRAY [CANDIDATES] OF BOOLEAN ;
```

```
      BEGIN
      VALID := TRUE ;
      FOR CHOICE := 1 TO NMROFCANDIDATES DO
         ALREADYCHOSEN[CHOICE] := FALSE ;
      FOR PLACE := 1 TO NMROFCANDIDATES DO
         BEGIN
         READ (CHOICE) ;
         IF (CHOICE < 1) OR
               (CHOICE > NMROFCANDIDATES) THEN
            VALID := FALSE
         ELSE IF ALREADYCHOSEN[CHOICE] THEN
            VALID := FALSE
         ELSE
            BEGIN
            BALLOT[PLACE] := CHOICE ;
            ALREADYCHOSEN[CHOICE] := TRUE
            END
         END ;
      READLN
      END (* READONEBALLOT *) ;

   BEGIN (* READALLBALLOTS *)
   NMROFVALIDBALLOTS := 0 ;
   REWRITE (BALLOTFILE) ;
   WHILE NOT EOF(INPUT) DO
      BEGIN
      (* read a single ballot *)
         READONEBALLOT(BALLOT,VALID) ;
      IF VALID THEN
         BEGIN
         NMROFVALIDBALLOTS := NMROFVALIDBALLOTS + 1 ;
         WRITE (BALLOTFILE, BALLOT)
         END
      END
   END (* READALLBALLOTS *) ;

BEGIN (* TRANSFERABLEVOTES *)
READLN (NMROFCANDIDATES) ;
(* read all the ballots, storing the valid ones *)
   READALLBALLOTS (NMROFVALIDBALLOTS) ;
(* count the votes *)
   (* consider all candidates as still in contention *)
      FOR CONTENDER := 1 TO NMROFCANDIDATES DO
         ELIMINATED[CONTENDER] := FALSE ;
   COUNTVOTES(LEADER,TRAILER,OVERALLMAJORITY,ALLTIED) ;
```

```
WHILE NOT OVERALLMAJORITY AND NOT ALLTIED DO
    BEGIN
    (* eliminate the candidate with fewest votes *)
        ELIMINATED[TRAILER] := TRUE ;
    (* recount the votes, ignoring eliminated candidates *)
        COUNTVOTES(LEADER,TRAILER,OVERALLMAJORITY,ALLTIED)
    END ;
IF OVERALLMAJORITY THEN
    (* declare the winner *)
        WRITELN ('WINNER IS CANDIDATE ', LEADER:2)
ELSE
    (* report an exact tie *)
        BEGIN
        WRITE ('TIE AMONG THE FOLLOWING CANDIDATES: ') ;
        FOR CONTENDER := 1 TO NMROFCANDIDATES DO
            IF NOT ELIMINATED[CONTENDER] THEN
                WRITE (CONTENDER:2, ' ') ;
        WRITELN
        END
END .
```

20.4 SOME GENERAL PRINCIPLES

Let us see what lessons we have learnt from the case studies, and what
general principles can be stated about the practice of programming by
stepwise refinement. Refer back to the case studies to see what these
principles mean and how they are applied.

Design decisions and refinements

Whenever we choose a particular algorithm to perform some task, and
whenever we introduce a variable and/or choose a type for a variable, we
are making what is called a design decision. All but the most trivial
programming problems involve a number of design decisions. Moreover,
these design decisions are generally inter-dependent, so it is important
that design decisions be taken, and documented, in a systematic manner.
That is what programming by stepwise refinement is all about.

When we refine a command, we are deciding how the command is to be
performed, having previously been interested only in what the command
was supposed to do. Refinement consists of breaking the command down
into simpler commands, some of which may be Pascal statements. How we
refine the command will depend on the nature of the command.

(a) We may refine the command into a sequence of simpler commands to be
    executed one after the other. Here the appropriate notation is the
    compound statement. An example of this is Refinement 2.4 of Case
    Study II.
(b) We may refine the command into some sort of selective action. Here

the appropriate notation is the IF statement or the CASE statement. This can be seen in Refinement 1.1 of Case Study II.

(c) We may refine the command into a loop in which some simpler command(s) are performed repeatedly. Here the appropriate notation is the WHILE statement, the FOR statement, or the REPEAT statement. Usually the loop must be preceded by some sort of initialization. The introduction of a loop can be seen in Refinement 1.2 of Case Study III (one of many examples).

When you choose a refinement of form (a), be sure that the simpler commands really can be executed strictly one after the other. A common mistake is (for example) to make the following initial refinement of the text formatting problem (Case Study II):

```
BEGIN
read the line width and make sure it is sensible ;
read the input text ;
write the output text left- and right-justified
END .
```

which would imply that the whole of the input text is to be read and stored before anything is written. If it is intended to store only one word at a time, then the reading and writing must be interleaved, so a loop is more appropriate in this case.

The decision to introduce a variable and to choose a type for it may seem to be so minor that you might take it almost unconciously, especially if it is a simple variable. Probably you will be more careful about the selection of a data structure, such as an array. Yet all such decisions may be highly significant, and they deserve to be considered carefully.

An example of a design decision of this kind was the decision, in Case Study II, to keep each line of output in store until it was (almost) filled, and for this purpose to introduce a string variable, LINE, accompanied by a count of the number of characters in the line, POSITION. This decision influenced the refinements of all the commands concerned with output (Refinements 2.1-2.6).

Data structures can be subjected to successive refinement in the same way as commands. Case Study III provided a good example of this. After studying Level 2 of that program, we decided that the most satisfactory way to store the ballots would be in a file, and on this basis we made Refinements 2.1 and 2.2. It was neither necessary nor desirable at that stage to decide on the representation of the individual ballots, i.e. to decide the component type of the file. If we had made the latter decision prematurely, we would have introduced too many details into Level 3.

Introducing details too early is always to be avoided. The whole point of programming by stepwise refinement is to delay every design decision as long as possible. It is often possible, for example, to refine many commands without making any commitment on how to store the data on which these commands operate. This allows us to delay choosing the best way of storing the data until we can see exactly what operations are to be performed on the data. Again Case Study III offers a good illustration of this point. If we had rushed into a premature decision about how to store the set of ballots, we might well have chosen a two-dimensional array. By delaying this decision until Level 2, we were able to see clearly that the ballots would be examined one at a time, in an arbitrary order, and so to decide that a serial file would be perfectly satisfactory.

As another example, suppose that the text formatting problem were modified so that the output lines were not to be right-adjusted, but were still to be restricted to the specified line width. Even with this modification, Level 1 and Level 2 would be unchanged (except for a re-wording of one of the commands). At this point, however, we should realize that there is no need to keep the current output line in store; we can write the words as soon as they are designated for output. This, a decision not to introduce a variable, is a design decision just as important as any other!

Backtracking and thinking ahead

In Case Study II we saw an example of a situation in which we had to choose between alternative refinements. When it is not immediately clear which refinement is preferable, it is best to try each possibility in turn, refining one or two levels down in each case. This should make it clear which refinement is to be preferred.

Actually, you will often be able to avoid this extra work by thinking ahead a level or two, visualizing roughly the consequences of each alternative refinement, and thus choose the most suitable refinement without trying out inferior refinements on paper. Your ability to think ahead successfully will improve as you accumulate programming experience.

No amount of programming experience, however, guarantees against making refinements which later prove to be unsatisfactory in some respect, for example leading to a program which is wasteful of time or storage space. Then it is necessary to backtrack, to isolate the design decision which has proved to be inappropriate and to undo all the refinements consequent upon that decision.

The time spent in backtracking and improving on earlier design decisions should not be regarded as having been wasted; it is part of the essential experience of every programmer. Even the most skilled programmers often find that, having solved a problem apparently satisfactorily, they can devise a better solution by starting again from scratch!

Documentation

When you have completed the development of a program, you will have on paper a complete record of the various levels of your program and the refinements of individual program fragments. This material forms a part of the documentation of the program, and if well done it will prove valuable to other programmers who wish to understand your program, perhaps with a view to modifying it. The same applies to the comments in the program, which should reflect the way in which the program was refined.

Correcting errors

Suppose that you have "completed" your program, but testing reveals a logical error, e.g. the program terminates prematurely, or it produces incorrect results. Or perhaps, more fortunately, you discover the error at an earlier stage, by hand-testing your program at a higher level.

It is as important to be systematic in correcting an error as in developing the program in the first place. Always backtrack to the level at which the error was introduced, and systematically correct the error at each level down to the final program.

What you must not do is to attempt to correct the error by chopping and changing the final program without regard to the way the program was developed. At best, you will succeed in correcting the error but you will leave the documentation of the program (the refinements written on paper and the comments in the program itself) out-of-date. This documentation will then be useless to anyone else, and even to yourself when you need to modify the program again. At worst, by unsystematic corrections you will delay correcting the error properly, or you may even introduce further errors. See below for an illustration of the dangers of unsystematic modifications to a program.

Modifications

Working programs often have to be modified to meet a changed specification. Indeed, professional programmers spend a large proportion of their time doing just that. For example, the programs used by a tax authority will require frequent modification in response to changes in the tax laws.

It is also common for a programmer to find that a new programming assignment bears some resemblance to a program previously written, either by himself or by another programmer. In such a case, judicious adaptation of the older program can save a lot of work.

Such modifications must be made in the same systematic manner as correcting errors, and for exactly the same reasons. The following example should illustrate the dangers of ignoring this advice.

Suppose that the specification in Case Study II were modified in such a way that the output text is to start with a new paragraph, even though the input text does not start with a paragraph marker. Then we might be tempted simply to replace the statement STARTLINE, in the initialization sequence of the final program, by the statement NEWPARAGRAPH. If we did so, the program would misbehave because the value of POSITION is undefined on the first entry to NEWPARAGRAPH. The truth is that NEWPARAGRAPH was never intended to be the first output procedure to be invoked; it was designed to terminate a previous paragraph as well as start a new one.

260

To be systematic in our modification, we should go right back to Level 1, which should be modified as follows:

```
BEGIN
read the line width and make sure it is sensible ;
start a paragraph ;
attempt to read a word ;
WHILE we have a word DO
    ..........
    ..........
END .
```

Subsequently, at Level 2, "start a paragraph" should be refined to

```
PROCEDURE STARTPARAGRAPH ;
    CONST
        INDENT = 6 ;
    BEGIN
    FOR POSITION := 1 TO INDENT DO  LINE[POSITION] := BLANK ;
    POSITION := INDENT
    END (* STARTPARAGRAPH *)
```

Thus the initialization sequence of the final program will contain the statement STARTPARAGRAPH rather than NEWPARAGRAPH.

The error in this example was rather obvious, perhaps, but more subtle examples could be given where unsystematic modifications at the level of the final program introduce errors which become more and more perplexing.

Practice!

No-one has ever become a good programmer simply by reading about programming methods (or, for that matter, by writing about them!). There is no substitute for experience, obtained by solving your own programming problems, all the time consciously practicing the methods advocated here. You will find a number of programming exercises at the end of this chapter to allow you to practice these methods.

Do not be tempted to cast off these methods when you come to the end of your computer programming course. Even if you choose not to specialize in computing science and your subsequent programming is done in some application area, such as commercial data processing or numerical analysis, perhaps using a programming language other than Pascal, the same methods will continue to pay off. Good luck!

20.1. Systematically enhance program TEXTFORMATTER to support the following features:
(a) the special "word" /BREAK/ is to start a new line, the current line being written without right-adjustment;
(b) the special "word" /SPACE/ is to have the same effect as /BREAK/ and, additionally, to leave a single blank line;
(c) the special "word" /PAGE/ is to have the same effect as /BREAK/ and, additionally, to start a new page;
(d) the program is to read, in addition to the line width, the maximum number of lines per page, and each page is to be headed by a page number.

{This book was prepared using a text formatting program, admittedly rather more sophisticated than TEXTFORMATTER.}

20.2. If you have read Chapter 19, systematically modify program TRANSFERABLEVOTES to store the valid ballots in a linked list rather than a file.

PROGRAMMING EXERCISES 20

20.3. Write a program to plot the results of an experiment roughly on a line-printer page. Pairs of x- and y-values are supplied as input, one pair per line. The plot must include both the x- and y-axes. The positions of the axes and the x- and y-scale-factors must be chosen so as to use as much of the page as possible. The scales need not be marked on the axes, but the x- and y-scale-factors must be printed on the same page.

20.4. A text file TITLES contains a list of book titles separated by line boundaries. A number of "keywords" are supplied as input data, each left-justified on a line. Write a program which, for each keyword, writes a list of all the titles which contain that keyword, aligned such that the keyword always starts in a fixed column, e.g.:

```
         COMPUTER PROGRAMMING FOR ENGINEERS
                  PROGRAMMING IN PASCAL
              SYSTEMATIC PROGRAMMING
AN INTRODUCTION TO DYNAMIC PROGRAMMING
                  PROGRAMMING AND PROGRAMMING
          PROGRAMMING AND PROGRAMMING
```

If a keyword occurs more than once in a title, the title should be repeated, as illustrated above.

20.5*. Disk files are often used for permanent storage of programs, texts, documents, mailing lists, etc. A program called an editor is needed to amend such files as required. Write an editor which reads a text file, ORIGINALFILE, and writes an edited copy of this file to a second text file, UPDATEDFILE. The input data contains <u>editing directives</u>, one per line, whose effect is specified below (where xyz and uvw stand for any character sequences):

Directive   Effect

C"xyz"   Copy the current line and subsequent lines up to the next
            line containing the character sequence xyz. This line
            becomes the new "current line".
S"xyz"   Skip to the next line containing the character sequence xyz
            (i.e. do <u>not</u> copy the preceding lines). This line becomes
            the new "current line".
R"xyz"uvw" Replace the first occurrence of the character sequence xyz
            in the current line by the character sequence uvw.

The "current line" is initially the first line of ORIGINALFILE. When all the editing directives have been processed, the current line and all remaining lines of ORIGINALFILE are to be copied to UPDATEDFILE.

Appendix 1 Collected syntax diagrams

Syntax diagrams defining the entire syntax of Pascal, including certain minor features not covered in the main text, are collected together here.

1.1 THE PROGRAM

Program :

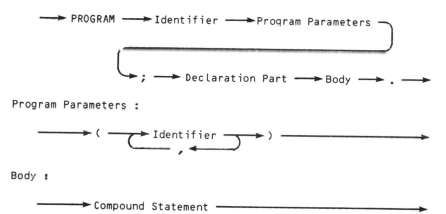

Program Parameters :

Body :

1.2 STATEMENTS

Statement :

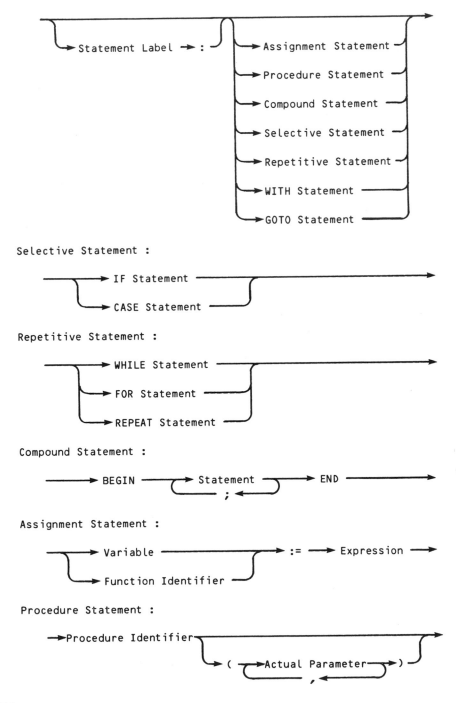

Selective Statement :

Repetitive Statement :

Compound Statement :

Assignment Statement :

Procedure Statement :

IF Statement :

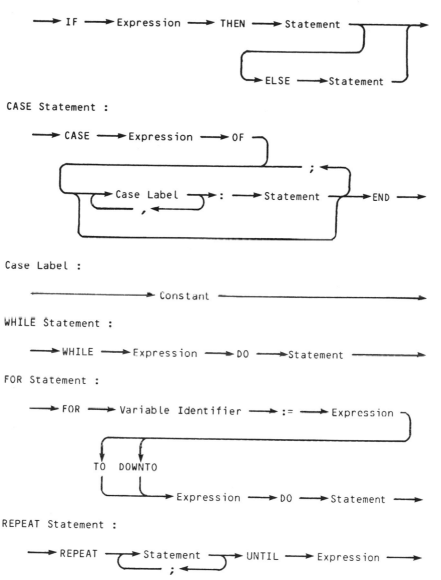

CASE Statement :

Case Label :

WHILE Statement :

FOR Statement :

REPEAT Statement :

WITH Statement :

GOTO Statement :

Statement Label :

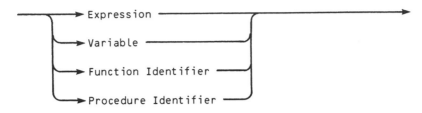

Actual Parameter :

1.3 EXPRESSIONS

Expression :

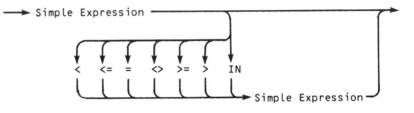

Simple Expression :

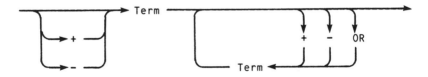

Term :

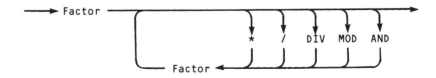

268

Factor :

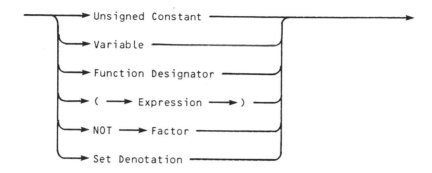

Function Designator :

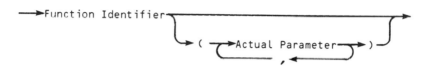

Set Denotation :

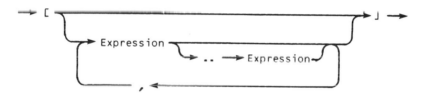

1.4 VARIABLES

Variable :

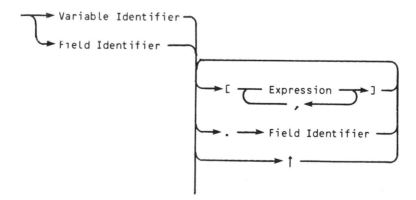

1.5 DEFINITIONS AND DECLARATIONS

Declaration Part :

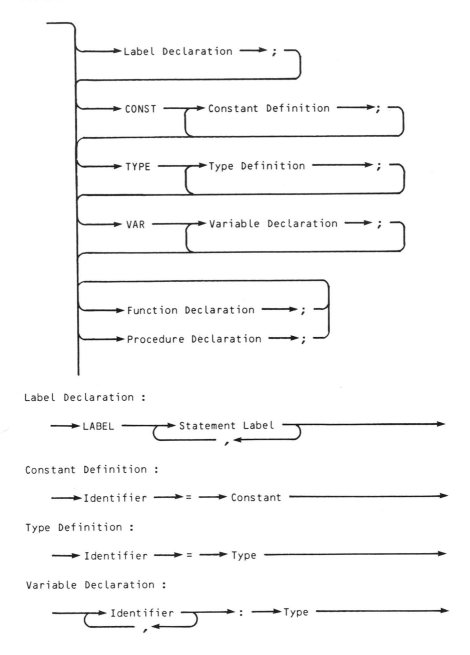

Label Declaration :

LABEL ──► Statement Label ──►
      ,◄──

Constant Definition :

──► Identifier ──► = ──► Constant ──►

Type Definition :

──► Identifier ──► = ──► Type ──►

Variable Declaration :

──► Identifier ──► : ──► Type ──►
      ,◄──

Function Declaration :

→ FUNCTION → Identifier → Formal-Parameter Part

: ←

→ Type Identifier → ; → Declaration Part → Body

→ FORWARD

Procedure Declaration :

→ PROCEDURE → Identifier → Formal-Parameter Part

; → Declaration Part → Body

FORWARD

Formal-Parameter Part :

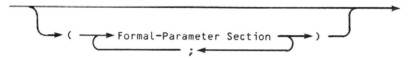

(→ Formal-Parameter Section →)

;

Formal-Parameter Section :

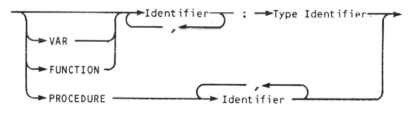

→ Identifier → : → Type Identifier

,

VAR

FUNCTION

PROCEDURE → Identifier

,

1.6 TYPES

Type :

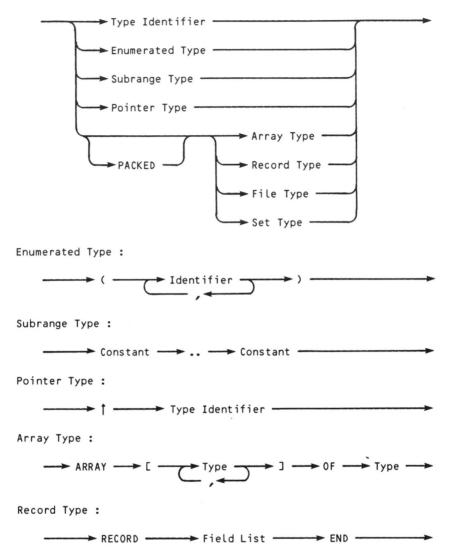

Enumerated Type :

Subrange Type :

Pointer Type :

Array Type :

Record Type :

Field List :

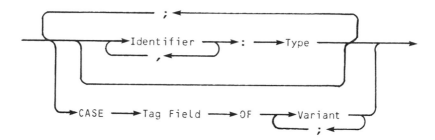

Tag Field :

Variant :

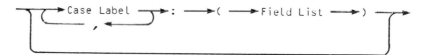

File Type :

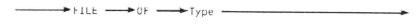

Set Type :

1.7 CONSTANTS

Constant :

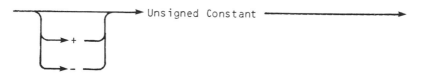

Unsigned Constant :

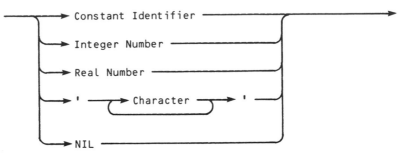

Integer Number :

Real Number :

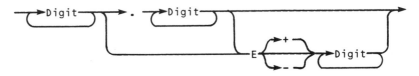

1.8 IDENTIFIERS

Identifier :

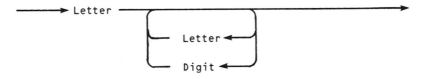

Appendix 2   Reserved words and special symbols

2.1 RESERVED WORDS

A reserved word is a word which has a special meaning and cannot
therefore be used as an identifier. Here is a complete list of the
reserved words of Pascal:

AND	DOWNTO	IF	OR	THEN
ARRAY	ELSE	IN	PACKED	TO
BEGIN	END	LABEL	PROCEDURE	TYPE
CASE	FILE	MOD	PROGRAM	UNTIL
CONST	FOR	NIL	RECORD	VAR
DIV	FUNCTION	NOT	REPEAT	WHILE
DO	GOTO	OF	SET	WITH

2.2 SPECIAL SYMBOLS AND THEIR REPRESENTATIONS

Here is a complete list of the special symbols of Pascal, as represented
in this book:

```
+    -    *    /
=    <>   <    <=   >=   >
(    )    [    ]    (*   *)
:=   .    ,    ;    :    ↑    '
```

Some of these symbols have alternative representations, depending on
the particular character set in use:

Symbol:	[	]	↑	(*	*)
ASCII representation:	[	]	^	{ or (*	} or *)
EBCDIC representation:	(.	.)	@	(*	*)

Strictly speaking, "{" and "}" are the standard representations of the
comment brackets, rather than "(*" and "*)". The latter representations
have been used in this book because they are available in all character
sets.

Appendix 3   Predeclared entities

CONST

    MAXINT = the largest positive integer which can be stored
            in a particular computer (* see INTEGER *) ;

TYPE

    BOOLEAN = (FALSE,TRUE) ;

    CHAR   = a particular character set ;

    INTEGER = the set of whole numbers, or integers,
            which can be stored in a particular computer
            (* in effect, -MAXINT..+MAXINT *) ;

    REAL   = the set of real numbers which can be represented
            in a particular computer ;

    TEXT   = FILE OF CHAR ;

VAR

    INPUT : TEXT ;   (* the standard input file *)

    OUTPUT : TEXT ;   (* the standard output file *)

(* Arithmetic functions *)

FUNCTION ABS (A : any arithmetic type) : same arithmetic type ;
          returns the absolute value of A ;

FUNCTION SQR (A : any arithmetic type) : same arithmetic type ;
          returns the square of A ;

FUNCTION ARCTAN (X : REAL) : REAL ;
          returns the arctangent, in radians, of X ;

```
FUNCTION COS ( X : REAL ) : REAL ;
          returns the cosine of X, which must be expressed in
          radians ;

FUNCTION SIN ( X : REAL ) : REAL ;
          returns the sine of X, which must be expressed in radians ;

FUNCTION EXP ( X : REAL ) : REAL ;
          returns the value of e raised to the power of X ;

FUNCTION LN ( X : REAL ) : REAL ;
          returns the natural logarithm of X ;

FUNCTION SQRT ( X : REAL ) : REAL ;
          returns the square root of X ;

FUNCTION ODD ( I : INTEGER ) : BOOLEAN ;
          returns TRUE if and only if I is odd ;


(* Type transfer functions *)

FUNCTION TRUNC ( X : REAL ) : INTEGER ;
          returns the value of X truncated to its integral part ;

FUNCTION ROUND ( X : REAL ) : INTEGER ;
          returns the value of X rounded to the nearest integer ;

FUNCTION ORD ( S : any ordinal type ) : INTEGER ;
          returns the ordinal number of S ;
          (* The values of an enumerated type, including BOOLEAN, have
          ordinal numbers 0, 1, 2, etc., in order of their
          enumeration. The ordinal numbers of CHAR values depend
          on the character set: see Appendix 5. *)

FUNCTION CHR ( I : INTEGER ) : CHAR ;
          returns the character whose ordinal number is I, if such a
          character exists ;

(* Successor and predecessor functions *)

FUNCTION SUCC ( S : any ordinal type ) : same ordinal type ;
          returns the successor value of S, if S has one ;

FUNCTION PRED ( S : any ordinal type ) : same ordinal type ;
          returns the predecessor value of S, if S has one ;
```

(* File handling procedures and functions *)

PROCEDURE RESET (VAR F : any file type) ;
          resets F's file position to the beginning of F, and assigns
          to F↑ the first component of F, if it exists ;

PROCEDURE REWRITE (VAR F : any file type) ;
          makes F ready to be written from scratch ;

PROCEDURE GET (VAR F : any file type) ;
          advances F's file position to the next component, and
          assigns to F↑ this next component, if it exists ;
          (* permitted only if EOF(F) is FALSE *)

PROCEDURE PUT (VAR F : any file type) ;
          appends the value of F↑ to F ;
          (* permitted only if EOF(F) is TRUE; EOF(F) remains TRUE *)

PROCEDURE READ (VAR F : any file type ;
                VAR V : component type of F) ;
```
   BEGIN
   V := F↑ ;
   GET(F)
   END ;
```

PROCEDURE WRITE (VAR F : any file type ;
                  V : component type of F) ;
```
   BEGIN
   F↑ := V ;
   PUT(F)
   END ;
```

PROCEDURE PAGE (VAR T : TEXT) ;
          forces subsequent output on T to continue on a new page ;

FUNCTION EOF (F : any file type) : BOOLEAN ;
          returns TRUE if and only if F's file position is at end-of-
          file ;

FUNCTION EOLN (T : TEXT) : BOOLEAN ;
          returns TRUE if and only if T's file position is at a line
          boundary ;

(* For procedures READ, READLN, WRITE, WRITELN with text files, see
Appendix 4. *)

(* Dynamic storage allocation procedure *)

PROCEDURE NEW (P : any pointer type) ;
        allocate a fresh anonymous variable and assign to P a
        pointer to this variable ;
        (* If this variable is to be a variant record with <u>fixed</u>
           tag-field values T1, T2, ..., then the statement
           NEW(P,T1,T2,....) allocates an amount of storage which
           will be sufficient for this combination of variants. *)

(* Packing and unpacking procedures *)

   (* Here it is assumed that UNPACKEDARRAYS and PACKEDARRAYS are array
     types (unpacked and packed respectively) with the same element
     type, and that INDEX is the subscript type of PACKEDARRAYS. *)

PROCEDURE PACK (U : UNPACKEDARRAYS ;
                I : INDEX ;
         VAR P : PACKEDARRAYS) ;
        copies U[I], U[SUCC(I)], ... into all the elements of P ;

PROCEDURE UNPACK (P : PACKEDARRAYS ;
         VAR U : UNPACKEDARRAYS ;
            I : INDEX   ) ;
        copies all the elements of P into U[I], U[SUCC(I)], ... ;

Appendix 4 Legible input and output

Legible input and output is achieved through text files, which are character files subdivided by line boundaries. (See Section 17.3.)

The standard file handling procedures RESET, REWRITE, GET, PUT, READ and WRITE, and the function EOF, as described in Appendix 3, are all applicable to text files. However, READ and WRITE are much more flexible when used with text files, and the additional procedures READLN and WRITELN, and the function EOLN, are provided to deal with line boundaries.

When the file position in a text file t is moved to a line boundary, by RESET, GET, READ or READLN, a blank is stored in t↑ and EOLN(t) becomes TRUE.

4.1 THE PROCEDURE READ

In this and the following section, t denotes a text file, and v, v1, v2, ... denote variables of type CHAR, INTEGER (or a subrange thereof), or REAL.

(1) READ(v1,v2,....) means READ(INPUT,v1,v2,....).

(2) READ(t,v1,v2,....) means:

BEGIN READ(t,v1); READ(t,v2) .... END

(3) If the type of v is CHAR, then READ(t,v) means:

BEGIN v:=t↑; GET(t) END

as described in Appendix 3. If the type of v is arithmetic, then the effect of READ(t,v) is to read a sequence of characters from t: blanks and line boundaries are skipped until a number (possibly signed) is recognized, and the value of this number is assigned to v.

4.2 THE PROCEDURE READLN

(1) READLN(v1,v2,....) means READLN(INPUT,v1,v2,....).

280

(2) READLN(t,v1,v2,....) means:

      BEGIN READ(t,v1); READ(t,v2); .... READLN(t) END

(3) READLN(t) advances the file pointer of t just beyond the next line boundary, i.e. to the beginning of the next line.

4.3 THE PROCEDURE WRITE

In this and the following section, t denotes a text file, and p1, p2, ... denote write-parameters. A write-parameter has one of the forms

      e:w   e   e:w:d

where e is an expression whose value is a character, a character array, a number, or a Boolean value, and where w and d are INTEGER expressions.

(1) WRITE(p1,p2,....) means WRITE(OUTPUT,p1,p2,....).

(2) WRITE(t,p1,p2,....) means:

      BEGIN WRITE(t,p1); WRITE(t,p2) .... END

(3) The effect of WRITE(t,e:w) is to write to t a representation of the value of e, preceded by as many blanks as necessary to ensure that at least w characters are written. The effect of WRITE(t,e) is similar, except that a suitable default value is taken for w. The effect of WRITE(t,e:w:d), where e must be REAL, is to write the value of e as a decimal fraction with d digits after the point. (If d is omitted, the value of e is written in scientific notation.)

4.4 THE PROCEDURE WRITELN

(1) WRITELN(p1,p2,....) means WRITELN(OUTPUT,p1,p2,....).

(2) WRITELN(t,p1,p2,....) means:

      BEGIN WRITE(t,p1); WRITE(t,p2); .... WRITELN(t) END

(3) The effect of WRITELN(t) is to append a line boundary to t.

4.5 OTHER PROCEDURES AND FUNCTIONS

(1) The effect of PAGE(t) is to force subsequent output on text file t to begin on a new page, should t subsequently be printed.

(2) The BOOLEAN function EOLN(t) returns TRUE if and only if the file position of text file t is at a line boundary.

Appendix 5 Character sets

The two most common computer character sets, the ASCII (or ISO) character set and the EBCDIC character set, are tabulated below, each in lexicograhic order across the rows. In each table "ƀ" denotes the blank character, and empty slots are "control characters", which cannot be printed. The ordinal number of each character may be determined by adding the numbers of its row and column.

5.1 THE ASCII CHARACTER SET

	0	1	2	3	4	5	6	7	8	9	10	11	12	13	14	15
0																
16																
32	ƀ	!	"	#	$	%	&	'	(	)	*	+	,	-	.	/
48	0	1	2	3	4	5	6	7	8	9	:	;	<	=	>	?
64	@	A	B	C	D	E	F	G	H	I	J	K	L	M	N	O
80	P	Q	R	S	T	U	V	W	X	Y	Z	[	\	]	^	_
96	`	a	b	c	d	e	f	g	h	i	j	k	l	m	n	o
112	p	q	r	s	t	u	v	w	x	y	z	{	|	}	~	

5.2 THE EBCDIC CHARACTER SET

	0	1	2	3	4	5	6	7	8	9	10	11	12	13	14	15
0																
16																
32																
48																
64	ƀ										¢	.	<	(	+	|
80	&										!	$	*	)	;	¬
96	-	/									,	%	_	>	?	
112											:	#	@	'	=	"
128		a	b	c	d	e	f	g	h	i						
144		j	k	l	m	n	o	p	q	r						
160			s	t	u	v	w	x	y	z						
176																
192		A	B	C	D	E	F	G	H	I						
208		J	K	L	M	N	O	P	Q	R						
224			S	T	U	V	W	X	Y	Z						
240	0	1	2	3	4	5	6	7	8	9						

Answers to selected exercises

Specimen solutions to more than half of the exercises (but not the programming exercises) are given here. Many of the exercises have alternative, equally satisfactory, solutions.

ANSWERS 1

1.1. (a), (b), (c), (e) and (g) are valid. However many Pascal compilers will ignore all but the first eight characters of an identifier, so (g) may be treated as if it were written ABCDEFGH.

1.3. (a) and (f) are valid.

1.4. For example: C1H4, Li1H1, B1H3, He99, C2H4, (C2H2)4C1Li2.
Note that (e.g.) CH4 is <u>not</u> allowed by the syntax given; every Component must end with an Integer Number.

ANSWERS 3

3.1.

```
CONST
    DAYSINWEEK   = 7;
    YARDSPERMILE = 1760;
    METRESPERKM  = 1000
```

3.2.

```
VAR
    GROSSPAY, TAX, UNIONDUES, NETTPAY : INTEGER
```

3.3.

UNIONDUES [20]   GROSSPAY [4800]   TAX [1600]

NETTPAY [3180]

```
3.4.
        VAR
            SUM, FIVERS, POUNDS : INTEGER;
            P50, P10, P5, P2, P1 : INTEGER;
            (* This answer assumes payment in Sterling *)
        FIVERS := SUM DIV 500;
        SUM := SUM MOD 500;
        POUNDS := SUM DIV 100;
        SUM := SUM MOD 100;
        P50 := SUM DIV 50;
        SUM := SUM MOD 50;
        (* ..... and so on ..... *)
```

ANSWERS 4

4.1.

8000	-3000	-1000	9000

4.3. For example:

```
        WRITELN ('Hugh McSporran') ;
        WRITELN ('13 Auchenshuggle Road') ;
        WRITELN ('Campbeltown') ;
        WRITELN ('Scotland')
```

4.4.

```
        PROGRAM POWERS ( INPUT, OUTPUT ) ;
        VAR
            NUMBER, SQ : INTEGER ;
        BEGIN
        READ (NUMBER) ;
        SQ := SQR(NUMBER) ;
        WRITELN ('    NUMBER    SQUARE      CUBE  4TH POWER') ;
        WRITELN (NUMBER:11, SQ:11, SQ*NUMBER:11, SQR(SQ):11)
        END .
```

4.5.

```
        PROGRAM DATE ( INPUT, OUTPUT ) ;
        VAR
            DAY, MONTH, YEAR : INTEGER ;
        BEGIN
        READ (DAY, MONTH, YEAR) ;
        WRITE (DAY:2, '/', MONTH:2, '/', (YEAR MOD 100):2)
        END .
```

5.1.
```
        POSITIVE := NUMBER>0;
        ZERO := NUMBER=0;
        NEGATIVE := NUMBER<0
```

5.2.   Either:
```
        LEFT := NOT ODD(PAGENMR)
```
or equivalently:
```
        LEFT := PAGENMR MOD 2 = 0
```

5.3.   Either:
```
        CELT := (SCOT AND NOT IRISH)  OR  (IRISH AND NOT SCOT)
```
or equivalently:
```
        CELT := SCOT <> IRISH
```

5.4.
```
        PROGRAM GREATER (INPUT, OUTPUT);
        VAR
           I,J : INTEGER;
        BEGIN
        READ (I,J);
        WRITE (I>J)
        END.
```

5.5.
```
        PROGRAM CHRISTMAS (INPUT, OUTPUT);
        CONST
           DECEMBER = 12;
        VAR
           MONTH, DAY : INTEGER;
        BEGIN
        READ (MONTH, DAY);
        WRITE ((MONTH=DECEMBER) AND (DAY=25))
        END .
```

5.6.   (a)
```
        LEAPYEAR := YEAR MOD 4 = 0
```

(b) The following answers are equivalent. Can you see why?
```
        LEAPYEAR := ((YEAR MOD 4 = 0) AND (YEAR MOD 100 <> 0))
                    OR (YEAR MOD 400 = 0)
```

```
          LEAPYEAR := (YEAR MOD 4 = 0) AND
                      ((YEAR MOD 100 <> 0) OR (YEAR MOD 400 = 0))
```

5.7.

```
    x < y    is equivalent to   NOT x AND y
    x >= y      "    "     "     x OR NOT y
    x > y       "    "     "     x AND NOT y
    x = y       "    "     "     NOT x AND NOT y  OR  x AND y
    x <> y      "    "     "     (x OR y)  AND  (NOT x OR NOT y)
```

5.8.

```
    x = TRUE     is equivalent to  x
    x = FALSE       "    "     "   NOT x
    x <> TRUE       "    "     "   NOT x
    x <> FALSE      "    "     "   x
```

Conclusion — use the simplified forms only, they are easier to read, to write and to compute.

5.9. (a) (a AND b AND c) OR x
      (b) TRUE
      (c) (a OR b OR c) AND (x OR y OR c)
           {Hint: use the fact that c is equivalent to (c AND c) to make the expression symmetrical.}

ANSWERS 6

6.1.
```
           *****
        -73
           *********
           ******
          0
           *
```

6.2. Assume the declaration "FACTORIAL, I : INTEGER".

```
      FACTORIAL := 1 ;
      I := 2 ;
      WHILE I <= N DO
         BEGIN
         FACTORIAL := FACTORIAL * I ;
         I := I+1
         END
```

6.3. Assume the declaration "POWEROF10, NMROFDIGITS : INTEGER".

```
            NMROFDIGITS := 1 ;
            POWEROF10 := 10 ;
            WHILE POWEROF10 <= N DO
               BEGIN
               NMROFDIGITS := NMROFDIGITS + 1 ;
               POWEROF10 := POWEROF10 * 10
               END
```

6.4.

```
            IF N > 0 THEN
               WRITE ('POSITIVE')
            ELSE IF N < 0 THEN
               WRITE ('NEGATIVE')
            ELSE
               WRITE ('ZERO')
```

6.5. Assume the declaration "THISDAY, THISMONTH, THISYEAR, BIRTHDAY,
      BIRTHMONTH, BIRTHYEAR, AGE : INTEGER".

```
            IF (BIRTHMONTH < THISMONTH) OR
               (BIRTHMONTH = THISMONTH) AND (BIRTHDAY <= THISDAY) THEN
               AGE := THISYEAR - BIRTHYEAR
            ELSE
               AGE := THISYEAR - BIRTHYEAR - 1
```

6.6. (a)
```
            PROGRAM LARGESTOFN ( INPUT, OUTPUT ) ;
            VAR
               NUMBER, LARGEST, N, COUNT : INTEGER ;
            BEGIN
            READ (N) ;
            LARGEST := 0 ;
            COUNT := 1 ;
            WHILE COUNT <= N DO
               BEGIN
               READ (NUMBER) ;
               IF NUMBER > LARGEST THEN
                  LARGEST := NUMBER ;
               COUNT := COUNT+1
               END ;
            WRITELN ('LARGEST NUMBER READ WAS ', LARGEST)
            END .
```

      (b)
```
            PROGRAM LARGESTOFALL ( INPUT, OUTPUT ) ;
            VAR
               NUMBER, LARGEST : INTEGER ;
```

```
BEGIN
LARGEST := 0 ;
READ (NUMBER) ;
WHILE NUMBER >= 0 DO
    BEGIN
    IF NUMBER > LARGEST THEN
        LARGEST := NUMBER ;
    READ (NUMBER)
    END ;
WRITELN ('LARGEST NUMBER READ WAS ', LARGEST)
END .
```

Compare this with Example 6.4, and make sure you understand the difference.

ANSWERS 7

7.1.   TRAFFICB is more efficient because the interval processing is only done between runs, rather than at every signal.

7.2.   Both versions correctly count the vehicles and report a survey period of zero. This is quite adequate.

7.3.   If there is no vehicle signal TRAFFICA does not update LONGEST and gives the longest vehicle-free interval as zero, regardless of the length of the survey period. TRAFFICB deals correctly with this situation.
       In fact this is just a special case of a serious mistake in TRAFFICA: if it so happens that the data ends with a vehicle-free interval and this is the longest such interval, the output will be incorrect. This failure is directly attributable to the lack of modularity in TRAFFICA. To correct it the end-of-interval processing would have to be repeated just before the output section, thus reducing the localization of the program and making it even less modular.

7.4.   TRAFFICA completely ignores data errors. This is unsatisfactory: a program should warn the user if it detects invalid data, even if it cannot take any more positive action.
       TRAFFICB goes into an infinite loop! This is completely unreasonable behaviour: programs should never be written in such a way that they will fail or loop indefinitely, no matter how garbled the input data.
       See Programming Exercise 7.6.

7.7.

```
PROGRAM EXAMMARKS ( INPUT, OUTPUT ) ;
CONST
    PASSMARK = 50 ;
```

```
      VAR
         MARK              : INTEGER ;
         PASSES, FAILURES : INTEGER ;
      BEGIN
      PASSES := 0 ;
      FAILURES := 0 ;
      WHILE NOT EOF(INPUT) DO
         BEGIN
         READLN (MARK) ;
         IF MARK >= PASSMARK THEN
            PASSES := PASSES + 1
         ELSE
            FAILURES := FAILURES + 1
         END ;
      WRITELN ('NUMBER OF PASSES:  ', PASSES) ;
      WRITELN ('NUMBER OF FAILURES: ', FAILURES)
      END .
```

ANSWERS 8

8.2.   Assume the constant definition "BLANK = ' '" and the variable
       declaration "THIS, PREVIOUS : CHAR".

```
      PREVIOUS := '*' ;     (* any non-blank character would do *)
      WHILE NOT EOLN(INPUT) DO
         BEGIN
         READ (THIS) ;
         IF (THIS <> BLANK) OR (PREVIOUS <> BLANK) THEN
            WRITE (THIS) ;
         PREVIOUS := THIS
         END ;
      WRITELN
```

8.3.   (a)
```
      FACULTY : (SCIENCE,MEDICINE,LAW,ARTS)
```

       (b) Assume the declaration "CODE : CHAR".

```
      READ (CODE) ;
      IF      CODE = 'S' THEN FACULTY := SCIENCE
      ELSE IF CODE = 'M' THEN FACULTY := MEDICINE
      ELSE IF CODE = 'L' THEN FACULTY := LAW
      ELSE IF CODE = 'A' THEN FACULTY := ARTS
      ELSE
         WRITELN ('INVALID FACULTY CODE: ', CODE)
```

(c)
```
IF      FACULTY = SCIENCE  THEN WRITE ('SCIENCE ')
ELSE IF FACULTY = MEDICINE THEN WRITE ('MEDICINE')
ELSE IF FACULTY = LAW      THEN WRITE ('LAW     ')
ELSE                            WRITE ('ARTS    ')
```

8.5.   Assume the declaration "NMROFDAYSINMONTH : 28..31".

```
(* determine the number of days in this MONTH and YEAR *)
   IF MONTH = FEB THEN
      IF YEAR is a leap year (* see Exercises 5 *) THEN
         NMROFDAYSINMONTH := 29
      ELSE
         NMROFDAYSINMONTH := 28
   ELSE IF (MONTH = APR) OR (MONTH = JUN) OR
           (MONTH = SEP) OR (MONTH = NOV) THEN
      NMROFDAYSINMONTH := 30
   ELSE
      NMROFDAYSINMONTH := 31 ;
(* update DAY, MONTH and YEAR to tomorrow's date *)
   IF DAY < NMROFDAYSINMONTH THEN
      DAY := DAY+1
   ELSE
      BEGIN
      DAY := 1 ;
      IF MONTH < DEC THEN
         MONTH := SUCC(MONTH)
      ELSE
         BEGIN
         MONTH := JAN ;
         YEAR := YEAR+1
         END
      END
```


ANSWERS 9

9.3.   A+B+C evaluates to 0.00. B+C+A evaluates to 0.004. (In the
        former case, a significant digit is lost by cancellation.)
            X*Y/Y evaluates to 3.89. (The value of X*Y, 15.054, is
        rounded to 15.1 before division.)
            Z+Z+Z+Z+Z+Z+Z+Z+Z+Z evaluates to 3.31. 10*Z evaluates to
        3.33. (Cumulative rounding error occurs in the former case.)

9.5.   Assume the declaration "S, AREASQUARED : REAL".

```
       S := (A+B+C)/2 ;
       AREASQUARED := S*(S-A)*(S-B)*(S-C) ;
       IF AREASQUARED >= 0.0 THEN
          WRITELN ('AREA OF TRIANGLE IS ', SQRT(AREASQUARED))
       ELSE
          WRITELN ('NO SUCH TRIANGLE EXISTS')
```

9.6. Assume the declaration "INCOME, ALLOWANCES, TAXABLEINCOME, TAX :
      REAL".

```
       READ (INCOME, ALLOWANCES) ;
       IF INCOME < ALLOWANCES THEN
          TAXABLEINCOME := 0.0
       ELSE
          TAXABLEINCOME := INCOME - ALLOWANCES ;
       TAX := 0.30 * TAXABLEINCOME ;
       IF TAXABLEINCOME > 10000.00 THEN
          TAX := TAX + 0.10 * (TAXABLEINCOME-10000.00) ;
       WRITELN ('INCOME:    ', INCOME     :10:2, ' GROATS') ;
       WRITELN ('ALLOWANCES:', ALLOWANCES:10:2, ' GROATS') ;
       WRITELN ('INCOME TAX:', TAX        :10:2, ' GROATS')
```

ANSWERS 10

10.1. (a)
```
          FREE : ARRAY [1..NMROFROOMS] OF BOOLEAN
```

       (b) Assume the declaration "NMRFREE, ROOM : INTEGER".

```
       NMRFREE := 0 ;
       ROOM := 1 ;
       WHILE ROOM <= NMROFROOMS DO
          BEGIN
          IF FREE[ROOM] THEN
             NMRFREE := NMRFREE+1 ;
          ROOM := SUCC(ROOM)
          END
```

10.3. Assume the declarations "L, H : LOW..HIGH; TEMP : CHAR".

```
       L := LOW ;  H := HIGH ;
       WHILE L < H DO
          BEGIN
          (* interchange TEXT[L] and TEXT[H] *)
             TEMP    := TEXT[L] ;
             TEXT[L] := TEXT[H] ;
             TEXT[H] := TEMP ;
          L := L+1 ;  H := H-1
          END
```

10.6. (a) Assume the declarations "SYMMETRIC : BOOLEAN; ROW, COL : INTEGER".

```
SYMMETRIC := TRUE ;
ROW := 2 ;  COL := 1 ;
WHILE SYMMETRIC AND (ROW <= N) DO
   IF MATRIX[ROW,COL] <> MATRIX[COL,ROW] THEN
      SYMMETRIC := FALSE
   ELSE
      BEGIN
      IF COL < ROW-1 THEN
         COL := COL+1
      ELSE (* about to hit main diagonal: go on to next row *)
         BEGIN  ROW := ROW+1 ;  COL := 1  END
      END
```

(b) Similar to (a).

ANSWERS 11

11.2. Assume the declaration "GROUP : 1..5".

```
IF WEIGHT > 60 THEN
   GROUP := 5
ELSE
   GROUP := (WEIGHT+14) DIV 15 ;
CASE GROUP OF
   1: CHARGE := 12 ;
   2: CHARGE := 22 ;
   3: CHARGE := 31 ;
   4: CHARGE := 36 + 2 * (DISTANCE DIV 1000) ;
   5: CHARGE := 40 + 3 * (DISTANCE DIV 1000)
END
```

11.6. Assume the constant definition "MAXSTARS = 42" and the variable declarations "MAXCOUNT, N : INTEGER; STAR : 1..MAXSTARS".

```
(* determine the greatest vote-count of any candidate *)
   MAXCOUNT := COUNT[1] ;
   FOR CANDIDATE := 2 TO NMROFCANDIDATES DO
      IF COUNT[CANDIDATE] > MAXCOUNT THEN
         MAXCOUNT := COUNT[CANDIDATE] ;
(* determine how many votes one asterisk should represent *)
   N := MAXCOUNT DIV MAXSTARS + 1 ;
```

```
                (* write the vote-counts in the form of a histogram *)
                   FOR CANDIDATE := 1 TO NMROFCANDIDATES DO
                   BEGIN
                   WRITE ('CANDIDATE ', CANDIDATE:2, '        ') ;
                   FOR STAR := 1 TO COUNT[CANDIDATE] DIV N DO
                      WRITE ('*') ;
                   WRITELN
                   END
```

11.7.

```
           PROGRAM TRIM ( INPUT, OUTPUT ) ;
           VAR
              CH : CHAR ;
           BEGIN
           WHILE NOT EOF(INPUT) DO
              BEGIN
              (* skip characters up to and including the colon *)
                 REPEAT READ (CH) UNTIL CH = ':' ;
              (* copy remainder of input line to output *)
                 WHILE NOT EOLN(INPUT) DO
                    BEGIN
                    READ (CH) ;
                    WRITE (CH)
                    END ;
              WRITELN ;
              READLN
              END
           END .
```

ANSWERS 12

12.2.

```
           FUNCTION FOURTHPOWER ( X : REAL ) : REAL ;
              BEGIN
              FOURTHPOWER := SQR(SQR(X))
              END (* FOURTHPOWER *)
```

12.3. (a)

```
           FUNCTION PRIME ( NUMBER : INTEGER ) : BOOLEAN ;
              VAR
                 DIVISOR  : INTEGER ;
                 NOFACTOR : BOOLEAN ;
```

```
            BEGIN
            DIVISOR := TRUNC(SQRT(NUMBER)) ;
            NOFACTOR := TRUE ;
            WHILE NOFACTOR AND (DIVISOR > 1) DO
               IF NUMBER MOD DIVISOR = 0 THEN
                  NOFACTOR := FALSE
               ELSE
                  DIVISOR := DIVISOR-1 ;
            PRIME := NOFACTOR
            END (* PRIME *)


    (b) Assume the declaration "N : INTEGER".

       READ (N) ;  WRITE (N) ;
       IF PRIME(N) THEN
          WRITE ('PRIME')
       ELSE
          WRITE ('NON-PRIME')
```

12.5. Assume the type definition "NAMES = ARRAY [1..LENGTH] OF CHAR".

```
        FUNCTION INITIAL ( NAME : NAMES ) : CHAR ;
        CONST
           BLANK = ' ' ;
        VAR
           INDEX : 1..LENGTH ;
        BEGIN
        (* locate the end of the surname *)
           INDEX := LENGTH ;
           WHILE NAME[INDEX] = BLANK DO
              INDEX := INDEX-1 ;
        (* locate the beginning of the surname *)
           WHILE NAME[INDEX] <> BLANK DO
              INDEX := INDEX-1 ;
        INITIAL := NAME[INDEX+1]
        END (* INITIAL *)
```


ANSWERS 13

13.2.
```
        PROCEDURE READBOOLEAN ( VAR B : BOOLEAN ) ;
        CONST
           BLANK = ' ' ;
        VAR
           CH : CHAR ;
```

```
            BEGIN
            (* skip any blanks preceding the Boolean representation *)
               READ (CH) ;
               WHILE CH = BLANK DO
                  READ (CH) ;
            IF CH = 'F' THEN
               B := FALSE
            ELSE IF CH = 'T' THEN
               B := TRUE
            ELSE
               WRITELN ('INVALID INPUT ON READING BOOLEAN: ', CH)
            END (* READBOOLEAN *)
```

13.4.   (a) Assume the type definition "PROFILES = ARRAY [CENTRES] OF REAL".

```
         PROCEDURE MAXMIN (      PROFILE              : PROFILES ;
                           VAR MAXCENTRE, MINCENTRE : CENTRES   ) ;
            VAR
               CENTRE : CENTRES ;
            BEGIN
            MAXCENTRE := FRANKFURT ;  MINCENTRE := FRANKFURT ;
            FOR CENTRE := LONDON TO ZURICH DO
               IF PROFILE[CENTRE] > PROFILE[MAXCENTRE] THEN
                  MAXCENTRE := CENTRE
               ELSE IF PROFILE[CENTRE] < PROFILE[MINCENTRE] THEN
                  MINCENTRE := CENTRE
            END (* MAXMIN *)
```

   (b) Assume the declaration "SELLCENTRE, BUYCENTRE : CENTRES".

```
         MAXMIN(CURRENCYVALUE[STERLING],SELLCENTRE,BUYCENTRE);
         WRITELN ('PROFIT ON STERLING DEAL IS ',
                  ((CURRENCYVALUE[STERLING,SELLCENTRE]
                   /CURRENCYVALUE[STERLING,BUYCENTRE]
                   - 1.0) * 100) :5:1, '%')
```

13.5.
```
         PROCEDURE SEARCH (      LIST     : LISTS ;
                                 TARGET   : ITEMS ;
                           VAR LOCATION : INDEXRANGE ;
                           VAR FOUND    : BOOLEAN     ) ;
            VAR
               INDEX : INTEGER ;
```

```
            BEGIN
            INDEX := 1 ;
            FOUND := FALSE ;
            WHILE NOT FOUND AND (INDEX <= N) DO
                IF LIST[INDEX] = TARGET THEN
                    BEGIN
                    LOCATION := INDEX ;
                    FOUND := TRUE
                    END
                ELSE
                    INDEX := INDEX+1
            END (* SEARCH *)
```

ANSWERS 14

14.2. (a)
```
        FUNCTION MINIMUM ( FUNCTION F          : INTEGER ;
                           LOWLIMIT, HIGHLIMIT : INTEGER ) : INTEGER ;
        VAR
           ARG, FVALUE, MINVALUE : INTEGER ;
        BEGIN
        MINVALUE := F(LOWLIMIT) ;
        FOR ARG := LOWLIMIT+1 TO HIGHLIMIT DO
           BEGIN
           FVALUE := F(ARG) ;
           IF FVALUE < MINVALUE THEN
              MINVALUE := FVALUE
           END ;
        MINIMUM := MINVALUE
        END (* MINIMUM *)
```

   (b)
```
      FUNCTION QUADRATIC ( P : INTEGER ) : INTEGER ;
         BEGIN
         QUADRATIC := SQR(P) - 2*P - 3
         END
```

   Call: WRITE (MINIMUM(QUADRATIC,-4,+4))

ANSWERS 15

15.1.   (a) Similar to the declaration of ONEEMPLOYEE in Example 17.4.

(b)
```
    WITH ONEEMPLOYEE DO
       BEGIN
       WRITE (NAME, NUMBER:8, '    ') ;
       CASE GRADE OF
          MANUAL:      WRITE ('MANUAL    ') ;
          SKILLED:     WRITE ('SKILLED   ') ;
          CLERICAL:    WRITE ('CLERICAL  ') ;
          MANAGERIAL: WRITE ('MANAGERIAL')
       END ;
       WRITELN ('    $', PAYRATE:7:2)
       END
```

15.2. (a)
```
    PROCEDURE WRITEDATE ( DATE : DATES ) ;
       BEGIN
       WITH DATE DO
          WRITE (DAY:2, '/', MONTH:2, '/', (YEAR MOD 100):2)
       END (* WRITEDATE *)
```

(b) Assume the declaration "TODAY, THATDAY : DATES", and assume that TODAY contains today's date.

```
    WRITEDATE(TODAY) ;  WRITELN ;
    (* determine the date exactly nine months hence *)
       THATDAY := TODAY ;
       IF THATDAY.MONTH <= 3 THEN
          THATDAY.MONTH := THATDAY.MONTH+9
       ELSE
          BEGIN
          THATDAY.MONTH := THATDAY.MONTH - 3 ;
          THATDAY.YEAR := THATDAY.YEAR + 1
          END ;
    WRITEDATE(THATDAY) ;  WRITELN
```

15.4. (a)
```
    SHAPES  = (CIRCLE,RECTANGLE,TRIANGLE) ;
    FIGURES = RECORD
                 CASE SHAPE : SHAPES OF
                    CIRCLE:
                        ( RADIUS : REAL ) ;
                    RECTANGLE:
                        ( X, Y : REAL ) ;
                    TRIANGLE:
                        ( A, B, C : REAL )
              END
```

(b)
```
    FUNCTION AREA ( FIGURE : FIGURES ) : REAL ;
       CONST
          PI = 3.14159265 ;
       VAR
          S : REAL ;
       BEGIN
       WITH FIGURE DO
          CASE SHAPE OF
             CIRCLE:    AREA := PI * SQR(RADIUS) ;
             RECTANGLE: AREA := X * Y ;
             TRIANGLE:  BEGIN
                        S := (A+B+C)/2 ;
                        AREA := SQRT(S*(S-A)*(S-B)*(S-C))
                           (* ... assuming the triangle exists! *)
                        END
          END (* CASE *)
       END (* AREA *)
```

ANSWERS 16

16.2.
```
       FUNCTION LENGTH ( STRING : STRINGS ) : INTEGER ;
          CONST
             BLANK = ' ' ;
          VAR
             TRAILING : BOOLEAN ;
             INDEX    : 0..MAXLENGTH ;
          BEGIN
          INDEX := MAXLENGTH ;
          TRAILING := TRUE ;
          WHILE TRAILING AND (INDEX > 0) DO
             IF STRING[INDEX] = BLANK THEN
                TRAILING := FALSE
             ELSE
                INDEX := INDEX-1 ;
          LENGTH := INDEX
          END (* LENGTH *)
```

16.3. Assume the type definition "DECIMALS = PACKED ARRAY [1 .. NMROFDIGITS] OF CHAR".

```
       PROCEDURE ADDDECIMAL (     OPERAND1, OPERAND2 : DECIMALS ;
                             VAR SUM                  : DECIMALS ;
                             VAR OVERFLOW             : BOOLEAN  ) ;
          VAR
             PLACE  : 1..NMROFDIGITS ;
             COLUMN : 0..19 ;
             CARRY  : 0..1 ;
```

```
BEGIN
CARRY := 0 ;
FOR PLACE := NMROFDIGITS DOWNTO 1 DO
   BEGIN
   COLUMN := (ORD(OPERAND1[PLACE]) - ORD('0')) +
              (ORD(OPERAND2[PLACE]) - ORD('0')) +
              CARRY ;
   SUM[PLACE] := CHR (COLUMN MOD 10 + ORD('0')) ;
   CARRY      := COLUMN DIV 10
   END ;
OVERFLOW := CARRY <> 0
END (* ADDDECIMAL *)
```

ANSWERS 17

17.2. Assume the type definition "ITEMFILES = FILE OF ITEMS".

```
PROCEDURE SEARCHFILE ( VAR ITEMFILE : ITEMFILES ;
                           TARGET   : ITEMS ;
                           VAR FOUND    : BOOLEAN    ) ;
   VAR
      ITEM : ITEMS ;
   BEGIN
   RESET (ITEMFILE) ;
   FOUND := FALSE ;
   WHILE NOT (FOUND OR EOF(ITEMFILE)) DO
      BEGIN
      READ (ITEMFILE, ITEM) ;
      IF ITEM = TARGET THEN     (****************)
         FOUND := TRUE
      END
   END (* SEARCH *)
```

The comparison marked above is not valid if ITEMS is an record or
array type (unless it is a string type).

17.4.

```
PROGRAM NUMBERLINES ( TEXTFILE, OUTPUT ) ;
VAR
   TEXTFILE  : TEXT ;
   LINECOUNT : INTEGER ;
   CH        : CHAR ;
```

```
            BEGIN
            LINECOUNT := 0 ;
            RESET (TEXTFILE) ;
            WHILE NOT EOF(TEXTFILE) DO
               (* read and write a line of TEXTFILE, with numbering *)
                  BEGIN
                  LINECOUNT := LINECOUNT+1 ;
                  WRITE (LINECOUNT:6, '    ') ;
                  WHILE NOT EOLN(TEXTFILE) DO
                     (* read and write a single character of TEXTFILE *)
                        BEGIN
                        READ (TEXTFILE, CH) ;
                        WRITE (CH)
                        END ;
                  WRITELN ;
                  READLN (TEXTFILE)
                  END
            END .
```

17.6.

```
            PROGRAM INTERSECTION
                    ( DRINKERSFILE, TEMPERANCEFILE, OUTPUT ) ;
            TYPE
               MEMBERS = RECORD
                            NAME    : PACKED ARRAY [1..16] OF CHAR
                         (* ........................
                            address and other details
                            ........................ *)
                         END ;
            VAR
               DRINKERSFILE, TEMPERANCEFILE : FILE OF MEMBERS ;
            BEGIN
            RESET (DRINKERSFILE) ;
            RESET (TEMPERANCEFILE) ;
            WHILE NOT (EOF(DRINKERSFILE) OR EOF(TEMPERANCEFILE)) DO
               IF DRINKERSFILE↑.NAME < TEMPERANCEFILE↑.NAME THEN
                  GET (DRINKERSFILE)
               ELSE IF DRINKERSFILE↑.NAME > TEMPERANCEFILE↑.NAME THEN
                  GET (TEMPERANCEFILE)
               ELSE
                  BEGIN
                  WRITELN (DRINKERSFILE↑.NAME, ' IS A MEMBER OF BOTH.') ;
                  GET (DRINKERSFILE) ;
                  GET (TEMPERANCEFILE)
                  END
            END .
```

18.3. The following solution assumes that the set type SET OF CHAR is available, and that the upper-case letters are contiguous and the lower-case letters likewise. Assume the type definition "CHARCLASSES = (LETTER,DIGIT,BLANK,PUNCTUATION,OTHER)".

```
FUNCTION CLASS ( CH : CHAR ) : CHARCLASSES ;
  BEGIN
  IF CH IN ['A'..'Z', 'a'..'z'] THEN
     CLASS := LETTER
  ELSE IF CH IN ['0'..'9'] THEN
     CLASS := DIGIT
  ELSE IF CH = ' ' THEN
     CLASS := BLANK
  ELSE IF CH IN ['.', '!', '?', ':', ';', ',',
                 '(', ')', '"', '''', '-']    THEN
     CLASS := PUNCTUATION
  ELSE
     CLASS := OTHER
  END (* CLASS *)
```

19.2.

```
PROGRAM REVERSE ( INPUT, OUTPUT ) ;
TYPE
   LINKS = ↑ NODES ;
   NODES = RECORD
                  CHARACTER : CHAR ;
                  NEXT      : LINKS
              END ;
VAR
   FIRST, THIS : LINKS ;
   CH          : CHAR ;
BEGIN
(* make the list of characters empty *)
   FIRST := NIL ;
WHILE NOT EOLN(INPUT) DO
   BEGIN
   READ (CH) ;
   (* insert CH at the front of the list *)
      NEW (THIS) ;
      THIS↑.CHARACTER := CH ;
      THIS↑.NEXT := FIRST ;
      FIRST := THIS
   END ;
```

```
(* write all characters in the list *)
    THIS := FIRST ;
    WHILE THIS <> NIL DO
        BEGIN
        WRITE (THIS↑.CHARACTER) ;
        THIS := THIS↑.NEXT
        END
END
```

19.3. Replace the variable declaration LISTHEAD : ITEMPOINTERS by

LISTHEAD : ARRAY ['A'..'Z'] OF ITEMPOINTERS

Replace all three occurrences of LISTHEAD in procedure INSERTITEM by LISTHEAD[NEWITEM[1]]. Insert the variable declaration INITIAL : 'A'..'Z' into procedure WRITEITEMS, and replace its body by

```
BEGIN
FOR INITIAL := 'A' TO 'Z' DO
    BEGIN
    ENTRY := LISTHEAD[INITIAL] :
    WHILE ENTRY <> NIL DO
        ........
        ........
    END
END (* WRITEITEMS *)
```

Replace the statement LISTHEAD := NIL in the program body by

```
FOR INITIAL := 'A' TO 'Z' DO
    LISTHEAD[INITIAL] := NIL
```

and insert the variable declaration INITIAL : 'A'..'Z'.

Index

304